Discourse Processing

Synthesis Lectures on Human Language Technologies

Editor
Graeme Hirst, *University of Toronto*

Synthesis Lectures on Human Languages Technologies is edited by Graeme Hirst of the University of Toronto. The series consists of 50- to 150-page monographs on topics relating to natural language processing, computational linguistics, information retrieval, and spoken language understanding. Emphasis is on important new techniques, on new applications, and on topics that combine two or more HLT subfields.

Discourse Processing
Manfred Stede
2011

Bitext Alignment
Jörg Tiedemann
2011

Linguistic Structure Prediction
Noah A. Smith
2011

Learning to Rank for Information Retrieval and Natural Language Processing
Hang Li
2011

Computational Modeling of Human Language Acquisition
Afra Alishahi
2010

Introduction to Arabic Natural Language Processing
Nizar Y. Habash
2010

DiscourseProcessing

Manfred Stede

ISBN: 978-3-031-01016-3   paperback
ISBN: 978-3-031-02144-2   ebook

DOI 10.1007/978-3-031-02144-2

A Publication in the Springer Nature series
SYNTHESIS LECTURES ON ADVANCES IN AUTOMOTIVE TECHNOLOGY

Lecture#15
SeriesEditor:GraemeHirst,*UniversityofToronto*
SeriesISSN
SynthesisLecturesonHumanLanguageTechnologies
Print1947-4040 Electronic1947-4059

Discourse Processing

Manfred Stede
University of Potsdam

SYNTHESIS LECTURES ON HUMAN LANGUAGE TECHNOLOGIES #15

ABSTRACT

Discourse Processing here is framed as marking up a text with structural descriptions on several levels, which can serve to support many language-processing or text-mining tasks. We first explore some ways of assigning structure on the document level: the logical document structure as determined by the layout of the text, its genre-specific content structure, and its breakdown into topical segments. Then the focus moves to phenomena of local coherence. We introduce the problem of coreference and look at methods for building chains of coreferring entities in the text. Next, the notion of coherence relation is introduced as the second important factor of local coherence. We study the role of connectives and other means of signaling such relations in text, and then return to the level of larger textual units, where tree or graph structures can be ascribed by recursively assigning coherence relations. – Taken together, these descriptions can inform text summarization, information extraction, discourse-aware sentiment analysis, question answering, and the like.

KEYWORDS

text structure, document structure, topic segmentation, coreference, anaphora resolution, coherence relation, discourse parsing

Contents

Acknowledgments

The author is grateful to the anonymous reviewers and to the series editor for their thoughtful and constructive suggestions to improve an earlier version of the manuscript. Also, thanks are due to several readers who provided comments on earlier versions of individual sections: Heike Bieler, Markus Egg, Thomas Hanneforth, Manfred Klenner, Constantin Orasan, Maite Taboada, and Sebastian Varges.

Manfred Stede
November 2011

CHAPTER 1

Introduction

Discourse processing, in a nutshell, is language processing beyond the sentence boundary: We compute information about a text in order to supplement the results of sentence processing (e.g., when supplying a referent for a pronoun from context), or we combine sentence-level information to larger units (e.g., when inferring a causal relationship to hold between two sentences). Since 'discourse' is a somewhat vague term, note that in this book it is meant to denote merely monologue written text, in contrast to its usual meaning, which also includes spoken language and thus dialogue as an object of study. So, for our purposes here, 'discourse' and 'text' are largely synonymous. Sometimes, however, the words are used to emphasize their respective specific facets of meaning, with 'discourse' referring to a purposeful activity of language production and reception, and 'text' rather to a static object of study.

Research on discourse processing generally revolves around the assumption that a text is more than the sum of its parts: It is not enough to collect some arbitrary sequence of sentences in order to obtain a text. Rather, a text covers a particular topic, usually addressing a range of subtopics while it progresses, and it is linearized in a way that enables the reader to process the information in a logical way. In short, a text is expected to be *coherent*.

Coherence: A coherent text is designed around a common topic. In the reading process, the individual units of information enter meaningful relationships to one another. Understanding the text implies uncovering those relationships, which on the one hand result from coreference between referring expressions, and on the other hand from semantic and pragmatic relations (e.g., Cause) between adjacent units. The text *coheres* and is not just a sequence of sentences to be interpreted in isolation.

This book is, on the one hand, an introduction to the various problems of discourse processing, as they are subsumed by the definition above. The phenomena are explained in such a way that no prior knowledge of discourse is required. On the other hand, in addition to the general introductions, we provide an overview of common methods to computationally solve the various tasks of discourse processing. Here, we assume some acquaintance with concepts and techniques in computational linguistics (or 'language technology'). The typical reader thus will be a student with some background in linguistics and computational linguistics, who has not received an education on discourse problems yet, and wants to know how (and to what extent) these problems can be tackled for advanced natural language processing tasks.

So, what are the central tasks of discourse processing? We briefly address them here by introducing the structure of the book.

Chapter 2   We examine how a text document can be broken into meaningful parts from a top-down perspective. As a first step (which can be regarded as 'preprocessing' for the others), we infer the *logical document structure*: What clues does the mere layout give on the hierarchical structure of the document? Next, we look at the situation where building blocks are induced by the *genre* that the text belongs to. Roughly speaking, an instruction manual for an MP3 player consists of an ensemble of sections (which is relatively predictable when you are familiar with manuals of technical gadgets) that is very different from that of, say, a scientific paper. The idea is that the sections each play an identifiable role for the function of the document as a whole, and this function is determined by the genre. Certain genres, of course, might not display any such functional structure at all.

Another important type of top-down division is an analysis of the *topic structure* of a text document, or some part of it. Again, this is more or less relevant depending on the genre; it tends to be important for longer news reports, essays, or stories, which move from one (sub-)topic to another, and thereby create a layer of structure.

Chapter 3   For many discourse theoreticians, the central defining criterion of 'textuality' is continuous reference to the same entities: The author of a text keeps talking about the same things (for a while, at least, before moving on to others). *Coreference* comes in many forms, with anaphoric pronouns probably the most prominent one (for linguists, at least). This is a very wide-ranging issue, but our general introduction in that chapter has to be relatively brief. Being able to compute coreference is important for two different reasons: On the one hand, it is necessary to complete the information that a single sentence (e.g., *They didn't read it*) might fail to convey when interpreted in isolation. On the other hand, the full set of coreference *chains* (expressions referring to the same entity, with each one pointing to the previous one in the discourse) once again provides information on the structure of the text, because the "things being talked about," of course, reflect the topics and their points of change. We explain both linguistically-motivated, rule-based approaches to coreference resolution and corpus-based statistical ones, which have become popular over the last ten years.

Chapter 4   In some sense the most exciting aspect of discourse coherence is the notion of *coherence relation*, which provides a label for the "extra" information that may be conveyed by juxtaposing two portions of text—in the simple case, just two clauses or sentences. Consider Example 1.1 below, where most readers would naturally infer a causal relationship, even though no explicit signal to that effect is present. This distinguishes the phenomenon of coherence relation from coreference, where at least we always get an overt "invitation" to search for a suitable entity being referred to. On the other hand, languages also offer a wide range of signals for relations, called *connectives* or *cue phrases*. They can be seen as instructions for the reader to combine the meaning of the adjacent units in some specific way; cf. Example 1.2, where the connective is underlined.

Example 1.1   Suddenly the kitchen door opened. Paul looked up.

Example 1.2   <u>Although</u> the lake was really cold, we swam for some twenty minutes.

The issue of coherence relations, and a text structure resulting from their recursive application, can be (and has been) addressed from the viewpoint of grammar, with the goal of extending sentence syntax and semantics to the text level. In this book, however, we largely put the grammatical perspective aside, and instead approach the task more from the perspectives of pragmatics and that of robust analysis, looking at the text as a whole, and figuring out how it breaks down into meaningful units that are related to one another. An influential account, to be discussed at length in Chapter 4, is *Rhetorical Structure Theory* [Mann and Thompson, 1988], which posits that adjacent minimal units of a text are linked by a semantic/pragmatic relation (to be chosen from a set of about 25), and that the resulting larger text spans are recursively also subject to this relational linking. The resulting tree then has to cover the whole text, with no overlaps and no crossing edges. Figure 1.1 shows an example analysis of a short text.[1] In Chapter 4, we will study the various subproblems involved in building such trees automatically. These trees can be useful in many applications such as question answering (e.g., in order to find responses to *Why-* questions) or summarization (in order to distinguish the more important from the less important information).

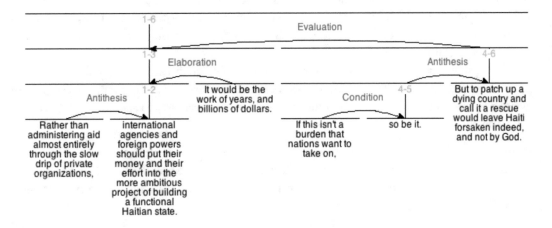

Figure 1.1: Sample analysis according to Rhetorical Structure Theory.

Chapter 5   We conclude the book by summing up our overall approach to discourse processing, which emphasizes computing different kinds of structural information about a text document, which then constitute distinct (but related) layers. This contrasts with more narrow views that aim at finding "the one and only discourse structure" at one particular level of description.

---

[1]Image created with RSTTool (www.wagsoft.com/RSTTool, Nov 20, 2010). The notational style follows that of Mann and Thompson [1988], but it could be re-drawn as a standard tree structure.

This multi-layer perspective originates largely from a practical viewpoint: When some information extraction task (in the widest sense: be it looking for a fact or an opinion, constructing a summary, or whatever) is applied to a text document, some preparatory work on the level of discourse can be of great help. For example, when looking for a factoid (e.g., *Who invented Rhetorical Structure Theory?*), the answer is not helpful when being extracted from a sentence containing as subject merely a pronoun (*they*). Anaphora resolution, i.e., the assignment of antecedent expressions to such pronouns, would be required here. Consider another case, where the task is to extract the personal opinions offered by the author of a text. A non-discourse-aware approach would look for a subjective linguistic expression—such as a 'loaded' adjective—and then extract the particular chunk of information containing it, as for instance *Dire Straits are a dull rock band*. However, if in the source text this string were preceded by *My brother always said that*, then the system would not have done justice to the author and her views; it failed to recognize the *attribution* of the view to the author's brother. Further, suppose the extracted string were in the text followed by *But one doesn't have to see it that way*. This does not contain any 'loaded' word and thus is likely to be missed by a simple sentiment analysis system, which thus would produce as output a position that is not only *not* held by the author, but actively called into doubt by her. A solution is to perform an analysis in terms of coherence relations: The conjunction *but* would have to be recognized as signaling a coherence relation of Contrast, which here could "warn" an opinion extractor that a dissenting view might in fact follow. This might just be a local analysis at this portion of the text, without aiming at a complete 'rhetorical structure'.

In short, querying text documents for information is made difficult by a number of complications belonging to the realm of discourse. Methods of discourse processing such as discussed in this book try to accomplish as much automatic text analysis as necessary to alleviate these problems as far as possible.

> **Discourse processing:** The acquisition of information *about* a text, including assigning structural descriptions to it, so that the extraction of information *from* a text becomes more interesting, more fruitful, or more simple.

For implementing a "pluralistic", multi-layered view on discourse processing, one needs a technical framework that allows for invoking different, specialized analysis modules, and integrating their results. In this book, we will *not* address the issue of such frameworks. Instead, the reader is referred to the volume *Introduction to Linguistic Annotation and Text Analytics* [Wilcock, 2009] in this same book series, which provides a practical introduction to well-established frameworks of this kind.

Organization of the book   The chapters occasionally point to one another, but they do not build upon each other. Therefore, the book can also be read selectively, as distinct short introductions to the three central topics.

At various points, we will provide working definitions for some key notions under discussion. These will appear in boxes, as already exemplified with two definitions above.

Typographical convention: We use *italics* for technical terms when being first introduced, sometimes for emphasis, and also for linguistic examples when they appear in running text. Single quotes mark technical terms in other places, while double quotes signal a "so to speak" reading. `Typewriter` font is reserved for code-like terminology.

Gender convention: Personal pronouns, used especially when referring to the reader, appear randomly in their masculine or feminine form.

Throughout the book, we will repeatedly make reference to an authentic sample text, which serves to illustrate many of the phenomena we will be discussing. It is given in Appendix A, with paragraph/sentence numbers inserted for easy reference. For brevity, the text will henceforth be referred to by its headline, printed in smallcaps: SUFFERING.

CHAPTER 2

Large Discourse Units and Topics

This chapter discusses the coarse-grained structure of text as a sequence of building blocks that 'hang together' in different ways that we will explore. Often, such blocks are a direct consequence of the text's belonging to a particular *genre*, which imposes a conventional—more or less strict—order of functional units. In other cases, long stretches of running text can sensibly be broken into smaller segments whose 'hanging together' is motivated by their dealing with a common *topic*. We will look at different algorithms for finding topic breaks, some based on building so-called *lexical chains*, others based on tracking the distribution of words across the text.

Why is breaking a text into its large, topic-induced blocks a relevant task? Among the beneficiaries are text summarizers, which can try to make sure that all subtopics or aspects mentioned in the text are being covered in the summary. And, for many purposes, information extraction or question answering, as well as sentiment analysis, can be made more precise when it is known from which part of a document an information unit is taken; some examples of this scenario will be given in this chapter. And finally, text segmentation can support a different subtask of language processing, anaphora resolution, under the assumption that local anaphoricity is partly determined by high-level segments; this will be discussed later in Chapter 3.

2.1 GENRE-INDUCED TEXT STRUCTURE

A text is not a free-floating entity: It originates as an instance of a particular class of texts, commonly called *genre*, and it is being received by the reader with certain expectations triggered by her knowledge about that genre (see, e.g., Biber [1989], Martin [1984]). When looking up the weather report in the newspaper, we expect a brief list of information, usually not in an arbitrary but in some specific order. When we open a cookbook, we expect for each recipe a list of ingredients and the steps necessary for preparing the dish. And so forth.

Some branches of discourse research have spent a lot of effort on the problem of finding "the" inventory of text genres, and on providing hierarchical classifications in terms of features shared by more or less specific genres. In information retrieval and computational linguistics, the task of *text classification* is mostly geared towards separating texts of different topics, but sometimes it specifically targets genre classification, e.g., when web pages are classified into groups like private homepage, company site, newsmedia, and so on (see, e.g., Mehler et al. [2010]).

> **Genre:** A class of texts that fulfill a common function, are being used for a common communicative purpose, and are potentially subject to conventions on various levels of description: length, layout, internal organization, lexical and syntactic choices.

For our purposes here, we are only interested in the text-structuring aspect of genres. Texts belonging to the same genre play some particular role in communication, and often this is achieved by means of a conventionalized set of building blocks that contribute to the text function; we call these building blocks *content zones*. The obligatoriness or optionality of the content zones, and the order they appear in, can differ considerably between genres. From this viewpoint, we can broadly distinguish three groups of documents with different degrees of structure imposed by their genre:

- *Unstructured* documents show no particular breakdown into identifiable pieces with a clear functional role. SUFFERING is an example. It is taken from the *Talk of the Town* section of *The New Yorker* magazine, which assembles essayistic pieces that sometimes tell little curious stories, and sometimes are more politically-minded and argumentative. A common structure is hardly identifiable.

- *Structured* documents display a relatively strict order of a rather fixed set of content zones. The conventional scaffolding of scientific papers is an example (never mind certain differences between the scientific disciplines), as they typically consist of title matter, abstract, introduction, related work, main sections, conclusion, and bibliography; some but not too much variation in ordering these zones is allowed.

- *Semi-structured* documents occupy the grey zone in the middle: There usually is a fixed range of necessary zones, but there may be a variety of optional ones, and the linear order among the zones is only partially fixed. One example, to be discussed below, is that of film reviews: Zones such as film title, story description, author's comments, overall evaluation are basically mandatory; others such as cast and credits, author biography, background on the director, are optional. As for the linear order, there are some clear tendencies (title in the beginning, credits and overall rating either toward the beginning or at the end, etc.) but no strict sequence is prescribed.

Why is it important to analyze the content zone structure when processing a text document? For instance, information extraction often can profit from focusing on particular zones, as in the following two cases. When looking for main results of a scientific paper (such as in the biomedical domain), it helps to check just the abstract and the conclusions, in order to avoid pitfalls of finding older and possibly outdated results that are cited in the related work section. In analyzing film reviews, when the goal is to determine the author's evaluation of the film, one can attend to that specific content zone (usually numerical information or a number of stars) if present; if there is no such crisp overall judgement, the orientation of the review can be computed more reliably when considering only the subjective *comment* zones, leaving the story *description* zones aside (as shown by Taboada et al. [2009]).

How, then, is the content zone structure determined? A good strategy is to first identify the *logical document structure* on the grounds of layout information, and then to compute content zones on its basis.

2.1.1   LOGICAL DOCUMENT STRUCTURE

As soon as a text document is more complex than a sequence of a few sentences, issues of global structure become relevant. The first relevant level of document structure is the one that is readily observable: The *physical document structure* means the document's appearance on paper (or elsewhere) as we perceive it independently of the reading process. Consider this book, which is fundamentally broken into *pages*. A page is a well-defined segment on the level of physical structure, but as far as the content organization of the book is concerned, the majority of page breaks are entirely accidental. Also, things like page headers and page numbers merely serve to organize the physical structure, but are not part of the content of the document. Next, consider the role of different font sizes or of boldface used for headlines. Such attributes are also not relevant to the content proper, but they operate on the interface to the level we are interested in here: They can serve as clues to the *logical document structure*. This level defines the internal, hierarchical organization of the document into sections, paragraphs, bullet lists, and the like. Thus, while the physical document structure is basically arbitrary (and for most practical purposes need not be preserved when a document is processed), the logical structure represents the "backbone" of its content.

Again, the genre plays a central role for the shape of the logical structure. Many hand-written notes and many private emails do not have any, or merely a trivial one. Newspaper articles may display a headline and a breakup in paragraphs as the sole features of logical structure. This is the case with SUFFERING, which—despite its being relatively long—does not offer any intermediate headlines. Books are typically structured in chapters, sections, subsections, paragraphs, etc. For illustration, Figure 2.1 shows a representation of the upper portion of the logical structure tree for this book; it omits the more fine-grained structural units such as paragraphs, figures, and bullet lists. Notice that the standard document pre-processing tasks of *sentence splitting* and *tokenization* can sensibly be integrated into the determination of logical document structure, so that the leaves of the tree would be constituted by sentences or tokens, respectively, as well as by non-textual objects such as figures.

Logical document structure has two important properties: It is *hierarchical* (segments are meaningfully embedded into one another), and it is signalled by properties of the layout of the document, whereas the words, i.e., the semantic content, do not matter. For illustration, Figure 2.2 provides a demagnified view of a page of this book. We see the corresponding part of the physical document structure, and we immediately notice that it provides clues to the logical document structure. Just by interpreting vertical and horizontal spacing, color, and font size, we can infer the boundaries of paragraphs, headlines operating at different levels of the hierarchy, and bullet point lists.

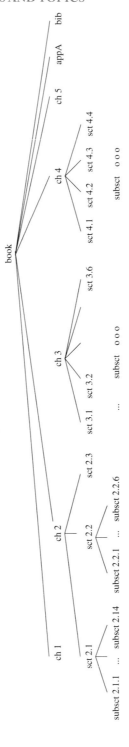

Figure 2.1: Logical document structure of this book (upper part only).

Figure 2.2: Demagnified view of a page of this book.

Logical document structure: "A hierarchy of segments of the document, each of which corresponds to a visually distinguished semantic component of the document. Ancestry in the hierarchy corresponds to containment among document components." [Summers, 1998, p. 2]

Readers familiar with the LATEX document preparation system will have no difficulty in grasping the notion of logical document structure. While text processors such as Microsoft Word allow users to prepare their documents on the level of physical structure ("what you see is what you get"), with LATEX the user specifies the logical structure and largely leaves computation of the physical structure to the processor.[1] Also, early HTML had been criticized for offering an irritating mixture of logical and layout-oriented tags, which then spurred developments in XML technology toward cleaner separation of 'content' and 'presentation'.

For discourse processing, the computation of logical structure for an input document involves two tasks:

- Map the *technical format* of the particular document to some standard XML format, so that subsequent processing modules do not need to worry about different formats. (This also includes a standardization of character encoding.)

- Derive the logical structure as a first representation of document structure.

While these aspects might be kept distinct, it often makes sense to use logical document structure as the 'base layer', whereupon subsequent analysis tasks operate, i.e., add further information. Several approaches (e.g., [Bärenfänger et al., 2006, Göcke and Witt, 2006]) use a subset of the *DocBook*[2]

---

[1] Of course there are exceptions, such as the `vspace` or `newpage` instructions, which directly affect physical structure.
[2] `www.docbook.org`

```
<?xml version='1.0'?>
<article>
  <info>
    <title>Suffering</title>

<author><firstname>George</firstname><surname>Packer</surname></author>
  </info>
  <para>The night after the earthquake, ...</para>
  <para>The earthquake seemed to follow ... </para>
  ...
  <para>But if Haiti is to change, the ... </para>
</article>
```

Figure 2.3: Skeleton of a (lightweight) DocBook representation of the SUFFERING article.

standard [Walsh and Muellner, 1999] for this purpose. DocBook was originally designed for technical documentation but is now being used for books and articles in a wide variety of genres. Its idea is quite similar to LaTeX, but it is XML-based. Hence, the well-formedness of a document is specified by means of a Relax NG[3] schema and Schematron[4] rules (older versions of DocBook used DTDs). For the purposes of automatic text analysis, some portions of the schema will usually not be needed (e.g., much of the metadata), and common practice therefore is to define a subset that is relevant for the application scenario. For illustration, Figure 2.3 shows the skeleton of a lightweight DocBook representation for SUFFERING.

Deriving the logical document structure can be relatively straightforward when the source document already contains explicit layout information in HTML or some XML format. In the "worst case", text processing has to actually start with a paper document that is subjected to OCR software. Then, all aspects of identifying the logical structure need to be inferred from a representation of physical structure, and irrelevant aspects of physical structure must be filtered in the process. Recall our discussion of Figure 2.2. For this task, Summers [1998] described an algorithm that inspects the vertical and horizontal spacings on the page, as well as other visual clues, in order to identify central aspects of logical document structure.

In case the input is a plain text file, as may for instance result from certain PDF converters, heuristics can be employed for tasks like trying to identify headings and distinguish them from paragraphs. Such rules can consider the proportional length of lines in context; for instance, a short line in between two paragraphs is likely to be a headline, whereas a short line immediately followed by more short lines is not a headline but part of a paragraph that uses hard line breaks for some reason.

---

[3]relaxng.org
[4]www.schematron.org

2.1.2   CONTENT ZONES

Computing the logical document structure may not be very interesting in its own right, but as explained above, for many text genres it is a useful or even necessary step in discovering the structure of the document's *content* as it may be induced by the genre. When the document can be sensibly broken into units that contribute to the overall function of the text, we speak of *content zones*.[5]

Content zone: A continuous portion of a text document that fulfills a functional role for the text as a whole, contributing to the overall message or purpose, as it is characteristic for the genre of the text.

For certain genres, the set of content zones is essentially part of their definition. For example, the vast majority of cooking recipes has two central zones: list of ingredients, and steps of preparing the dish. Most user manuals, rules of the game, or maintenance instructions are similarly schematic, possibly extended by some background information, hints, or warnings. With other genres, specifying content zones in a meaningful way is much more difficult: For articles in magazines, for instance, the variety might be too large to define a sensible inventory of zones that would provide a useful document structure.

For genres where zone analysis makes sense, a decision on recursion is to be made: Are the texts to be characterized just by a flat list of zones, or is a hierarchical structure (by analogy to logical document structure, recall Figure 2.1) appropriate? For instance, in German court decisions, one can find an inventory of four 'global' zones (caption, facts of the case, operative provisions, reasons for the judgement), which in turn are composed of a number of clearly distinguishable 'local' zones (viewpoint of the plaintiff, viewpoint of the defendant, etc.), whose order may vary, though.

From the perspective of the genre theoretician, a text should be completely divided into zones, which is an important aspect of its belonging to that genre. For many practical purposes, however, it might not be necessary to compute a zone label for each and every unit of the text; instead, finding only a limited set of relevant zones (e.g., for information extraction or summarization) may be sufficient. To some extent, the difficulty of finding zones is influenced by the relationship between logical structure and content structure: For "rigid" genres, the logical structure will largely pre-determine the content structure, at least on the abstract level of the zone hierarchy. This is the case for the court decisions mentioned above, since their overall structure is fairly standardized. In the following, we briefly look at two examples where the logical structure is of some help but clearly not decisive for finding content structure.

2.1.3   EXAMPLE: SCIENTIFIC PAPERS

Many text analysis efforts have centered on the genre of scientific papers; we focus here on the work by Teufel and Moens [2002], who aimed at recovering relevant content zones from conference

---

[5]In other work, the same phenomenon is referred to by different terms. Zones have been called *moves* [Swales, 1990] and *stages* [Martin, 1984]; the resulting structure is labeled *text type structure* by Bärenfänger et al. [2006].

papers in computational linguistics (which can be seen as one particular sub-genre). Specifically, they identified the following zones that are worth distinguishing, for example for purposes of automatic summarization:

- Aim: research goal of the paper

- Textual: statements about section structure

- Own: description of the authors' work (methodology, results, discussion)

- Background: generally accepted scientific background

- Contrast: comparison with other work

- Basis: statements of agreement with other work

- Other: description of other researchers' work

For annotating a corpus of 80 articles, the instruction was that each sentence had to be given exactly one of the labels, no matter in what section of the paper the sentence appears. It follows that in this case, there is no correspondence between logical document structure and content structure: There will in the end be tendencies for labels appearing in different sections, but the section structure is not an a priori constraint on the task.

To support the annotators, a decision tree was provided where the questions, which para-phrased and extended the short characterizations given above, should lead an annotator transparently to the leaf nodes corresponding to the zone labels. The agreement among the annotators was around 90%, hence quite good.

Given the annotated corpus, naive-Bayes classifiers were built for automating the labeling task. The authors used 16 different features that on the one hand capture surface aspects like the position of the sentence within its section and paragraph, length of the sentence, co-occurrence with words appearing in headlines, 18 categories of formulaic expressions (e.g., *when compared to, following the argument in*), the presence of citations (including a distinction between self-citation and other), and the presence of 'significant' terms according to a *tf.idf* measure. Further, three syntactic features were evaluated: voice, tense, and the presence of modal auxiliaries. The context was modeled with a feature giving the most likely category of the preceding sentence. Finally, as an approximation of a semantic analysis, a hand-crafted verb lexicon was used to determine the action type expressed in the sentence (from an inventory of 20 classes), as well as the agent performing it. This is meant to distinguish between the authors themselves and other researchers, in 13 different verb categories.

The performance of the classifier differs widely between the zones: F-measure ranges from 26% for Contrast to 86% for Own. For a practical application, one would often want to specifically extract particular zones. Some can be identified with fairly good precision and recall, e.g., for the goal of the paper with 57%/79%, and for criticism/contrast sentences with 57%/42%.

2.1.4   EXAMPLE: FILM REVIEWS

Most newspapers and a variety of websites[6] regularly publish film reviews, which have a number of obligatory content zones (such as the title of the film, the director, a description of the story, comments on the film, the overall rating assigned by the author, etc.) and several optional ones (such as the cast, runtime, opening date, etc.). See Figure 2.4 for illustration. There are certain tendencies for ordering the zones, but not very many. Hence, instances of this text genre belong to the class of semi-structured text.

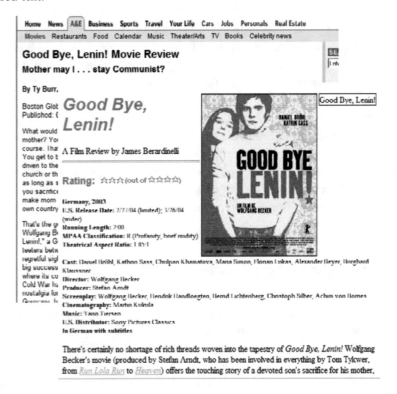

Figure 2.4: Examples of online film reviews.

Bieler et al. [2007] describe an approach for breaking such documents down into their content zones. Based on a corpus study involving 213 texts from seven different (German) websites, they built an inventory of 24 *formal* zones (short elements that frequently or always occur in this genre) and several *functional* zones (paragraphs that serve the author's communicative purpose). These functional zones are further divided into *describe* and *comment* zones: The former contain neutral descriptions of the story or other aspects of the film, whereas the latter contain the authors' subjective

---

[6]We are referring here not to user-generated reviews (e.g., www.epinions.com) but to (semi-) professional reviews that appear in somewhat standardized formats (e.g., www.filmcritic.com).

evaluations. In the corpus, it turned out there was usually no mixture of describing and commenting within the same paragraph. The describe- and comment-paragraphs, however, appear in widely different orderings in the texts.

The formal zones are identified by weighted, symbolic rules that combine simple keyword search via regular expressions (for zones such as cast or copyright notice) with information about likely positions of the zones, both in absolute and in relative terms, i.e., which zones tend to be adjacent to one another, as determined from the corpus. Some of the formal zones can be identified perfectly, because they always have unique keywords (rating, audience restrictions), others are much more difficult: The title of the film, for instance, regularly appears somewhere at the top of the review but can easily be confused with a tagline or short teaser; the program yielded merely a precision of 61% and recall of 65% for this zone. However, the implementation described in the paper does not evaluate HTML tags but takes the input as plain text—clearly, taking the markup into account is very likely to improve the accuracy.

The distinction between describe- and comment-paragraphs, on the other hand, was performed by supervised machine learning. There were no features used other than the plain text. Instead of word tokens or lemmas, character 5-grams as obtained with a moving-window approach were used as terms. With a support vector machine classifier, an accuracy of 79% for making the basic distinction between 'subjective' and 'objective' paragraphs was achieved, i.e., the finer distinctions as to what aspect was described or commented on were not targeted.

2.2   TOPIC-BASED SEGMENTATION

2.2.1   INTRODUCTION: "WHAT IS THIS ALL ABOUT?"

Logical document structure and content zones are often useful for segmentation, but sometimes they turn out to be not really applicable: Documents characterized by long passages of running text can have little (or, occasionally, no) layout-induced or functional structuring. SUFFERING is an example – the only means of structuring to be found are the headlines at the beginning, and the paragraph breaks. Still, just like any other coherent text, SUFFERING has its internal structure on the basis of *topics* and *subtopics* that the reader can recognize and relate to one another, and that collectively render the text a unified whole. In this case, the text begins with observations of individual people in various places (paragraph 1), followed by a more general description of what had happened (§2). Then the text turns to the role of God in Haiti, citing views of a journalist and a housekeeper (§3), that of an American televangelist (§4), and that of U.S. President Obama (§5). This in turn leads on to an examination of humanitarianism and the goals of helping Haiti (§6), which contrasts with an assessment of the political situation (§7), leading in the end to a call for a new approach toward rebuilding the country (§8). Altogether, in SUFFERING the topic structure corresponds quite nicely to the paragraph structure.

In general, however, recognizing the (sub-) topics and the boundaries between the text segments corresponding to them, is not an easy task, and moreover the notion of topic is not easy to define. First of all, some formal decisions have to be made. It is sensible to assume that a topic structure covers the text completely, i.e., we do not want some portions of the text be left out of that structure. Next, from a computational perspective, we prefer not to allow overlap among segments. For the reader (or the literary scholar) this might become problematic since some texts might very well display a more interwoven topic structure, with one topic only slowly giving way to the next. For our purposes, though, we assume fixed boundaries between neighboring segments. Finally, an important question is whether a topic structure should be hierarchical or flat; that is, whether a topic segment may recursively include smaller segments devoted to subtopics. This includes "envelope" structures where the topic temporarily shifts to a subtopic (or a completely separate one) and then reverts to the original one. Here is an example from the MUC-4 corpus, quoted by Manning [1998]:

Example 2.1   (a) A bomb exploded last night in downtown Bogota. (b) Three people were injured, none seriously. (c) This comes after an incident 3 days ago when a police station was damaged. (d) Two vehicles were also destroyed. (e) Yesterday's attack was condemned by officials. (f) Police are searching for two hooded men.

Observing that sentences (c-d) are devoted to a subtopic that is embedded in the main topic of the report, Manning concluded that for information extraction purposes, a hierarchical topic structure should be computed, and several general theories of discourse structure do indeed argue for the necessity of hierarchies (to which we will turn in Chapter 4). However, the vast majority of computational approaches to topic-based segmentation opt for a flat structure, for the simple reasons that a hierarchy is considerably more difficult to determine automatically, and for many practical purposes a flat partitioning of the text is sufficient. In the following, we will largely adhere to this view, and only toward the end, in Section 2.2.5, mention a recent approach to hierarchical modeling.

> **Topic-induced text structure:** A sequence of non-overlapping text segments that completely covers the text, i.e., a partitioning. Each unit consists of one or more sentences that address a common topic.

Experiments and evaluation   The fact that we have not given a definition for 'topic' yet is not an accident. The research literature offers little more than describing the topic of a text (segment) as the entity that the text (segment) "is about", which is hardly more precise. When writing guidelines for human annotators, it therefore is common practice to merely briefly appeal to their intuition, rather than trying to compile extensive instructions. In an early study by Rotondo [1984], students were given a 2866-word excerpt from a Biology textbook, as printed with the original layout, and Rotondo asked them to mark those points in the text where they felt one 'complete thought' ended and another began. Rotondo does not offer any quantitative analysis, but states that—on the encouraging side—each subject tries to segment at a consistent level of analysis, and there also appears to be a fair amount of hierarchical consistency: "If subject i marks fewer boundaries than subject j then there is a tendency for the set of subject i's boundaries to be a subset of the boundaries marked by subject j." [Rotondo, 1984, p. 84] On the whole, though, he also noted considerable variety in segment sizes and locations. Stark [1988] asked subjects to re-instate paragraph breaks in texts where they have been removed. This is a slightly different task, but since the texts were expository essays, the 'complete thought' criterion seems to apply here quite well. For three different essays, the overall accuracy achieved by the subjects ranged from 22% to 60%, indicating that the task is rather difficult; agreement was also relatively low. Kan et al. [1998] had several judges segment 20 news articles and found that the average agreement of judges with the majority opinion is only 62.4%. Working with very different data, spoken monologue narratives that are broken into prosodic phrases, Passonneau and Litman [1997] asked annotators to mark boundaries with the criterion that a segment correspond to an informal notion of a single 'speaker intention'; the instructions did not mention any linguistic features as hints for possible boundaries. The authors provide a comprehensive discussion of the quantitative evaluation task and conclude that, with their somewhat 'special' data, and using an atheoretical notion of speaker intention, they achieve highly significant agreement on segment boundaries across subjects.

Topic segmentation thus is largely a matter of intuition, and so it is not easy to create a human-annotated gold standard against which algorithms can be evaluated. Some influential studies (e.g., [Hearst, 1997, Litman and Passonneau, 1995]) took a majority-vote approach, postulating that a segment boundary is to be set at a particular position when at least three out of seven annotators marked a boundary there. Obviously, this is a costly procedure, and thus no large human-annotated corpora with topic breaks are available so far. Instead, data is usually created by concatenating a number of different articles into one long file, so that the task of the algorithm is to re-create the original boundaries. This can be made more or less difficult by taking the texts from the same or from different domains and genres. From a purely technical viewpoint, this is a clever way out of the data dilemma, but it has only limited value for our understanding of topic change signals *within* a text.

Assuming, anyway, the existence of gold standard data, one can evaluate an algorithm using the usual measures of precision (how many postulated boundaries also appear in the gold standard) and recall (how many of the gold standard boundaries have been found). However, as Beeferman et al. [1999] pointed out, this method has a severe disadvantage, as it fails to differentiate between a "near miss" and a totally-misplaced segment boundary. Sometimes, topics don't change very abruptly; instead, there may be a sentence that simultaneously closes off the old topic and initiates a new one, so that the boundary may be marked before or after it. (To some extent, this is the case for sentence 5.4 in SUFFERING, which finishes the White House/Obama episode but at the same time provides a link to the role of humanitarianism in allocating foreign aid.) But when an algorithm postulates a boundary one segment beside a gold standard boundary, this will reduce both the precision and the recall result. An algorithm that misses the boundary altogether, on the other hand, gets penalized only on the recall side and hence will achieve better results. Thus, precision and recall do not seem to be optimal measurements for most segmentation tasks where assigning a near-miss boundary is to be preferred over assigning no boundary at all.

As an alternative evaluation metric, Beeferman et al. [1999] suggest to move a window across the text, stepping from one sentence to the next, and, for each pair of sentences constructed from the two ends of the window, to count whether they are correctly placed in the same segment or not. That is, the placement of the pair as assigned by the algorithm (same segment or different segments) is compared to the pair in the gold standard, and for each disagreement, a counter is increased by one. As window size, the authors suggest half of the average length of the segments in the corpus. In the end, the counter is divided by the number of probes taken and thus normalized to a value between 0 and 1; if the algorithm yields 0, all segment pairs were correctly handled and therefore all boundaries were correctly identified.[7]

Even though topics are difficult to define in linguistic terms, and settling on an evaluation method is not straightforward, deriving a topic-based segmentation automatically is an attractive goal. It has been argued to be useful, for example, in information retrieval (leading to improved measures for document relevance, see [Reynar, 1997]) or for text summarization (e.g., [Barzilay and Elhadad, 1997, Farzindar and Lapalme, 2004]), where the idea is that all the important topics addressed in the text should in some way be mentioned in the summary.

2.2.2   EXPLOITING SURFACE CUES

Cohesion   From the linguistic perspective, the phenomenon of local discourse "continuity" is that of *cohesion*: Sentences are connected to one another not only underneath the surface (by coherence, thus requiring understanding and interpretation) but also by more-readily identifiable linguistic signals.[8] The most prominent ones are the following:

- **Connectives:** *Jim went over to the garage. And then the door opened.*
  Causal (e.g., *thus, therefore*), additive (e.g., *moreover, also*), temporal (e.g., *afterwards, later*), and contrastive (e.g., *but, still*) connectives create strong cohesive ties. (They will be explained in detail in Section 4.3.1.)

- **Word repetition:** *Jim went over to the garage. What does he need a garage for, anyway?*
  When the same word shows up again in the text, this creates a cohesive link and can be interpreted as topic continuity.

- **Related words:** *Jim went over to the garage. He opened the door slowly.*
  While repetition amounts to the *identity* relation between two words, other important relations that create *lexical cohesion* are *synonymy*, *hyponymy* (the meaning of one word subsumes that of another), or *meronymy* (part-whole), as in the example just given.

- **Pronouns:** *Jim went over to the garage. He opened the door slowly.*
  Interpreting a pronoun means identifying its antecedent expression, which is most often found in the same or the previous sentence; thus a pronoun can create a strong link to the previous

---

[7]For an in-depth study of this metric and a proposed modification, see [Pevzner and Hearst, 2002].
[8]The classical linguistics textbook on cohesion is [Halliday and Hasan, 1976].

discourse. (The task of pronoun resolution will be covered in Chapter 3.) When material is *elided*, the effect is even stronger—but more difficult to recognize automatically.

Cohesion: A central phenomenon of 'textuality': Sentences and clauses are connected to one another by a variety of linguistic means that can be identified at the text surface. Thus, noting cohesion does not require deep understanding of the text.

So the basic hypotheses are that (i) signals of cohesion in text serve as indicators of topic continuity (with certain exceptions, as noted), and conversely, that (ii) the absence of cohesive ties indicates a topic shift. All four types of signals mentioned above will be taken up in this and the following subsections; for connectives, we will notice that their role for topic dis/continuity is not quite as straightforward as for the others. But before we turn to lexical signals of topic structure, we briefly consider a non-lexical one that immediately follows from logical document structure: paragraph breaks. At first sight, they appear to be very relevant for topic segmentation, but their contribution is not always clear, as the rules or tendencies for breaking text into paragraphs can differ widely between genres and also between authors.[9] In newspapers, for instance, decisions on paragraph breaks depend not solely on content, but also on goals of rhetorical effect, and on layout constraints. In general, topics can easily span across more than a single paragraph, and hence a break is obviously not a *sufficient* criterion for a topic shift. For genres with highly-conventionalized paragraph structure, they could be regarded as a *necessary* criterion, though (i.e., topic shift positions amount to a subset of the paragraph breaks); SUFFERING, as pointed out earlier, is actually a good example.

Cue words   For a number of genres, one can identify a set of specific words or phrases that are quite typically used to close off a topic, or to start a new one. Reynar [1997], for instance, works with transcriptions of broadcast news, and his list of genre-specific cues includes the phrases *joining us, good evening, welcome back* as indicators of topic opening, and *brought to you by, this is (person name)* as indicators of topic closing. Given an annotated corpus, such terms can be extracted and then used for the segmentation task.

Moving a step beyond such very specific cues, Kauchak and Chen [2005] analyzed various *narratives* and found that, on the one hand, no single word could serve as a reliable cue of a segment beginning or end. On the other hand, certain *groups* of words occur significantly at the beginning of segments. These include groups that are intuitively plausible: months, days, temporal phrases, and country names. We would expect that these often serve to indicate a shift of scene in a story. Other groups mentioned by the authors, however, e.g., military rankings, seem to be quite specific to particular story domains.

More challenging is the problem of finding largely genre-neutral cues that can help in segmenting a larger variety of texts. One proposal to this end was made by Passonneau and Litman

---

[9]See [Stark, 1988] for a linguistic-pragmatic overview of the "paragraph problem". She points out that some scholars in fact regard paragraph breaks as essentially arbitrary and unpredictable. (Again, such statements ought to consider dependency on genres.)

Table 2.1: Excerpt from cue word list by Hirschberg and Litman [1993].

actually	also	although	and	basically	because
but	essentially	except	finally	first	further
generally	however	indeed	like	look	next
no	now	ok	or	otherwise	right

[1997] who used a list of cues from work by Hirschberg and Litman [1993]. An excerpt from that list is shown in Table 2.1. The genre to which Passonneau and Litman applied this list was a bit unusual, though: transcripts of oral narrations of a given story. The narrations were broken down into units corresponding to prosodic phrases (hence: usually shorter than sentences). Then, the cue word feature was set to 1 if and only if one of the cues appeared as the very first word in a phrase. In this setting, an algorithm that reconstructs topic breaks from the cue words alone yielded a recall of 72% and a precision of 15%. This means that most topic segments indeed start with a cue but that the cues are much too frequent to yield an acceptable precision.

The role of connectives   It is not straightforward to see how this cue-based approach could generalize to written text genres. For one thing, notice the heterogeneity of the cue word list in Table 2.1: It includes connectives (in the narrow sense: closed-class lexical items that semantically denote two-place relations and serve to link two expressions usually denoting an eventuality—see Section 4.3), certain adverbials that semantically take only one argument (e.g., *essentially*), and discourse particles that are typical for spoken language (e.g., *ok*). The only group that could potentially be helpful with written text is the connectives. Next, there are problems with ambiguity: Many of these words have both a *discourse reading* and a *sentential reading* [Hirschberg and Litman, 1993], such as *right* (uptake particle versus direction adjective) or *further* (discourse structure marker versus ordinary adjective).

Regarding the connectives proper, there is temptation to treat them as indicators of cohesion and hence of topic continuity—which, interestingly, would amount to using them in the opposite way that Passonneau and Litman did (recall that they hypothesized a topic break right before one of their cue words). This results directly from the ambiguity problem: Many connectives can also be used as uptake particles (e.g., *so, because*) and thus in transcribed speech can serve a very different function from that of a connective in written text.[10] Still, in text, an adverbial connective linking to the preceding sentence (e.g., *therefore*) is clearly a strong cohesion marker. It is less clear, however, whether such adverbials indeed signal topic continuity in all cases. Thus, while a causal connective such as the one starting this sentence (i.e., *thus*) will usually indicate a strong link to the previous context and render a topic break unlikely, a contrastive or an additive connective such as *also* might very well be used in a sentence that initiates a new topic. Cohesion and topic continuity are related phenomena, but they are not identical: When a text moves to a different topic, there might still be cohesive signals present—in particular, as seen, certain connectives. Therefore, a thorough study

---

[10]We will address the problem of disambiguating potential connectives in Section 4.3.2.

Table 2.2: Personal pronouns and their antecedents in SUFFERING.					
Sentence number → Sentence number					
1.2 → 1.2	1.11 → 1.10 (3)	1.12 → 1.11	1.15 → 1.14	1.16 → 1.15 (2)	
2.2 → 2.1	2.3 → 2.2	2.4 → 2.3	3.1 → 3.1	3.3 → 3.3	3.5 → 3.5
4.2 → 4.2	4.3 → 4.2	5.1 → 5.1	5.4 → 5.3	6.3 → 6.3	6.6 → 6.6
7.2 → 7.2	7.3 → 7.3	8.3 → 8.2	8.5 → 8.5		

of connective behaviour at the beginning and end of topic segments, possibly resulting in relevant subcategories, would be needed before they can be trusted as segmentation features.

Pronouns   But connectives are not the only closed-class lexical items of relevance for topic segmentation. Definite *pronouns* have been used in various approaches (e.g., Passonneau and Litman [1997], Reynar [1997]) as indicators of cohesion. The idea is that their presence is a vote against stipulating a segment boundary right before the sentence including the pronoun (with the proviso that a complex sentence may contain both a pronoun and its antecedent). Both approaches mentioned above used the pronoun feature in combination with others, and unfortunately no results on the utility of the pronoun feature in isolation are provided.

For illustration, Table 2.2 shows the connections made by third-person personal pronouns in SUFFERING (thus omitting references to the speaker and to the addressee, and also omitting expletives, as in 8.4 *so be it*). A sentence number on the left of an arrow indicates the presence of a personal pronoun, and the sentence on the right of the arrow is the location of the antecedent.[11] Recall that for this text, we take paragraph boundaries to be the gold standard topic boundaries. The good news is that indeed all pronouns have their antecedents within the same paragraph (and, actually, either within the same sentence or in the immediately preceding sentence), so they function as cohesive devices in the expected way. However, we cannot exploit the mere presence of a pronoun for predicting a non-boundary between the current and the previous sentence because there are several within-sentence antecedents, also at the beginning of paragraphs (in 3.1 and 4.1). For topic segmentation, pronouns therefore need to be handled with care, as in principle they require being resolved to their antecedents in order to be maximally useful (see Section 3.5.2).

2.2.3   LEXICAL CHAINS

The closed-class items we just discussed can provide hints, but their frequency of occurrence is far too low for them to be decisive in a topic segmentation procedure. Accordingly, we have to look into exploiting the open-class, or *content* words for our task. The insight here is that content words in a text do not occur independently of one another but bear *semantic similarity*. To a large extent, this similarity is well-defined through a small set of lexical-semantic relations that dictionaries

---

[11]By convention, we take as antecedent always the *most recent* coreferent expression. See Chapter 3 for a general introduction to coreference.

Table 2.3: Content words from second paragraph of SUFFERING.

earthquake seem follow malignant design
strike metropolitan_area Haiti nine_million people live
flatten headquarter United_Nations mission lead coordinate relief kill U.N. employee report mission_chief
country building code wipe_out neighborhood shoddy concrete structure hospital wreck port airport control_tower action damage key institution Presidential_Palace National_Cathedral kill archbishop senior politician cut_off power phone service block passage street
heavy equipment capital use move debris trap survivor dig mass_grave
go_wrong hospital_manager say

(and semanticists) use to characterize the structure of our vocabulary, and which show up in many implemented thesauri and ontologies. Consider Table 2.3, which lists the content words of the sentences of the second paragraph of SUFFERING, grouped by their sentences. Examples of instances of standard lexical-semantic relations to be found there are:

- (Near-)Synonymy: *United_Nations – U.N.; wipe_out – wreck*

- Hyponymy: *country – Haiti; building – control_tower*

- Meronymy: *airport – control_tower; country – capital*

Other word pairs are similar due to their belonging to the same 'semantic field', but the relation is less regular than in the cases shown above. Examples are *politician – archbishop, wreck – debris*, or *kill – survivor*.

Obviously, the fact that we find such word pairs in a text, and more precisely, within certain portions of a text, is due to the fact that portions of a text deal with a common topic. Turning this observation around then leads to the idea that we can exploit the presence of lexical-semantic relations for our present task: finding the topic-induced text structure.

One way to operationalize this, first proposed by Morris and Hirst [1991], extends the notion of the word pair to that of a *lexical chain*: a sequence of words, taken in linear order from the text, whose neighbors are semantically related. Such a chain would capture not just an arbitrary snapshot of the topicality phenomenon (like the individual word pair does) but in fact serve as a record of a topic's (or subtopic's) presence in a text. Looking again at Table 2.3, we can extract the sequence of words belonging to the lexical field 'disaster':

earthquake - strike - flatten - relief - wipe_out - wreck - damage - kill - cut_off - block - go_wrong

Now, the idea is that determining all such lexical chains for a text will allow us to compute segment boundaries on the basis of chain boundaries: Intuitively, a point in the text where certain chains stop and certain chains begin is much more likely to constitute a topic segment boundary than a point where a number of chains pass through. To make this more precise, we need to consider several details: (i) where does information on lexical relations come from; (ii) how exactly are chains formed; and (iii) how are the segment boundaries computed from the chains? As a prerequisite, note that when speaking about 'words' in the rest of this chapter, we are referring to morphologically-analyzed units (lemmas or stems), and not to individual word forms.

Resources for lexical-semantic relations   In their pioneering experiment, Morris and Hirst [1991] used *Roget's Thesaurus* for their manual analyses that demonstrated the utility of lexical chains for text segmentation. The thesaurus offers a structured account of the vocabulary of English, grouping it into 1042 categories, with three levels of hierarchy above them. For example, the path to the word *viability* is: Matter — Organic Matter — Vitality — Life: life, living, vitality, viability, ... The categories themselves are further structured into words belonging to different syntactic parts of speech, and also into subgroups that are considered particularly similar; such subgroups may then contain pointers to related categories or to subgroups. Finally, the thesaurus offers an index that for any word lists its various readings (word senses), which are identified by a category and the position therein. So, Roget's Thesaurus (unlike similar printed resources such as guidebooks to synonyms or antonyms) does not name any specific lexical relations, but simply offers an account of 'relatedness' by means of its hierarchical structure plus the pointers between categories. The two most useful configurations exploited by Morris and Hirst were (i) two words having a category in common in their index entries (e.g., both *residentiality* and *apartment* have category 189 in their respective lists); and (ii) one word in its index having a category that contains a pointer to the category of the other word. These, and three other less frequently used configurations, served for making the decision on whether two words are related and thus should participate in a lexical chain.

For actually implementing such an approach, the obvious resource nowadays is WordNet[12] or any of its various adaptations to other languages. Several researchers have described algorithms for deriving lexical chains with the help of WordNet. Since it offers a fairly wide range of lexical relations between *synsets* (sets of words with very similar meaning), it is not trivial to decide whether two given words are related and thus should take part in a chain. In essence, the problem is to compute the shortest path between the words and then to classify that path as un/related. This invites experimentation, and for that purpose, Teich and Fankhauser [2005] describe a tool that allows for flexibly annotating texts with WordNet chains, based on configurable settings that allow for specifying maximum path lengths and relations to be used (synonymy, hyperonymy, hyponymy, antonymy, and various kinds of meronymy). Thus, the effects of different settings can be explored easily by inspecting the resulting chains in the text under scrutiny.

---

[12]wordnet.princeton.edu

Building lexical chains   The task of building chains essentially breaks down into three questions: Which words are to be considered as candidates at all? Under what circumstances should two candidate words be classified as 'related'? Which of the existing chains is chosen for a new word to attach to, and in what way is that word integrated into the chain?

As for candidate words, most researchers limit their attention to nouns (the class that WordNet has the most information on). A pre-processing step thus is to identify all the noun lemmas (or stems) in a text, which then constitute the search space for chain building. We ignore here the issue of handling multi-word expressions (compound nouns, complex named entities).

The question when to consider two words as 'related' on the one hand requires a threshold on the allowed distance in the text. Hirst and St-Onge [1998], for example, set this threshold depending on the strength of the computed semantic relatedness to three sentences (for weakly related words), seven sentences (for strongly related words), and unlimited (for the special case of word repetition). The issue of deciding on their semantic relatedness, on the other hand, is more intricate than it might appear at first sight because it subsumes the problem of word sense disambiguation: For deciding whether *keyboard* is related to *screen*, one needs to determine whether the keyboard is a "device consisting of a set of keys on a piano ... or a computer or the like" or a "holder consisting of an arrangement of hooks on which keys or locks can be hung" (WordNet 3.0), and whether a screen is indeed one of the things the reader will probably have in mind now, or maybe the thing described in WordNet sense 4 as "a covering that serves to conceal or shelter something". WordNet is notorious for usually giving rather many word senses (for $screen_{noun}$, it offers nine), so disambiguation is in fact a severe problem. The solution proposed by Barzilay and Elhadad [1997] is to maintain a search space of alternative 'interpretations' of the text, where an interpretation is defined as an assignment of a single word sense to each word that has been processed so far, with links between those word senses that according to a WordNet path computation are considered as related. Relatedness can be of different strength, and the authors have experimentally settled on three weight categories: 10 for word reiteration and synonymy; 7 for antonymy; and 4 for hyperonymy and meronymy. The sum of the link weights then defines the overall score of an interpretation: The more and the stronger the links between word senses, the higher ranked is the interpretation. To control the exponential growth in the number of interpretations when moving through the text and adding new word senses to interpretations (and creating new interpretations), weak interpretations are pruned from the search space. Still, the procedure is very costly, and a much more efficient variant of this algorithm, which is in fact linear in time and space, was later suggested by Silber and McCoy [2002].

Let us illustrate the basic idea with the beginning of paragraph 2 of SUFFERING. For computing relatedness, we use a simple length threshold on WordNet paths, as computed with the *WordNet Connect* tool[13], using all the semantic relations. We treat words as related when the shortest path has no more than 5 nodes; and we set the weight to 5−(length of the path). Then, the higher the overall weight, the more preferred is the interpretation.

---

[13] dingo.sbs.arizona.edu/~sandiway/wnconnect/ (Dec 20, 2010; notice that this application is based on an older version of WordNet)

The first eight nouns in the paragraph are, in this order: *earthquake, design, area, Haiti, people, headquarters, mission, lead*. The first word, *earthquake*, has two WordNet senses (geological, metaphorical), so we start with two alternative interpretations. *Design* has seven different readings, and the path to *earthquake* has 13 nodes, so the two words are not related. We build $2\times7=14$ interpretations with (unrelated) word sense pairs. The next word, *area*, has six readings, yielding a total of $14\times6=84$ interpretations. Path-length from *earthquake* to *area* is 12, and from *design* to *area* it is 5, singling out the readings (design/decoration/ornament) and (area/structure/construction). Thus, we establish an edge in the interpretations involving these readings, with weight $5-5=0$. *Haiti* has a single reading and is related to a sense of *area* (path length is 4, hence weight is 1), but not to any of the other words. The number of interpretations stays the same, *Haiti* is added to all of them, with weighted links for those involving the right sense of *area*. And so forth. With the next words, short paths are found between senses of *mission* (five senses in total) and *headquarters* (three senses in total), and between *mission* and *lead* (17 senses in total). Interestingly, WordNet (in the version provided with *WordNet connect*) offers no short path between *headquarters* and *lead*. Overall, we are clearly facing an enormous search space here, so that a clever implementation is needed, as mentioned above.

In summary, when moving through the text, for each candidate word we need to decide whether it should (potentially) start a new chain, or be attached to one of the chains already computed. A distance threshold needs to be defined for this decision, which ensures that chains can in fact come to an end, and a new chain with similar words might re-start later (the issue of so-called 'chain returns'). The linking decision depends on word sense disambiguation, and furthermore it should ideally not just be a local decision. When a word is compared only to the candidate predecessor and not to the other words in that chain, we may run into transitivity problems, as illustrated by Morris and Hirst [1991] with the example *cow – sheep – wool – scarf – boots – hat – snow*. While all adjacent words can be argued to be related in one way or another, *cow* and *snow* clearly should not.

Individual links may receive a weight, which depends for instance on linear distance between the words and between the length of the WordNet path. Often, word repetition is weighted higher than a semantic relation between distinct words. Other factors may be added; for example, Okumura and Honda [1994] in their work on Japanese increase the weight when a word bears the topic marker *wa*, under the assumption that the resulting chain will reflect the discourse topic better than others. So, on the basis of link weights, weights can be computed for the complete chains as well, reflecting chain length, density, and strength of the individual links.

Some implementations of lexical chaining modules have been made available by their developers, for instance one by Michael Galley at Columbia University.[14] Waltinger et al. [2008] describe an implemented chainer that is able to integrate different lexical resources for computing similarity. This tool is integrated into the *e-Humanities Desktop*[15] [Gleim et al., 2009] for text analysis. An excerpt of the WordNet-based graph for SUFFERING as computed by that tool is shown in Figure

---

[14]`www1.cs.columbia.edu/nlp/tools.cgi` (Jan 13, 2011)
[15]`hudesktop.hucompute.org` (Jan 13, 2011)

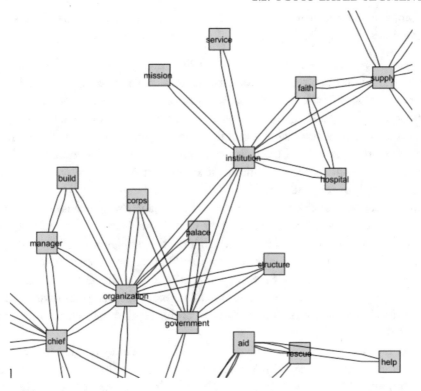

Figure 2.5: Excerpt from lexical-chain graph for SUFFERING, using software from Waltinger et al. [2008].

2.5. The nodes now need to be related back to the word positions in the text, and a decision on the linear-distance threshold has to be added, so that the linear chains for the text can be constructed.

Lexical chain: List of content words that appear sequentially in the text, with some maximum linear distance between adjacent words, and that bear a pairwise semantic relation to one another. A chain (possibly in conjunction with other chains covering the same span) can be taken to represent a (sub-)topic that is being discussed in the corresponding span of text.

The issue of word similarity and relatedness (which also includes antonymy and more indirect associations) is central to many tasks in language processing and has received much attention. For the interested reader, Pedersen et al. [2007] discuss the transfer of WordNet-based methods to a biomedical ontology; Budanitksy and Hirst [2006] provide a general overview of both WordNet-based and other methods for computing lexical similarity/relatedness and methods of their evaluation. A comparative implementation of various measures has been provided by Pedersen in the WordNet::Similarity package[16].

Determining chain-induced segment boundaries   When lexical chains have been built for a text, we are left with the task of determining topic boundaries. A fairly obvious measure here (applied by [Okumura and Honda, 1994, Stokes et al., 2004] and others) is to compute a 'boundary strength' at every sentence break by adding the number of chains ending in the sentence right before the break, and the number of chains beginning in the following sentence. Given the resulting ranking of sentence boundaries, the top n of them can be postulated as segment boundaries, where n can be set to the mean of all boundary scores. With this straightforward procedure, and the individual links computed quite simply by class membership in a thesaurus, Okumura and Honda [1994] reported a recall of 52% and precision of 25% for the genre of essays in Japanese, which is not really satisfactory. The measure can be extended by also accounting for the number of chains passing through the sentence boundary. Further, if chains have been weighted, these weights obviously would replace the mere counts. And the computed sentence boundary ranking can be mapped to a segment boundary ranking in more elaborate ways, too. Several approaches compare the sentence boundary's value to those of the neighboring boundary values in order to look at the *change* in values and thereby to avoid a merely local minimum. This follows the idea of the 'depth score', which will be explained in the next subsection.

The fact that a single lexical link might very well be misleading (similar to the issue with the cohesive connectives) was illustrated by Manning [1998] with the 'Bogota' text shown as Example 2.1 at the beginning of this section (page 17). There is clearly a semantic similarity between the expressions *3 days ago* and *yesterday*, and one between *injured* and *damaged*, yet establishing links between sentences (2) and (3) and between (3) and (4) would be somewhat misleading since different events are being described, which in Manning's view, should be reflected in the topic segmentation.

2.2.4   WORD DISTRIBUTIONS

The approaches to segmentation based on lexical chains presented in the previous section all rely on the availability of some lexical resource that provides the semantic relations. In this section, we turn to more surface-oriented methods that tackle the topic segmentation problem without relying on rich external resources, but still explore lexical cohesion as the key feature. The basic idea is quite straightforward: When an author stays on topic, we assume that she keeps using the same words; when she switches to a new topic, we assume that new words will be used. Thus, we have two potentially fruitful features: word repetition (as a simple variant of calculating semantic similarity between words), and the sudden appearance of new words.

Word repetition   Can the mere repetition of words (here: lemmas, stems) help with topic segmentation? Reynar [1994] had shown that at least for the task of separating different concatenated articles, this single feature can deliver promising results, using a technique of optimising the density

---

[16]www.d.umn.edu/~tpederse/similarity.html (Dec 10, 2010)

of regions in a *dotplot* of the text (see Figure 2.7 below, showing a plot resulting from a slightly different approach). In order to reduce noise, he removed from the text not only the function words but also certain high-frequency and semantically vacuous verbs like *to be* and *to have*. The task is to compute in the matrix the regions of high density that can be taken to represent a topic segment.

From a different viewpoint, determining repeated words is just a "degenerate" form of lexical chaining, and the above observations on determining boundaries apply here just as well. Since the number of links will be much smaller, one needs to adjust the distance threshold for chain inclusion, though. Galley et al. [2003], for example, experimentally found that with their data, a gap of 11 sentences or less should be allowed for adding a word to its predecessor, and otherwise a new chain is being started. These authors also experimented with different weighting functions for chains, and suggest that a chain containing more repeated terms and spanning a smaller number of sentences is more indicative of a topical unit. Their formula for thus combining frequency and *compactness* is:

$$weight(chain_i) = freq(t_i) * \log\left(\frac{length(text)}{length(chain_i)}\right) \qquad (2.1)$$

where t_i is the word of the underlying $chain_i$, and $length$ is computed as the number of sentences.

Interestingly, several researchers report that for relatively simple tasks, using merely word repetition yields results no worse than with the (computationally costly) step of adding WordNet relations (Kan et al. [1998] on classifying existing paragraph boundaries as topic boundaries) or even considerably better ones (Choi [2000], Stokes et al. [2004] on recreating breaks between articles in concatenations; Galley et al. [2003] on segmenting transcriptions of meetings, a somewhat more difficult task).

Vocabulary shifts   When we take the two hypotheses 'word identity = topic continuity' and 'word change = topic switch' a step further, we arrive at an idea that had already been formulated by Skorochod'ko [1972]: Divide the text into sentences, count the overlap in content words between neighboring sentences, and postulate topic boundaries on the basis of these overlap counts. In this vein, Youmans [1991] undertook a thorough descriptive (linguistic) study. He proposed to use a *type/token curve* to study vocabulary usage in narratives and essays, and found that a sharp upturn of that curve tended to correlate with a shift of information flow in the text (e.g., the narrative moves to a new scene). This idea was later implemented by Nomoto and Nitta [1994] and by Hearst [1997], who used the term *text tiling* for her procedure of dividing a text into a sequence of non-overlapping segments that are characterized by a common (sub-)topic. From information retrieval, Hearst borrowed the idea of representing a text as a high-dimensional vector space, and applied this to successive *portions* of the text, so that computing word overlap between these portions amounts to computing the distance between vectors. Hearst tested the method on *expository* text and hints at the possibility that other types (such as descriptive, instructive, narrative) might not be as amenable to the approach: The typical expository text explains or demonstrates a certain notion by successively exploring different aspects or parts of the notion, which often nicely correlates with shifts in vocabulary that the method can identify. Many narratives or descriptions, on the other hand, have a more subtly inter-woven structure.

The two phases of the text tiling algorithm are the same as in the lexical chaining approaches: Similarity determination is followed by boundary postulation.

Similarity determination   Hearst's algorithm does not work with sentences as minimal units, since the differences in length might skew the comparisons. Instead, 'pseudosentences' with a fixed size of w tokens are defined as the minimal units, where w is one parameter of the algorithm; Hearst states that $w = 20$ has been a good choice in her experiments. The second parameter k is the number of adjacent pseudosentences that are concatenated to form a 'block', which is the unit for computing lexical overlap. The recommendation is to set it to the average length of paragraphs in the text (measured in pseudosentences), and again, a value is given that fared good in experiments: $k = 6$. Hearst does not encourage reverting to the actual paragraph structure of the text, since they can differ in length and thus skew the distributions (the same argument that was used against sentences).

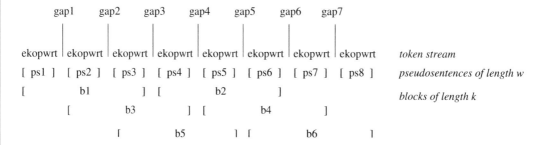

Figure 2.6: Text tiling [Hearst, 1997].

For every gap between two pseudosentences, a similarity measure is computed for the blocks that meet at that gap—see Figure 2.6. In effect, a window with the length of $2 * k$ pseudosentences is moved through the text, and at each step (pseudosentence), the similarity score is determined between the two blocks: The more words the blocks have in common, the higher the score for the gap. In this moving window approach, each pseudosentence is used in $2 * k$ comparisons.

For the comparison itself, Hearst experimented with different formulas. Her proposal is to compute word overlap via a normalized inner product, the *cosine metric*:

$$score(gap_i) = \frac{\sum_t w_{t,b1} w_{t,b2}}{\sqrt{\sum_t w_{t,b1}^2 \sum_t w_{t,b2}^2}} \tag{2.2}$$

where t ranges over all the content words in the text (function words are not being considered) and $w_{t,b}$ is the weight assigned to the word in the block $b1$ or $b2$, respectively. In the simple form of the algorithm, this weight is equal to the plain frequency of the word in the block. The normalization maps the score to the interval between 0 and 1. Other researchers have explored more intricate weighting functions. For example, Dias et al. [2007] argue that word relevance should also depend on inverse document frequency *idf*, as known from information retrieval, thus factoring in the word's frequency in a collection of reference documents. Furthermore, they propose to look at the distribution of the word across the complete individual document instead of making only a local comparison (a point that has also been made by Choi [2000]) and to that end, they suggest a variant of the *tf.idf* measure for sentences. The intuition is to "punish" a word that occurs frequently all over the text, because its distribution in two adjacent blocks can be expected to be less informative than that of words occurring only in the region under investigation. Their *tf.isf* measure considers the frequency of a word in a sentence (or a Hearst-type pseudosentence) *s* in relation to its frequency in other sentences:

$$tf.isf(word) = \frac{stf(word, s)}{|s|} * \ln \frac{Ns}{sf(word)} \tag{2.3}$$

Here, $stf(word, s)$ is the frequency of *word* in *s*, $|s|$ the number of words in *s*, $sf(word)$ the number of sentences in which *word* occurs, and Ns the number of sentences in the document. A word occurring in every sentence of the document will have a *tf.isf* value of 0, whereas a word that is frequent in one sentence but rare in the other sentences gets a high score. Dias et al. proceed to calculate the weight of a word from various factors including *tf.idf* and *tf.isf*; the overall weight can then be used, for instance, in Hearst's scoring function for block gaps.

Hearst [1997] had compared her scoring function to a variant of Youmans's method (vocabulary introduction, mentioned above). Here, the score of gap *i* results from adding the number of first usages of words in the two pseudosentences *p*1 and *p*2 meeting at the gap, and normalizing by the overall size of the two pseudosentences, so that the result is again a number between 0 and 1.

$$score(gap_i) = \frac{NumNewWords(p1) + NumNewWords(p2)}{w * 2} \tag{2.4}$$

Hearst found that in general, the algorithm using the block comparison achieved somewhat better results than the version with vocabulary introduction.

Boundary postulation   With scores assigned to each gap between two adjacent pseudosentences, the second task is to decide which of these gaps should be regarded as a topic boundary. Intuitively, when plotting the gap scores, we are looking for 'valleys', because they are characterized by a low lexical overlap between the blocks, while on either side there is a high overlap. The significance of a valley is expressed by its 'depth score', which Hearst computes as the sum of the differences in the y coordinates of the neighboring peaks in the plot:

$$depth(gap_i) = (y_{i-1} - y_i) + (y_{i+1} - y_i) \tag{2.5}$$

Several special cases need to be considered here, such as the role of "plateau valleys", where the depth score might need adjustment—the reader is referred to the discussion in [Hearst, 1997, p. 50]. At any rate, some formula for (modest) smoothing is to be applied, in order to remove small dips. Other methods for computing the significance of gaps can be conceived, such as looking at the steepness of the function surrounding a valley; see, e.g., [Dias et al., 2007].

When each gap has been assigned a significance (here: a depth score), the n top-ranked gaps are being postulated as topic boundaries for the text. Hence, we have a final parameter for the procedure, n. Hearst advises against simple thresholds depending solely on text length or something similar, and instead suggests defining the cutoff as a function of the depth score range, using their average $\bar{s}$ and standard deviation σ (under the assumption that they have a normal distribution). One such function would assign a boundary only if the depth score exceeds $\bar{s} - \sigma$. When making the boundary decisions, it usually makes sense to avoid creating very short topic segments, i.e., to enforce a minimum distance between the boundaries.

As the final step, we have to revert the initial decision of using 'pseudosentences': Our computed topic boundaries will usually be in the middle of actual sentences of the text, so we have to calculate for each boundary the closest "real" sentence break to the right or left of the pseudo-boundary we found.

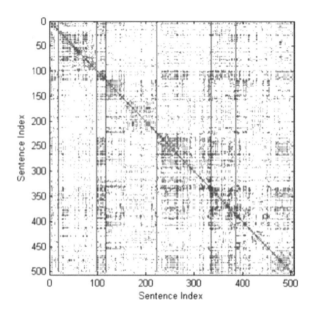

Figure 2.7: Sentence similarity plot (from [Malioutov and Barzilay, 2006, p. 26]).

Hearst's pioneering work on knowledge-free and hence genre- and domain-independent topic segmentation has initiated a lot of later research, which resulted in slight variations of text tiling, and also in some rather different approaches, of which we briefly mention a few here. Choi [2000] took up the idea of Reynar [1994], mentioned above, who represented the text with a similarity matrix (Figure 2.7). In Choi's framework, both axes represent the sequence of sentences, and the cells are filled with similarity values for the corresponding two sentences. Choi's procedure for boundary detection is quite similar to Reynar's; he uses a divisive clustering algorithm that maximises the density of topical text segments. Working with concatenated news stories, Choi reports that his algorithm delivers better results than Hearst's.

As an alternative, Malioutov and Barzilay [2006] argue that methods that perform well on concatenated-story data are less powerful when it comes to segmenting individual, coherent documents, where topic changes tend to be marked in more subtle ways. The authors propose a *graph-based* approach and emphasize the point noted earlier, that similarity should be computed not only locally between adjacent segments but between segments throughout the text or at least in the surrounding region. In their graph, nodes correspond to sentences and weighted edges to sentence similarity, which is computed over word vectors, similar to Hearst's cosine measure, plus a weighting in the spirit of *tf.isf* as mentioned above. In principle, all sentence pairs are investigated (as in a dotplot approach, see Figure 2.7), so one would build a complete graph; to speed up performance, sentence pairs whose linear distance exceeds a certain threshold, are being ignored. Now, the graph-theoretic method to be employed is the *minimum cut*, which splits the graph $G = (V, E)$ into two disjoint sets of nodes A and B, such that the sum of the weights of the edges that connect the two sets is minimized:

$$cut(A, B) = \sum_{u \in A, v \in B} w(u, v) \tag{2.6}$$

For our problem this means that the resulting sets of sentences are maximally different from each other. To add the constraint that each set is also maximally homogeneous, we normalize by the sum of the edges the subset has to the whole graph:

$$NormCut(A, B) = \frac{cut(A, B)}{\sum_{u \in A, v \in V} w(u, v)} + \frac{cut(A, B)}{\sum_{u \in B, v \in V} w(u, v)} \tag{2.7}$$

And since we are interested not just in a single split, we have to extend this to the k-way normalized cut, which will produce k segments, i.e., a partition $A_1 \ldots A_k$:

$$NormCut_k(V) = \frac{cut(A_1, V - A_1)}{\sum_{u \in A_1, v \in V} w(u, v)} + \ldots + \frac{cut(A_k, V - A_k)}{\sum_{u \in A_k, v \in V} w(u, v)} \tag{2.8}$$

where $V - A_i$ is the vertex set difference between G and partition i. Malioutov and Barzilay suggest solving this with a dynamic programming algorithm, exploiting the constraint that the segmentation has to respect linear order of the segments (all nodes between the leftmost and the rightmost nodes of a partition have to belong to that partition), so that the complexity of the general minimum-cut problem is reduced to $O(K, N^2)$, where N is the number of nodes in the graph. The evaluation demonstrated that indeed clear improvements can be achieved by taking long-distance similarities into account—except for the concatenated-news dataset produced by Choi [2000], where the big differences between the individual texts render any long-range comparisons largely futile.

2.2.5   PROBABILISTIC MODELS OF SEGMENTATION AND TOPICS

In recent years, text segmentation has often been tackled with probabilistic approaches, which we briefly introduce in this subsection. Such approaches often rely on dynamic programming (as did that of Malioutov and Barzilay above). Consider Figure 2.8, where a node in the graph represents a sentence break in the document, and an edge is a sequence of sentences, i.e., a segment. For illustration, the dotted line represents Seg_1^5, which includes sentences 2 to 5. In dynamic programming, scores for all possible segments are to be computed, which corresponds to $N \times (N+1)/2$ node pairs; the goal is to find the minimum-cost path connecting the first to the final node.

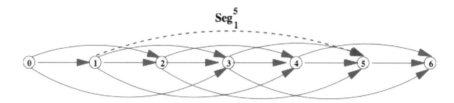

Figure 2.8: Text segmentation as shortest-path problem (from Misra et al. [2009]).

An early and influential probabilistic approach is that of Utiyama and Isahara [2001].[17] They seek to maximise the probability of a segmentation S given a word sequence W:

$$P(S|W) = \frac{P(W|S)P(S)}{P(W)} \tag{2.9}$$

Since $P(W)$ is constant for a text, maximization targets the numerator. The prior probability $P(S)$ may incorporate information about the text (such as average length of segments), but in the absence of such information, the authors suggest an information-theoretic measure (description length priors). To compute $P(W|S)$, the idea is to regard a topic as a word distribution, assuming that different topics have different distributions and that statistical independence holds between topics as well as between the words constituting an individual topic. With these assumptions, $P(W|S)$ can be rewritten to the following expression, where a segment S_i contains n_i words, and w_i^j denotes the jth word in S_i:

$$P(W|S) = \prod_{i=1}^{m} \prod_{j=1}^{n_i} P(w_i^j|S_i) \tag{2.10}$$

Then, Utiyama and Isahara use maximum-likelihood estimation and Laplace smoothing to compute the parameters with a dynamic programming algorithm. As in many approaches of this kind, stopwords are removed and Porter stemming is used to group related lexical items together.

---

[17]An implementation of the segmentation algorithm by Utiyama and Isahara [2001] is at `mastarpj.nict.go.jp/~mutiyama/software.html` (Jan 8, 2010)

Hidden topics The basic idea that topics correspond to sets of words with probabilities (i.e., to word distributions), and that texts in turn correspond to topic distributions, can be taken further to a generative probabilistic perspective on texts. For a moment, let *topic distribution* refer not to a segmentation but to the spreading of words that belong to common topics across the text. Also, imagine for a moment that we are dealing with an entire collection of texts rather than with just a single one. When the set of topics that are to show up in various places in the collection is given, then we can view each individual text as being generated by a two-step random process:

1. Select a topic distribution: Which topics are to be addressed in the new text, and how prominent shall they be?

2. Produce the text (whose length we assume to be fixed) word by word: For each new word, first draw a topic (from the topic distribution), and then draw a word (from the word distribution corresponding to that topic).

The result will be a text that reflects the topics according to the proportions selected in (1), and where for each topic, the words in the text reflect the lexical distribution corresponding to that topic; each word is drawn independently from the others. Thus, for our complete collection, texts share the same set of topics, but each text expresses those topics with different proportion.

Topic modeling aims at reversing this generative procedure, i.e., to infer the topics from a given set of texts. We observe the texts, but their topic structure (as described above) is *hidden*; the computational problem thus is to uncover this hidden structure. The distribution of topics across a text is called *Dirichlet distribution*, and it is used to *allocate* the words of the text to the various topics. Thus, the overall problem is named *latent Dirichlet allocation (LDA)*. Notice that LDA is an unsupervised technique: The texts in the input collection are neither labeled with topic keywords nor organized in any subgroups.

More formally, the computational problem of computing the posterior (the conditional distribution of the topic structure for K topics given D observed documents) is as follows [Blei, to appear]. The notation is:

- $\beta_{1:K}$ are the topics, where each β_k is a distribution over the vocabulary,

- θ_d are the topic proportions for the dth document, where $\theta_{d,k}$ is the topic proportion for topic k in document d,

- z_d is the topic assignment for the dth document, where $z_{d,n}$ is the topic assignment for the nth word in document d,

- w_d are the observed words for document d, where $w_{d,n}$ is the nth word in document d.

Then, the posterior to be computed is

$$p(\beta_{1:K}, \theta_{1:D}, z_{1:D}|w_{1:D}) = \frac{p(\beta_{1:K}, \theta_{1:D}, z_{1:D}, w_{1:D})}{p(w_{1:D})} \qquad (2.11)$$

See Blei, to appear for an introduction to LDA and an outline of algorithmic techniques for approximating this posterior, and Blei et al. [2003] for an in-depth application of LDA to various problems of text engineering.

LDA for text segmentation   LDA, as sketched above, adheres to the bag-of-words model: words are being drawn independently from another, and thus there is no assumption on consecutive words in a text being topically related qua their being neighbours. One way of transferring LDA to the segmentation problem, proposed by Shafiei and Milios [2008], is to assume a Markov structure on the topics of a sequence of sentences. To that end, sentences also receive topics, and a binary variable captures whether the topic of the current sentence is the same as that of its predecessor, or is new. Also, Eisenstein [2009] shows how LDA can be used for hierarchical topic modeling, thus allowing for embedded topic segments (recall the example from Manning [1998] given at the beginning of this section). The intuition is that word distributions corresponding to lower-level subtopics change rapidly, whereas higher-level topics are more stable; this seems appropriate for news stories that address various aspects of the story while continuously mentioning the same protagonists, for example. For inferring the segmentation with his "multi-scale lexical cohesion" model, Eisenstein also uses a dynamic programming algorithm.

2.2.6   COMBINING EVIDENCE

So far in this section, we have seen approaches to topic segmentation based on observing specific cue words, and approaches computing shifts in the distribution of content words, in various ways. A natural idea then is to use *both* kinds of evidence together. A number of researchers have explored this and reported that adding cue words to a purely-distributional method yields performance gains for their respective datasets. However, almost all of these approaches differ from those discussed above in that they require training data, i.e., they perform supervised learning. We provide only a short overview here.

The basic idea is to regard topic segmentation as a *classification* problem: Given a sentence boundary, it is to be decided whether it also constitutes a topic boundary or not. To this end, a set of features is defined, to be computed in a text window surrounding the potential boundary. These features are (usually automatically) annotated in a corpus that can then be used to train the statistical classifier.

The first to explore this direction were Passonneau and Litman [1997] in their early work on segmenting transcribed narratives. They used the C4.5 program [Quinlan, 1993] to induce decision trees from the corpus, evaluating three kinds of features: the presence of certain NP forms and cue words from a predefined list (as discussed earlier), plus the duration of prosodic pauses.

Later work concentrated on combining a word distribution analysis with cue word features, where *cue word* is meant in a different sense, though: These methods automatically acquired from the training corpus words that appear significantly frequently at or in the vicinity of the potential boundary. Beeferman et al. [1999], for example, report experiments with different window sizes for detecting those candidates, and then fuse the feature of their presence with a lexical distribution analysis in a maximum-entropy model. Also using maximum entropy, Reynar [1997] combined his word repetition model and genre-specific cues for broadcast news (both have been mentioned above) with pronoun presence and an account of lexical distribution; here, he proposed to use not single words but bigrams, in order to partially circumvent the word disambiguation task. The hope is that such a minimal context can sometimes differentiate between word readings and thus increase precision—but the drawback is that the data becomes sparse.

Galley et al. [2003], who targeted the segmentation of meeting transcripts (see above), followed Passonneau and Litman [1997] in looking for cue words at the beginning of boundaries, but they extracted them automatically from their corpus and then manually removed implausible candidates, which left as most significant cues the words *okay, anyway, allright, but, and, so*—very similar to those that Passonneau and Litman [1997] had used earlier. Galley et al. combined cue words, several aspects of prosody, and lexical distribution features, also inducing decision trees with C4.5. The idea of the 'first word cue' does not seem to easily carry over to written text, though; in medical textbooks, Eisenstein and Barzilay [2008] determined the words *the, this, it, these, a, on* as most frequently initiating a segment (only the first two with statistical significance), which is not very informative. These authors, who in addition also worked with the meeting corpus, proposed an unsupervised Bayesian approach, along the lines of LDA, for combining word distribution with the cue feature (and potentially other features).

For the narrative genre, finally, Kauchak and Chen [2005] built a classifier with support vector machines and used, besides word distribution and some of the features mentioned above, the presence of full proper names and of direct speech as indicators for the beginning of a new topic segment. Besides, they computed 'entity chains' of certain types of referring expressions and used them in analogy to lexical chains; this notion will be covered in more depth in the next chapter.

2.3 SUMMARY

In this chapter, we looked at document-level text structure from two viewpoints: The first moved from the (literally) obvious logical document structure to content zones, a representation that is decidedly specific for a particular text genre. Second, we saw methods for breaking a longer text span into topical segments, which are to some extent genre-independent, with the exception of some work accounting for genre-specific boundary cue words or phrases. Topic segmentation can in principle be applied to a complete (unstructured) document or to a portion of a document, e.g., after some major blocks in the logical or content structure have been identified and are to be further divided.

We noted that for human readers, finding topical segments is a difficult, subjective task that is hardly possible to define precisely, and usually does not lead to good inter-annotator agreement. From a methodological viewpoint, then, it is understandable when the research turns to synthetic data sets resulting from concatenating different news articles into a single document (which, at least, can be clearly evaluated) and explores the advantages and problems of various classification algorithms when applied to the same data. From a linguistic viewpoint, on the other hand, this is not really satisfying: There is a plethora of segmentation methods that deliver one or another performance, depending on whether they are applied to one or another data set. To illustrate this with just a few examples from research we have discussed above: Choi [2000] points out that his clustering approach on his (synthetic) data performs better than Hearst's text tiling. Dias et al. [2007] show that on their data, text tiling is better than Choi's clustering, and their own method is better still. Kauchak and Chen [2005] point out that for narratives, text tiling yields almost random results, and other standard methods are hardly better. Etc.

For authentic, non-synthetic text, ultimately we want to know more exactly *how* classes of text differ from each other and, accordingly, what means they employ to signal topic boundaries. References to text types[18] appear occasionally (e.g., Hearst pointed out that her approach was particularly geared to expository text; Kauchak and Chen noted that narrative text can hardly be captured with the standard methods), but more work is needed here. Cue words, for instance, have mostly been applied only as signals when they appear sentence- (or utterance-) initial, which for many genres is a simplification.

The word distribution approach, at any rate, implicitly provided us with a technical characterization for the notion of *topic*, which linguistically is so hard to describe: A topic as a property of a text segment is characterized by the particular distribution of content words in that segment, and the difference to the distribution in other segments.

---

[18]We will discuss the notion of text type in some detail in Chapter 5.

CHAPTER 3

Coreference Resolution

One essential characteristic of texts is, loosely speaking, that they "keep talking about the same things": Topics and subtopics are stable across spans of text, as discussed in the previous chapter, and in addition, many entities being referred to are being referred to more than once. Less loosely speaking now, the term *coreference* characterizes the fact that different *referring expressions* of a text point to the same entity in "the world". When an entity is mentioned several times, a *chain* of coreferent expressions is formed. Resolving coreference thus means uncovering these relationships and finding for a given text the set of coreference chains.

Why is discourse processing interested in coreference? For one thing, in the previous chapter we have pointed to the close connections between coreference resolution and topic segmentation, where the instrument of the lexical chain plays a role that the coreference chain could play as well, and possibly even better. After all, 'aboutness' in a stricter sense usually means the entities that are being referred to, the people and things that the author of the text reports on. But the relevance of coreference goes much further: Basically, any single text analysis task can profit from the capacity of replacing, for example, a pronoun with its antecedent. Sentences like *He did it* are not uncommon in language—and essentially void of content if the pronouns cannot be interpreted. Or consider extractive text summarization, where individual sentences are taken from different positions in the text and concatenated to constitute the summary. If a sentence in that summary contains a pronoun whose antecedent is not available (because the sentence containing it was not extracted), the summary can be hard to understand or even entirely misleading, if the reader resolves the pronoun to a "wrong" antecedent that is available in the summary. The easy solution is to remove sentences with pronouns from the summary, but replacing them with their antecedent could be much more helpful.

This chapter is structured as follows. After a brief overview of the linguistic phenomena involved, Section 3.2 explains an influential approach to manual corpus annotation, the 'MUC-7 Guidelines', which serves to further delineate the problem of coreference resolution. Section 3.3 discusses types of *transitions* between neighboring sentences, as resulting from the referring expressions in these sentences; in several models, such transitions serve to explain the *local coherence* of discourse. Turning then to automatic methods for handling nominal anaphora, Section 3.4 introduces work on determining anaphoricity and familiarity status, which is the first step toward solving the overall coreference problem. Coreference resolution as such is discussed in Sections 3.5 (rule-based, heuristic methods) and 3.6 (corpus-based, statistical methods).

3.1   REFERENCE AND COREFERENCE: AN OVERVIEW

Given the breadth of the underlying problems on the one hand and the enormous amount of research that has been dedicated to coreference on the other, a fairly short chapter can only give a relatively rough exposition. In this first section, we provide an overview of the various problems associated with coreference and introduce the terminology. Thereafter, we will look at methods for solving the different subtasks involved. However, neither the linguistic aspects of (co-)reference nor the range of computational solutions can be surveyed in their entirety—we are merely scratching the surface here.[1]

At the center of our attention are *referring expressions*: Linguistic forms that refer to entities in the world or, more precisely, in the mental models of writer and reader, because we can have common conceptions of entities that do not actually "exist", or have existed a long time ago, etc. Henceforth we will call the entities that are being referred to *discourse referents*. When two referring expressions point to the same discourse referent, they are *coreferent*, and when writing examples, we follow the practice of denoting coreferent expressions with the same index. The sequence of all expressions referring to the same entity forms the *referential chain* for that entity. For illustration, sentence 1.7 from SUFFERING, reproduced below, contains one chain of length 3, two chains of length 2, and two (trivial) chains of length 1.

Example 3.1   [A man named Lionel Gaedi]$_1$ went to [the Port-au-Prince morgue]$_2$ in search of [[his]$_1$ brother]$_3$, [Josef]$_3$, but was unable to find [[his]$_3$ body]$_4$ among [the piles of corpses that had been left [there]$_2$]$_5$.

The example also illustrates the complication that referring expressions need not be disjoint in the text but can be embedded in one another, as with possessive noun phrases or with restrictive relative clauses when they are seen as part of the governing NP (in order to simplify, one could generally cut off the relative clauses, irrespective of their being restrictive or non-restrictive).

As a shorthand, we occasionally call referring expressions pointing to a discourse referent *mentions* of that referent. In English, the most important types of referring expressions are the following:

- Indefinite noun phrases (henceforth: NPs). Example: *a man*

- Definite NPs: *the morgue*

- Proper names: *Lionel Gaedi*

- Demonstratives: *there / this man*

- Pronouns: *she / his*

---

[1]There is, not surprisingly, a vast literature on (co-)reference and anaphora in syntax, semantics, philosophy of language, computational linguistics and language technology. For a more comprehensive CL/LT-oriented introduction to the field, see the textbook by Mitkov [2002], even though it does not cover the latest, machine learning-oriented research.

Members of the last two groups, and many members of the second and the third group, are called *anaphors*. An anaphor is a referring expression that cannot be interpreted without considering the discourse context; specifically, the anaphor amounts to a "search instruction" for finding another referring expression that makes the intended discourse referent clear. The target of that search is called the *antecedent* of the anaphor. In Example 3.1, we have two anaphoric possessive pronouns, which have different antecedents: $[his]_1$ – [A man named Lionel Gaedi]$_1$ and $[his]_3$ – [Josef]$_3$. The last case illustrates that we follow the convention to mark as antecedent always the *most recent* co-referring expression (from the viewpoint of the anaphor), hence we choose 'Josef' rather than 'his brother', so that in fact a chain representation results.

Anaphora resolution: The task of finding an antecedent for each anaphor in a text. An anaphor is characterized by the fact that its discourse referent can only be identified when its antecedent is interpreted. 'Anaphora' is an irreflexive, non-symmetrical relation.

Coreference resolution: The task of partitioning the set of mentions of discourse referents in a text into classes (or 'chains') corresponding to those referents. Since referents are identical, 'coreference' is an equivalence relation (reflexive, symmetrical, transitive).

While the two relations 'anaphora' and 'coreference' most often correlate, they are, in principle, independent. Consider the sentence *That car is expensive because of the powerful engine*. The referent of *the powerful engine* can only be found when that of *that car* is known: *the powerful engine* thus is anaphoric. But it cannot be coreferent with *that car*, since the two entities are distinct (although they are related—we will return to this shortly). Likewise, two referring expressions can be coreferent without anaphora being present, as in *On Monday, the Pope went to Brazil, and on Wednesday, the plane with the Pope landed in Argentina*. Here, the two occurrences of *the Pope* can be interpreted in isolation—understanding the second mention does not depend on the first. From the viewpoint of Linguistics, anaphora is the interesting problem, as in the case of intra-sentential anaphora it interacts in systematic ways with syntactic analysis. From the viewpoint of text processing, on the other hand, the most important task is coreference, as it helps to complete the information found in single sentences.

Familiarity   Let us temporarily put text *understanding* aside and assume a *production* viewpoint instead. Then, the basic heuristic of forming referring expressions in text is to introduce a new discourse referent with an indefinite NP and subsequently to refer to it either with definite NPs or with pronouns. With named entities, there is a similar tendency to first use the full name, possibly extended with an apposition giving more information, and then to use shorter names, or definite NPs, or pronouns. Example 3.1 largely conforms to these rules, but with two exceptions, viz. the first mentions of referents 2 and 5 with definite NPs. The Port-au-Prince morgue has not been mentioned before in the text, yet it is marked with a definite article, which is unproblematic for the human reader on the grounds of world knowledge that a morgue can be supposed to be *unique* in a city of a certain size, in the same way as 'the mayor' or 'the center'. Notice that use of an indefinite determiner would suggest the presence of several alternative morgues in the city. In SUFFERING, there are several other examples of definiteness-qua-uniqueness, e.g., *the White House*. The definiteness of the first mention of referent 5 is licensed in a different way: Piles are not unique qua world knowledge, but the restrictive relative clause provides a description that renders the referent 'identifiable' to the reader.

The basic distinction between first and subsequent mentions, which needs to be signalled to the reader in order to shape his discourse model of entities being talked about is the *given/new* dichotomy. Many researchers, however, have proposed finer-grained inventories of *familiarity* labels. Prince [1992], for example, proposed that the relevant distinctions can be captured by two feature dimensions that characterize the familiarity status of a referent: It can be *discourse-old* or *discourse-new* on the one hand, and *hearer-old* or *hearer-new* on the other. The first feature pertains to the linguistic context, the second to the reader's general knowledge, which subsumes the contextual knowledge: Discourse-old referents are automatically hearer-old. A further feature to be added for the 'new' cases is whether a referent is *anchored* to another one—it is mentioned for the first time but overtly linked to another referent (often by means of a possessive) so that it need not be introduced with an indefinite article.[2] Thus, in Example 3.1:

- mention 1 of referent 1 (*A man named ...*) is discourse-new and hearer-new,

- mention 1 of referent 2 (*the ... morgue*) is discourse-new and hearer-old,

- mention 2 of referent 1 (*his*) is discourse-old and hearer-old,

- mention 1 of referent 3 (*his brother*) is discourse-new and hearer-new and anchored to referent 1,

- mention 2 of referent 3 (*Josef*): The referent is discourse-old and hearer-old (but the information that the name of the brother is *Josef* is new),

- mention 3 of referent 3 (*his*) is discourse-old and hearer-old,

- mention 1 of referent 4 (*his body*) is discourse-new and hearer-new and anchored to 3,

- mention 1 of referent 5 (*the piles ...*) is discourse-new and hearer-new and identifiable due to the relative clause,

- mention 2 of referent 2 (*there*) is discourse-old and hearer-old.

Beyond the few types of expressions mentioned in our heuristic rule for appropriate referring ("First indefinite, then definite or pronominal"), and beyond those types encountered in Example 3.1, the actual inventory of languages is much richer. It offers options for expressing nuances in familiarity, or in other words, ways of expressing different degrees of *salience* that discourse referents may have. In a nutshell, the more recently a referent was mentioned, the more salient it is at a certain point of

---

[2]Another feature that Prince discussed and generated some controversy in the literature is *inferable*, which we leave aside here.

processing the discourse; but salience is in fact affected by various factors, such as the grammatical role of the associated referring expression. In Section 3.3 below, we will discuss the mapping between familiarity statuses of discourse referents, salience, and their linguistic expression in more detail.

Some complications   So far, the problems of anaphora and coreference resolution might seem relatively benign, but in fact they offer a range of interesting complications. In the following, we will briefly mention the most important ones.

In English, we frequently encounter *one-anaphora*, as in *Tom bought a drink, and Sue got another one*. This is sometimes not easy to detect, since the word *one* has at least two other readings: the 'generic person' (*One never knows.*) and the numeral. It can be argued that an article reading also should be distinguished. One-anaphora has been studied extensively, for instance from the perspective of semantics [Webber, 1979] or by focusing on its various discourse functions [LuperFoy, 1991].

Closely related is *ellipsis*, which in English mostly occurs with verbs: *Tom bought a drink and Sue Ø a sandwich*. Ellipsis, i.e., the non-realization of a linguistic element, presumably indicates the highest degree of salience, because what can be left out entirely must be recoverable by the reader very easily. Other forms of verb phrase (VP) ellipsis in English are *Tom bought a drink, and so did Ø Sue* and *Tom bought a drink but he didn't know why Ø*.

A significant problem for automatic pronoun resolution is posed by pronouns that in fact do not refer properly, the so-called *expletive* or *pleonastic* pronouns. In constructions like *it is raining* or *it is clear that ...*, it must be inferred that no discourse referent should be sought for *it*. We will return to this problem at the beginning of Section 3.4.

Deictic pronouns point to a referent not inside the co-text but in the situation of utterance; accordingly, they typically occur in spoken language. Examples include personal pronouns (*I, you, ...*), as in *Let me tell you a story about her*, when being uttered in a group discussion.

Furthermore, there are pronouns that do have a discourse referent in the text, but it is not located in the preceding discourse. The *cataphoric* pronouns point forward to a coreferent noun phrase, so that the term 'antecedent' is not quite appropriate. Example: *When [she]$_i$ arrived in Toronto, [Ann]$_i$ immediately went to the Art Gallery of Ontario.*

Plural pronouns can be complicated to resolve, when a number of antecedents have to be collected possibly from different positions in the preceding sentence(s): *When [Sue]$_i$ went skating, she ran into [Tom]$_j$ and his friend [Joe]$_k$. [They]$_{i,j,k}$ all had a glass of mulled wine.*

One somewhat special type of anaphoric expression is the 'other'-anaphor (for a computational approach, see [Modjeska, 2003]). In SUFFERING, there is just one instance of it, viz. in sentence 6.4: *the harder task of figuring out what the United States and other countries can and ought to do for Haiti*. One frequent form is 'X and other Y', but there are many variants where the 'X' can appear at a greater distance from 'Y': *The unicorn decided to spend time looking for other animals*. The question is "other than what" and thus the NP is anaphoric, pointing to the antecedent *the unicorn*. This phenomenon is a good example for anaphora-without-coreference, as the whole point of such expression is that 'Y' is *not* the same as 'X'; it thus borders on the phenomenon to be discussed next.

Finally, both pronouns and full NPs may refer in somewhat unusual ways, namely when the referent is not a particular entity (as it was the case in all the examples we saw so far) but a concept—in which case the nominal is said to have a *generic* reading:

- *[Whales] are mammals.*

- *[The automobile] was invented by Carl Benz in 1885.*

- *I saw two Corgis and their seven puppies today. [They] are the funniest dogs.*

Bound anaphora   From the perspective of syntax and semantics, it is important to distinguish pronouns whose interpretation is governed by syntactic principles from those that can be related to their antecedent merely on the grounds of discourse pragmatics. Reinhart [1983, p. 49] illustrated the range of possibilities as follows:

- Obligatory coreference
  Zelda bores herself.

- Obligatory non-coreference
  Zelda bores her.
  She adores Zelda's teachers.

- Optional coreference
  Zelda adores her teachers.
  Those who know her adore Zelda.

When syntax imposes restrictions on interpretation, this is called *bound anaphora*, because in semantics, such pronouns are treated as bound variables rather than referring expressions. Several pronoun resolution algorithms (see Section 3.5.2), which assume syntactic structure as input, pay attention to the distinction and test for violations of syntactic binding principles in order to prune the set of antecedent candidates for a pronoun.

Indirect anaphora   When discussing Example 3.1, we mentioned 'uniqueness' as being responsible for the definite article in *the Port-au-Prince morgue*, and this uniqueness of the discourse referent is assumed by the writer to be either presupposed (the reader knows already that there is only one) or inferable (the reader learns, in passing, that there is only one). One way of describing this is that the reader can *accommodate* the referent in her text representation—there does not have to be an indefinite article as an explicit instruction to create the referent.

This uniqueness and ensuing accommodatability can result from world knowledge, but it can also involve anaphora, namely when a definite NP picks up some aspect of a previously introduced referent and enters into a relation with that referent other than identity. This is sometimes called *indirect* anaphora, whereas Clark [1977] used the term *bridging* for this phenomenon: A referring expression is definite because it builds a bridge to a previous one, without there being identity of the referents. Clark offered the following list of cases:

- Necessary parts: *I entered the room. The ceiling was high.*

- Probable parts: *I entered the room. The windows looked out to the bay.*

- Inducible parts: *I entered the room. The chandeliers sparkled brightly.*

- Necessary roles: *I went shopping. The time I started was 3pm.*

- Optional roles: *John was murdered. The knife lay nearby.*

- Relations like reason, cause, consequence: *An earthquake (...). The suffering people are going through (...).*

An alternative view on bridging from the perspective of language *processing* is to ask what sort of knowledge is required to resolve a bridging reference. Vieira and Teufel [1997], who subsume relatively many cases of anaphora under bridging, suggested the following classes:

- Bridging by well-defined lexical relations (synonymy, meronymy), as they can be found in WordNet (recall our discussion of lexical chains in Section 2.2.3):
  the unicorn – the head

- Bridging from an anaphoric common noun to a proper name – resolution requires inferring the type of the entity denoted by the proper name:
  Wittgenstein – the philosopher

- Bridging from a definite NP not to the head of an antecedent NP but to one of its modifiers:
  there were several plastic unicorns – the plastic

- Bridging from a definite NP to a referent introduced by a VP:
  my three unicorns keep making holes in the garden – the digging

- Bridging from a definite NP to an entity that was not explicitly introduced but is implicitly present as a discourse topic; for example, in a text about unicorns, the NP *the fable* may be used felicitously without having been explicitly 'anchored'.

- Bridging via more general common-sense knowledge, e.g., about causal relations, as mentioned above.

Coreference: a case of ambiguity resolution   As our brief discussion has shown, there is a wide range of referring expressions, and they can enter into an equally wide range of relations with discourse referents. Moreover, some expressions can easily be mistaken to be anaphoric but they are not, as with the expletive and the deictic expressions. On the whole, deciding when two expressions have the same discourse referent is a difficult task, because the ambiguity can be substantial. For the human reader, semantics and world knowledge usually serve to make the intended referents very clear, so that cases of doubt or even misinterpretation are rare. In the absence of deep knowledge, however, more surface-based factors need to be evaluated as hints: There are a few hard-and-fast rules for excluding certain candidates, especially with pronouns, but the remaining work is a matter of weighing the evidence.

For practical purposes, being able to resolve *nominal* anaphora is the most important challenge, since it is both the most frequent type (at least in written language) and the one that is needed for most tasks, be it information extraction, sentiment analysis, summarization, or something similar. VP anaphors, or pronouns referring to longer stretches of text, have been addressed in some computational work in recent years, but they are in general harder to resolve than nominals. In the following, we discuss some efforts in annotating corpora with coreference information, and then turn to the subtasks of coreference resolution for nominals, and the different methods for tackling them.

3.2   CORPUS ANNOTATION

Theoretical descriptions of types and problems with referring expressions are one side of the coin; the other is formed by the task of providing explicit guidelines for annotating coreference in authentic text. There, referential phenomena are encountered with all their subtleties and hard-to-define grey areas; and therefore, looking at efforts on producing guidelines serves to add some more precision to our brief account given so far.

The MUC-7 Guidelines   An influential early guideline of this kind originated with the MUC-7 *message understanding conference* and was compiled by Hirschman and Chincor [1997]. Many annotation efforts have been directly or indirectly based on this annotation scheme, but it has also drawn criticism (e.g., by van Deemter and Kibble, 2000). Nonetheless, we use it here as the leitmotif for the discussion. Many statistical approaches to coreference resolution (see Section 3.6) have been developed and evaluated on the MUC-7 data and its successors. A central decision made in the MUC-7 scheme is to restrict annotation to coreference in the narrow sense, that is to the relation *identity of reference*. This might at first seem to be a convenient simplification, but even the notion of identity has its problems, as we shall see.

In a way, writers of annotation guidelines are in a more difficult position than, say, semanticists. The latter have to measure their results merely with respect to what they consider "the truth"; the former have to prepare a document that fulfills a number of potentially conflicting goals [Hirschman and Chincor, 1997]: They have to enable or support some specific task or application; they have to be designed in such a way that high inter-annotator agreement results; they should lead to efficient (quick, and hence cheap) annotation; and moreover, the resulting corpus should be a useful resource for the research community (and hence be useful for similar, non-identical purposes as well). In MUC, priority was explicitly given to the first aspect: The corpus should serve as evaluation data for particular coreference resolution competitions with the genre *news*. This necessarily entails compromises—some difficult choices are made in essentially arbitrary ways, and the guidelines as a whole do not necessarily reflect the state of the art in theoretical research. And this becomes an

```
<COREF ID="1" TYPE="IDENT" REF="0">A man named Lionel Gaedi</COREF>
went to
<COREF ID="2" TYPE="IDENT" REF="0" MIN="morgue">the
Port-au-Prince morgue</COREF>
in search of
<COREF ID="3" TYPE="IDENT" REF="0">
   <COREF ID="4" TYPE="IDENT" REF="1">his</COREF>
   brother
      <COREF ID="5" TYPE="IDENT" REF="3">Josef</COREF></COREF>,
but was unable to find
<COREF ID="6" TYPE="IDENT" REF="0">
  <COREF ID="7" TYPE="IDENT" REF="5">his</COREF>
  body</COREF>
among
<COREF ID="8" TYPE="IDENT" REF="0" MIN="piles
of corpses">the piles of corpses that had
been left there</COREF>.
```

Figure 3.1: MUC-7-style coreference annotation of a sentence.

important matter when third parties—despite the "warnings"—take such guidelines for their own experiments on different data and under different circumstances. Annotation guidelines can trigger massive amounts of annotation work and research in the community, and a great many machine learning experiments may be based on the resulting corpus when it is made publicly available. Hence, the "roots" of such efforts should be on a solid foundation, so that everybody knows what they are doing, and what it is that their ML systems are learning.

On the technical side, an annotation scheme makes choices on the specific markup format. The minimum, obviously, is to have spans of text pointing to other, coreferent, spans. In addition, it needs to be decided whether any extra labeling is to be used. MUC-7 used an SGML format that is basically compatible with contemporary XML. Annotations are represented *inline*, that is the raw text is extended with XML tags. (This is in contrast to *standoff* annotation, where text and annotations are kept distinct). In MUC-7, a *markable* (an expression that is to receive a label) is marked up with the XML tag COREF, which has attributes ID (a unique identifier for the markable), TYPE (a string denoting the relation encoded; in this scheme, it is always set to IDENT), and REF (the identifier of the markable that the present one is coreferent with). Furthermore, there are two optional attributes: MIN gives a minimal string included in the markable, which can be used for evaluation purposes when a system identifies smaller markables, and the STATUS attribute can be set to OPT for 'optional' when the annotator is not sure whether the coreference holds. Thus, in this scheme, coreference is annotated pair-wise, but since IDENT is an equivalence relation, complete sets of coreferential markables can be computed via transitivity. As an illustration, Figure 3.1 shows a MUC-7 encoding of our Example 3.1. The markup does not exactly correspond to the bracketing we used earlier; the differences will be explained below.

Turning then to the content of the annotation, the first task for the guidelines is to define the range of markables: What strings in the text are to be marked as referring expressions and may enter into the IDENT relation with others? One aspect of this question is the decision whether to mark all referring expressions, i.e., things that *could* enter into an IDENT relation, or only those that actually *do* in the text, i.e., that have at least one coreferent markable. There are good arguments for doing it either way, but there ought to be a consistent procedure. MUC-7, as van Deemter and Kibble [2000] criticize, is not very clear on this issue; it seems that sometimes a markable is to be marked only when it is coreferent with another one, while on other occasions a broader view is taken.

The types of markables are, basically, nouns, noun phrases, and pronouns. As for the latter, personal, possessive, and demonstrative pronouns are covered; with possessives, embedding may occur (as in our example sentence: *his brother*; see Figure 3.1). Nouns and noun phrases are taken to include all kinds of proper names, as well as syntactically non-standard units such as dates, currencies, and percentage figures.

Following a distinction commonly made in semantics, the guidelines state that nouns and noun phrases can be either

- extensional descriptions: enumeration of the member(s) of a set by their names, or numerical values; or

- intensional descriptions: a predicate that is true of an entity or a set, such as *the prime numbers* or *the president of Chrysler Corporation*, or denotes a function, as in *the temperature*.

Example 3.2   The rate, which was 6 percent, was higher than that offered by the other bank.

In Example 3.2, the noun phrase *the rate* is a function expression, here instantiated by the predicate *6 percent*, so these two would be marked as coreferential. As for the pronoun *that*, it is coreferential at the function level with *The rate*. However, there are clearly two different rates being referred to, and therefore, *that* is not to be marked.

One source of complication, when annotation is restricted to nominal anaphora, concerns the handling of verbal expressions denoting not events but entities. In MUC-7, gerunds (*slowing the economy*) are generally not markables. On the other hand, present participles that are modified by other nouns or adjectives (*excessive spending*), are preceded by an article, or are followed by an *of* phrase (*slowing of the economy*) are to be considered noun-like and thus are seen as markables.

Similar choices occur with certain bare nouns. The scheme prescribes that prenominal modifiers (e.g., *ocean drilling* in *the ocean drilling company*) are considered markable only if either the prenominal modifier is coreferential with some named entity or with the syntactic head of a maximal noun phrase. This entails that any coreference chain must include a head or a name, that is, more than just a modifier.

Regarding conjunction, for NPs with two or more heads, the guidelines prescribe to first treat the entire maximal conjoined noun phrase as a markable. Then, the MIN attribute is to specify the span from the first head through the last head, including all material in between. Thus, the sentence *The sleepy boys and girls enjoyed their breakfast*, which includes a plural pronoun, is coded as follows:

```
<COREF ID="1" MIN="boys and girls">The sleepy boys and girls</COREF>
enjoyed <COREF ID="2" REF="1" TYPE="IDENT">their</COREF> breakfast.
```

In addition, if any of the individual conjuncts is coreferential with some other phrase, it constitutes a separate markable.

In general, the decision on the length of markables is directly influenced by the task that the corpus is designed for. In MUC-7, the MIN attribute is used to specify the head of the referring expression (which is the minimum that has to be found by coreference resolvers). The COREF tag itself is applied to the *maximal* noun phrase, which includes all its modifiers, such as appositional phrases, non-restrictive relative clauses, and prepositional phrases that may be viewed as modifiers of the noun phrase. In our Example 3.1, the annotator thus has to decide whether the relative clause *that had been left there* is to be read as restrictive, or as providing additional information. This is fairly often not an easy decision and prone to disagreement between annotators; in our original bracketing, it was treated as part of the noun phrase, in contrast to the MUC-7 version in Figure 3.1.

Similarly, a scoping decision has to be made for appositions. MUC-7 chooses to encode coreference between the apposition and the entire NP, so that the NP has scope over the apposition. This is another one of the arbitrary choices that just have to be specified for annotators; in our original bracketing of Example 3.1, we incidentally opted for the other way.

Identity   Finally, we take a step backward and briefly look at the IDENT relation a little more closely. One diagnostic that is sometimes offered for it is the replacement test: When the anaphor is replaced by the antecedent expression in the text, there should result an unproblematic sentence. This is, however, difficult with bound anaphora, as van Deemter and Kibble [2000] noted: In *Every TV network reported its profits*, the replacement does not work straightforwardly, even though coreference holds.

More important, however, are the cases where our intuitions on coreference are being challenged. An example from the MUC-7 guidelines is *The stock price fell from $4.02 to $3.85*. At one time, the stock price is coreferential with $4.02, and later on with $3.85. Once again, some encoding needs to be decided on: Is there no coreference to be marked at all, or with one of the two figures, or with both? The guidelines argue that the latter option would seriously jeopardize the notion of 'coreference set', since 4.02 and 3.85 are plainly not identical. The choice is to mark the more recent value ($3.85) as coreferential with *the stock price*. It is not clear on what grounds to systematically prefer one or the other option, though. The arbitrariness is pointed out also by van Deemter and Kibble, who discuss cases like *Higgins stepped down as CEO of Corporation X, and will become president of Corporation Y next month.* – Whether *Higgins* is marked as coreferential with CEO-of-X or with president-of-Y can hardly be decided systematically.

One plausible solution for examples like this one is to simply accept the ambiguity and have it encoded in the corpus annotation, as advocated by Poesio and Artstein [2008]. Their annotation scheme allows annotators to set multiple pointers from an anaphoric expression to possible antecedents. The authors discuss the consequences of this step for the evaluation of inter-annotator agreement, and conclude that allowing for ambiguity in the corpus on the whole leads to more reliable data.

While reference-to-A versus reference-to-B is a binary decision and thus a clear instance of *ambiguity* (between two separate alternatives), the IDENT relation also has problems of *vagueness*, i.e., issues of "grey zones" [Krasavina and Chiarcos, 2007]. Deciding on identity of referents, unfortunately, is often not an easy matter. Consider this example: *Germany had pursued a seat on the U.N. Security Council for several years. Last week, the Berlin government achieved at least a partial success.* The entity pursuing the seat was presumably not the entire country but the government—or maybe something in between, such as the government plus the majority of the population. Recasens et al. [2010] uncovered many examples of this kind in corpora, where many annotators would intuitively consider two entities "almost" identical. A "pragmatic" response to this situation would be for an annotation guideline to instruct annotators in case of doubt to always prefer option X (e.g., to not mark the coreference). This is what is being done in many guidelines, also for other annotation tasks. The quality and utility of the corpora is not increased by that step, though. The data purports clarity and allows for running training and evaluation sessions, but progress on the underlying linguistic or ontological problems is hindered, since the relevant instances in the data remain unmarked. Recasens et al. therefore take a different approach and suggest that coreference be regarded not as a binary decision but as a continuum with a middle zone of near-identity relations. Rather than merely allowing annotators to label such examples as *maybe* cases, they propose a full typology of near-identity relations (NIDENT), which covers four groups that are in turn decomposed into subgroups. We give just one (abridged) example for each group here:

- **Name metonymy** – e.g., location: the name of a location can serve to describe the physical place, the people living there, the government ruling them, etc.
  The Jordan authorities arrested, on arriving in <u>Iraq</u>, an Italian pilot who violated the air embargo to <u>this country</u>.

- **Meronymy** – e.g., stuff-object
  Council prohibited selling <u>alcoholic drinks</u> during night hours. Bars will not be allowed to sell <u>alcohol</u>.

- **Class** – e.g., more-general
  Diego looked for information about <u>his character</u> in the novel, forgetting that Saramago does not usually describe <u>them</u>.

- **Spatio-temporal function** – e.g., time: existence and location of objects are dependent on time; the different referents cannot coexist simultaneously
  <u>Postville</u> feels like Hometown, USA, but a look around this town shows it's become a miniature Ellis Island. For those who prefer <u>the old Postville</u>, Mayor John Hyman has a simple answer.

NIDENT clearly resembles what we discussed earlier as *bridging*, but the difference is that with NIDENT it is hard to discern any relation *other than* identity. In a typical bridging relation like standard meronymy (*the car – the powerful engine*), the point is that the two referents are distinct, yet related; with NIDENT, there are no clearly identifiable distinct referents.

Recasens et al. tested their taxonomy, which consists of 15 subgroups in total, in an annotation experiment and achieved a kappa value of 0.58. The evaluation result is being disturbed by just two problematic instances: When leaving out these two outliers and computing kappa for the remaining instances, the value increases to a very good 0.84.

Available Corpora   Besides the MUC-7 corpus and its predecessor MUC-6 (which consist of 60 documents each), the most popular corpora for machine learning work on coreference resolution (see Section 3.6) are the ACE corpora that originated with the Automatic Content Extraction conference[3], a successor of MUC. An ongoing effort in collecting coreference corpora is the Anaphoric Bank[4], which also extends to several European languages other than English. In addition, coreference annotation is available for some treebanks, hence in conjunction with other layers of annotation. For English, such a resource is the Ontonotes corpus [Hovy et al., 2006].

3.3   ENTITY-BASED LOCAL COHERENCE

One benefit of coreference-annotated corpora is the opportunity to obtain a complete picture of the development of referential chains in a text. We can study the ways in which new discourse referents are introduced and how their subsequent mentions are formulated—and all of this *in context*, so that the reasons for those formulations can be investigated. As we have indicated earlier when discussing the notion of familiarity status, there are regularities in the forms of referring expressions. This begins with the rule of using indefinite NPs for first mentions, but goes much further in providing rules for the interaction of referring expressions and sentence structure in adjacent sentences. Text can "flow" more or less well, and the form and position of referring expressions is a significant factor.

Pronouns, in particular, have a huge effect on information flow across sentences. As psycholinguistic research has demonstrated, pronouns play a rather special role in anaphora resolution: Since they are almost void of meaning (they only signal gender and number of the antecedent), the discourse referent to be picked up must be particularly salient, so that it can be readily identified by the reader. A stronger view of this basic insight is articulated by the *discourse center hypothesis* (e.g., Hudson et al., 1986), which states that at any point in discourse understanding, there is one single entity that is the most salient discourse referent at that point. This referent, the current focus of attention in the reader's mind, is called the *center*. The challenge is to explain what means a writer employs to steer the reader's focus of attention in a way that minimizes the processing effort for understanding. The writer thus should make it clear at any point what the center is, and in particular, when it shifts to a new referent. *Centering theory*[5] is a linguistic account of this process of steering

---

[3]www.itl.nist.gov/iad/mig/tests/ace (Jan 26, 2011)

[4]anawiki.essex.ac.uk/anaphoricbank/ (Jan 26, 2011)

[5]The first comprehensive introduction to Centering is due to Grosz et al. [1995], but a computational application to pronoun resolution had already been presented by Brennan et al. [1987]. Later, a seminal collection of papers was published by Walker et al. [1998]. A more recent overview of subsequent work on various versions of the theory is provided by Poesio et al. [2004].

(from the writer's perspective) and tracking (from that of the reader). The means the writer has at his disposal are to some extent language-specific. For English, the proponents of the original centering theory see the *grammatical role* as the most important device; specifically, the grammatical subject is taken to be the default position for the discourse center. Furthermore, there is a pronominalization rule that says whenever some discourse referent is referred to by a pronoun, then in the same sentence the center referent must *also* be pronominalized. Rather than going into more detail here, we illustrate the idea of centering with an example from [Grosz et al., 1995], where two sentences come in two different versions. First consider the following text only up to sentence (e).

Example 3.3   (a) Terry really goofs sometimes. (b) Yesterday was a beautiful day and he was excited about trying out his new sailboat. (c) He wanted Tony to join him on a sailing expedition. (d) He called him at 6 AM. (e) ?He/Tony was sick and furious at being woken up so early. (f) He told Terry to get lost and hung up. (g) Of course, ?he/Terry hadn't intended to upset Tony.

In (e), using the pronoun in subject position clearly signals center continuity, and the reader would initially interpret it as referring to Tony, which then turns out to be semantically incompatible. Thus, a full noun phrase (here: the proper name) is needed to mark the shift. Similarly, in (g) the semantics requires Terry to be the subject; and even though Terry is the most "recent" antecedent candidate in the previous sentence (in terms of word distance), we cannot refer to him with a pronoun, as the subject pronoun strongly suggests center continuity, i.e., a reference to Tony.

Depending on the configuration of grammatical roles in adjacent sentences, Brennan et al. [1987] distinguish four different types of *transitions*, which are supposed to capture the smoothness of the move from one sentence to another. When the second sentence basically stays on topic, the transition is *Continue*; the other types involve topic shifts: *Retain*, *Smooth Shift*, and *Rough Shift*. The phenomenon underlying such classifications is commonly called *entity-based local coherence*.

Entity-based local coherence: At any point in the text, the association between discourse referents, their corresponding referring expressions, and the syntactic positions they appear in is not arbitrary. When these configurations are chosen felicitously in adjacent sentences, the text at this point is locally coherent on the grounds that discourse entities can be easily identified by the reader; cognitive processing is not hindered.

Local coherence, as induced by entities, can be studied when combining all the referential chains, together with syntactic information, into a common representation. For illustration, Table 3.2 shows this representation for a sample text (given in Table 3.1) from Barzilay and Lapata [2008], who label this representation *entity grid*. Indices in the text record the grammatical roles, which are then used as fillers in the entity grid, where the rows correspond to the sentences. In case an entity appears twice in the same sentence, the highest-ranking role is recorded, following the hierarchy also used in Centering: subject (s) – object (o) – other (x). Barzilay and Lapata argue that the

Table 3.1: Sample text (abridged), annotated with grammatical roles [Barzilay and Lapata, 2008, p. 7].

1 [The Justice Department]$_S$ is conducting an [anti-trust trial]$_O$ against [Microsoft Corp.]$_X$ with evidence that [the company]$_S$ is increasingly attempting to crush [competitors]$_O$.

2 [Microsoft]$_O$ is accused of trying to forcefully buy into [markets]$_X$ where [its own products]$_S$ are not competitive enough to unseat [established brands]$_O$.

3 [The case]$_S$ revolves around [evidence]$_O$ of [Microsoft]$_S$ aggressively pressuring [Netscape]$_O$ into merging [browser software]$_O$.

4 [Microsoft]$_S$ claims [its tactics]$_S$ are commonplace and good economically.

Table 3.2: Entity grid for sample text in Table 3.1 [Barzilay and Lapata, 2008, p. 6].

	Department	Trial	Microsoft	Evidence	Competitors	Markets	Products	Brands	Case	Netscape	Software	Tactics
1	s	o	s	x	o	-	-	-	-	-	-	-
2	-	-	o	-	-	x	s	o	-	-	-	-
3	-	-	s	o	-	-	-	-	s	o	o	-
4	-	-	s	-	-	-	-	-	-	-	-	s

information for building up the grid can be obtained with sufficient quality from contemporary dependency parsers and NER modules; their work explicitly targets practical application rather than theoretical description. The idea is to then convert the grid into feature vectors recording the transitions for an entity across a number of sentences (which corresponds to the length of the vector). Then, probabilities for transition types can be determined by counting vectors in the grid, such as that of a transition from subject to null: [s −] occurs three times in our example, and the total number of transitions of length two is 36, so its probability is 8%. Mapping the entire grid to such vectors then enables machine learning of entity distribution patterns, which Barzilay and Lapata used for different applications. One is the ordering of sentences in extractive text summarization, where a "good" ordering is supposedly one that displays a probable entity transition distribution.

As for the kinds of referring expressions, Centering theory has clearly focused its attention on the conditions for pronominalization, that is on the choice between personal pronoun and full NP. But the spectrum of referring expressions in English is wide. When producing text, the choice among them is also not arbitrary, but the differences are much harder to pin down than for basic pronominalization (for which many interesting psycholinguistic results have been found). Anyway, some researchers have attempted to extend the 'salience ordering' of types of expressions to a broader coverage. One such proposal comes from Ariel [2001], who offers a hierarchy of referring expressions for named entities, ranging from 'inaccessible' to 'highly-salient':

full proper name > long definite description > short def. desc. > last name > first name > distal demonstrative > proximal demonstrative > stressed pronoun > unstressed pronoun

The 'stressed' feature indicates that the hierarchy is meant to cover spoken language as well. Such a series seems intuitively plausible, and to some extent it can be verified with psycholinguistic experiments, but it is difficult to demonstrate the validity with corpus evidence, since many of the forms are rare, and thus a large amount of fine-grained annotation of referential chains would be required.

3.4   DETERMINING ANAPHORICITY AND FAMILIARITY STATUS

We now begin to look at the computational problem of resolving anaphors in text. Here, the first subtask consists in finding out whether a noun phrase that on the surface seems to be anaphoric is indeed an anaphor. This problem stems from 'pleonastic' (or 'expletive') pronouns on the one hand, and first-mention definite NPs on the other: Both types of NP are mostly anaphoric, but sometimes they are not, and it is important to classify the instances correctly. Many approaches to anaphora resolution do not strictly see this as a pre-processing task but perform it in conjunction with anaphora resolution—and some ignore it altogether. Nonetheless, for making the concepts clearer, we cover it here separately. Furthermore, a natural extension of determining anaphoricity is to automatically detect the *familiarity status* of a discourse referent, which was mentioned above when we introduced the terms discourse-old/new and hearer-old/new from Prince [1992]. Being able to solve these tasks can be useful even when full anaphora resolution is not targeted, since the feature of anaphoricity already provides information on cohesive links between adjacent clauses and therefore can inform decisions on text segmentation.

Pleonastic pronouns   While pronouns are regarded as the anaphors *par excellence*, the most frequent pronoun in English, *it*, is quite often being used non-anaphorically. Li et al. [2009] worked with a portion of the Wall Street Journal corpus (from the Penn Treebank) and report that in fact 25% of all occurrences of *it* are non-anaphoric. In SUFFERING, the figure is similar: 11 of the 15 instances of *it* are anaphoric (note that two of those refer to a verb phrase rather than to a nominal: in 8.3 and 8.5). What, then, is the role of a non-anaphoric *it*? We can broadly distinguish four types of usages, the first three of which are commonly called 'pleonastic':

- Extraposition: A clause is extraposed, and its original position filled by *it*.
  It is clear that we have to sign the contract.

- Cleft: *It is the secretary, who is to be applauded.*

- Reference to the 'local situation': weather, time, etc.: *It is half past nine.*

- Idiom: *I couldn't make it.*

Three of the four non-anaphoric instances in SUFFERING are idiomatic (3.3, 4.5, 8.4), although in 4.5 it can be said to refer even though being part of an idiomatic expression (*People struck by disaster always had it coming*). The remaining one is a reference to the 'larger situation', which not surprisingly is part of quoted speech: *"I don't see him—it's a catastrophe," Gaedi said.* (1.8)

As with many of these semi-regular tasks, both rule-based and machine-learning approaches towards it have been developed. A set of hand-crafted rules is implemented in the RAP pronoun resolution algorithm [Lappin and Leass, 1994] (which will be explained in Section 3.5.2), building on the observation that pleonastic *it* typically appears with a modal adjective (*it is important to …*) or a cognitive verb in its passive participle form (*it has been suggested that*). RAP uses lists of both kinds of adjectives and verbs and checks for the presence of seven types of patterns, among them (it is MODAL-ADJ that S), (it is MODAL-ADJ (for NP) to VP), and (it seems/appears/means/follows (that) S). Obviously, such enumerations pose the problem of potentially missing complete patterns, or certain syntactic variations on them. Accordingly, several machine-learning approaches have been proposed, with an early and influential one being that by Evans [2001]. Using memory-based learning, Evans devised 35 features covering factors such as the linear position of the pronoun in the clause, and lemmas and parts of speech of verbs and NPs in the same clause. His system achieves an accuracy of 71% on the overall binary classification of non-/anaphoricity.

First-mention definite NPs   As stated earlier, the general rule for "well-behaved" noun phrases is that an indefinite NP serves to introduce a new discourse referent, whereas a definite NP (henceforth: defNP) refers back to a referent already introduced. Then there are, supposedly, exceptions, such as defNPs referring to entities known from the larger context. SUFFERING has several examples, including *the earthquake* at the very beginning of the text (which was published when the event was highly prominent in the news). Further, a defNP can easily refer to an entity that was not previously mentioned as such, but is systematically related to a known discourse referent. This relation can be overt in a complex noun phrase, such as *the night after the earthquake* in sentence 1.1, but it can also be left implicit.

Unfortunately, studies indicate that the phenomenon of 'first-mention defNPs' (i.e., definite NPs being used non-anaphorically) is by no means exceptional. Vieira and Poesio [2001] found that 50% of definite NPs in their corpus of newspaper articles are in fact not anaphoric but discourse-new. Bean and Riloff [1999] give the even higher number of 63% non-anaphoric defNPs (which according to their taxonomy appears to include bridging references, though). Therefore, an anaphora resolution module considering a defNP needs to know whether it should look for an antecedent at all.

Some of the first-mention NPs can be detected on structural grounds, that is without any world knowledge. This idea goes back to Hawkins [1978], who identified several correlations between discourse-new definite NPs and features of their syntactic environment. He thus suggests a list of 'special predicates' that license definiteness because they are semantically functional (e.g., *the fact that X, the conclusion that X*), or they contain superlatives or adjectives such as *first, last*, or *maximum*, or the nouns denote temporal entities (*morning, afternoon,* etc.) Further, Hawkins suggests some rules for distinguishing restrictive from non-restrictive modification, which is another major factor for the discourse-new/old distinction. An implementation of his observations was presented by Vieira and Poesio [2001], who defined syntactic patterns for their defNP resolution module (also adding some rules for appositions and proper names), and for their newspaper corpus achieved 72% precision and 69% recall in identifying discourse-new descriptions. In a similar effort of encoding structural patterns, Bean and Riloff [1999] proposed a procedure that learns from the annotated MUC-4 corpus, and achieved slightly better results. Several other researchers tackled the non-/anaphoricity problem with feature-based machine learning approaches. For example, Ng and Cardie [2002a] coded 37 different features with a decision-tree induction system, which applies to all types of nominals, not just to definite NPs. The features belong to four groups: lexical (string or head matching), grammatical (syntactic type of NP, various properties, some specific forms), semantic (lexical relationship), and positional (is the NP located at the beginning of the text). The authors report accuracies of 84% and 86.1% for two different data sets. Note that the figures cannot be compared to those given above, as Ng and Cardie also classified pronouns, which are almost always anaphoric.

Familiarity status   An intermediate step between deciding on anaphoricity and deciding on an antecedent is the task of determining the *familiarity status* of discourse referents, as investigated for instance by Prince [1992], mentioned above in Section 3.1. In this vein, Nissim et al. [2004] proposed a classification that combines elements from Prince's taxonomy and some new categories. The top-level distinction is between *old* (defined as both discourse-old and hearer-old), *mediated* (discourse-new but inferable), and *new*; the *old* class is then split into six specific subtypes, and *mediated* into nine. The first question for Nissim et al. was whether human annotators were able to reliably work with this fairly fine-grained tag set. To make the task easier, the annotation guidelines provide a decision tree that establishes priorities for cases where more than one tag seems to apply. With this provision, the authors report kappa values of 0.845 for the basic three-way distinction and 0.788 for the full taxonomy, which can be regarded as very good agreement. The data used are transcriptions of three dialogues from the *Switchboard* corpus of telephone conversations, and thus the results might not easily carry over to written text. The importance of the role of genre was in fact demonstrated by Ritz et al. [2008], who applied their annotation guidelines to three different German data sets. With seven categories, kappa ranged from a rather low 0.55 for newspaper commentary and 0.61 for 'maptask' dialogues to a more acceptable 0.73 for question-answer pairs elicited by a questionnaire.

Turning to the problem of automatically classifying familiarity status (again with transcribed dialogues), Nissim [2006] worked with the three-way distinction (old, mediated, new) and used only seven features to train her decision tree model, including a fairly "deep" one (grammatical role), the syntactic type of the NP and the determiner, and measurements of previous mentions. The overall accuracy achieved is 79.5%, which includes a rather bad performance on new referents (precision 62.3%; recall only 23.4%). Nissim then re-calculated the results with a conflation of the categories 'mediated' and 'new', which leads to a much higher accuracy of 93.1%; not surprisingly, the 'mediated' category is thus creating considerable difficulty for the automatic classification.

3.5   RULE-BASED METHODS FOR RESOLVING NOMINAL ANAPHORA

We now turn to the "kernel" problem of anaphora resolution (albeit restricted to nominal anaphora). In this section, a variety of heuristic, rule-based methods for four types of nominal anaphors is surveyed: proper names, pronouns, definite NPs, and 'other'-anaphora.

3.5.1   MATCHING PROPER NAMES

The names of persons, institutions, companies, etc. usually offer variants that a writer can use in order to avoid repetition or unnecessary complexity (in case the 'primary' name is rather long). An obvious case is the introduction of a person with both first and last name, and subsequent mention with only one of them (for an example in SUFFERING, see sentences 1.7 and 1.8). Institutions often have abbreviations—e.g., *the United Nations* and *U.N.*, both in sentence 2.3 of SUFFERING. Resolving proper names requires to first identify them; this is not so difficult in English, where capital letters are a quite reliable indicator, but potentially complicated in a language like German, which uses capital letters with every noun. For many "stable" named entities like countries, cities or companies, lists can be found at various websites and then used in gazetteers for named-entity recognition (NER). The names of people, on the other hand, are harder to enumerate. Their first mention can often be guessed in a particular context by a part-of-speech tagger, and subsequent references, possibly using variants of the name, are to be captured with relatively straightforward string-matching methods.

For example, Bontcheva et al. [2002] describe an "orthomatcher" module that applies a set of rules that in part apply to all types of NEs and in part only to NEs that have already been identified as having a specific type. The four general rules are (i) exact matching of the two strings; (ii) 'equivalent' matching based on a synonym list, which can cover nicknames such as *IBM / Big Blue*; (iii) possessive matching by appropriate morphological adjustments (covering *IBM / IBM's*); (iv) 'spurious' list for *not* matching names that are similar but should not be identified, such as companies and their daughter companies (e.g., *BT Cellnet / BT*).

Some of the rules applying only to organizations and persons are a 'word token match' that looks at sets of tokens, ignoring punctuation and word order, covering *Arnold Schwarzenegger / Schwarzenegger, Arnold*; a 'first-token' match handling *Arnold Schwarzenegger / Arnold*—which is the reason why the 'spurious' list is important. Further, a last-token match matches a long name with a single token, covering *Arnold Schwarzenegger / Schwarzenegger*, and an acronym list is applied to handle cases like *IBM / International Business Machines*.

3.5.2   PRONOUN RESOLUTION

The relation between a pronoun and possible antecedents is subject to a few hard constraints: There must be agreement in number and gender, and in the case of intra-sentential candidates there are syntactic binding rules, which determine that, for example, in *Tom saw him* the pronoun cannot refer to *Tom*, whereas it can in *Tom made sure that Sue could see him*. So, when reliable syntactic parsing with morphological analysis is available, a first filter on antecedents can be applied. An algorithm for resolving intra-sentential pronouns by walking the syntax tree was proposed by Hobbs [1978], which according to his manual evaluation on perfect syntax trees yielded an accuracy of 88%.

For the human reader, a highly decisive clue are the semantic *selectional restrictions*: constraints that are imposed by the verb on the semantic types of its arguments. Thus, in the following example the referent of *it* is clear: *John had his coffee in the bar. He drank it very slowly.* Sometimes, the constraints can also be imposed by an adjunct on the modified NP, as in this variant: *John had his coffee in the bar. He liked it with lots of sugar.* This type of knowledge is typically not available to a parser, though, and therefore other factors need to be considered when preferential decisions on antecedents are to be made.

In Section 3.3 above, we discussed Centering theory, which is built on the insight that pronouns play a special role in reference resolution and are subject to a specific ranking induced by grammatical roles. The theory clearly has a point there, but it has been developed largely on the basis of small, hand-crafted example discourses; it is not clear how the theory should be generalized and operationalized to process authentic discourse with more complex sentences and more intricate configurations of referring expressions. Thus, while Centering emphasizes the influence of grammatical roles, in more empirical approaches, a number of different factors have been suggested for obtaining an overall accessibility ranking of discourse referents. These factors include:

- Grammatical role: prefer the subject, as discussed by Centering and elsewhere

- Recency: entities mentioned recently are more salient

- Repeated mention: entities mentioned more frequently are more salient

- Current discourse topic: referents associated with the topic are more salient

- Parallelism: Syntactic structure can make a referent salient with respect to a specific position: *John bought coffee from Jim in the morning. Sue bought coffee from him in the evening.*

Such factors are obviously not independent (repeated mention will often correlate with recency; the discourse topic with subject position; etc.), but at the same time they can make conflicting predictions—note that in the parallelism example, the subject preference is overridden when resolving

Table 3.3: Salience update values for discourse referents [Lappin and Leass, 1994].

(1)	sentence recency	100
(2)	subject emphasis	80
(3)	presentational emphasis ("there are ...")	70
(4)	accusative (direct) object emphasis	50
(5)	indirect object and oblique emphasis	40
(6)	head noun emphasis	80
(7)	non-adverbial emphasis	50

him to *Jim*. So, such factors can hardly be arranged in a fixed evaluation order for finding the "best" antecedent for a pronoun. Instead, they can be operationalized as weighted preferences: Some factors seem to be particularly predictive, others are less important, and the accumulation of weights contributed by the factors decides on the optimal antecedent. This way of modeling the salience of discourse referents is implemented in the well-known RAP algorithm ('Resolution of Anaphora Procedure') by Lappin and Leass [1994] for resolving third-person singular pronouns. (A similar algorithm, which also covers some other types of anaphors, was presented by Stuckardt [2001]).

RAP builds on the output of a syntax parser and keeps track of discourse referents by analyzing each noun phrase and assigning an ID to the supposed referent. Each referent has an associated salience value, which is updated with every sentence. This updating first cuts all values in half, to model the decay of salience as the text progresses, and then adds new points to those referents that are mentioned in the sentence. The number of points reflects the influence of the various factors mentioned above: The increment in salience that a referent receives differs from factor to factor; see Table 3.3. Lappin and Leass determined these values by running their algorithm on a corpus of instruction manuals and finding the setting that yielded the best accuracy. (1) is a general boost for (re-)appearing referents, which gives them a large advantage over referents that are missing in this sentence; in this way, the preference for recent antecedents is realized. The importance of this factor is illustrated by SUFFERING: Consider again Table 2.2 on page 22, which lists the sentence numbers of personal pronouns and their antecedents. In this text, all pronouns have their antecedents either in the same or in the immediately preceding sentence.

The bonuses (2)-(7) are given only to selected candidates, based on grammatical role (2, 4, 5) or appearance in a particular construction—presentational constructions (3) such as *There was a unicorn in the garden* are treated as almost as salient as subjects. (6) and (7) assign additional points to syntactically prominent referents: (6) rewards head nouns and thereby punishes embedded nouns as *the garden* in *The unicorn in the garden was yellow*. Similarly, (7) grants additional points to referents that are being realized in non-adverbial constituents and thereby demarcates adverbials.

In this way, a discourse model of salience scores is maintained when moving through the text, and it serves as the basis for pronoun resolution. Upon encountering a pronoun, the algorithm first collects all referents that were mentioned in the previous four sentences. From this set of candidates, those not agreeing with the pronoun in number and gender are removed. A second filter applies syntactic binding constraints on the candidates appearing in the same sentence as the pronoun. Then, the salience ranking of the candidate referents determines the antecedent—but at this point, two additional weight modifications are applied (just locally for the antecedent decision, not in the discourse model): A candidate that appears in the same syntactic position as the pronoun receives an extra 35 points (to capture the parallelism preference), and the weight of referents that only show up after the pronoun in the sentence (amounting to a cataphoric use of the pronoun) is reduced by 175 points, so that cataphora is rendered less likely.

Table 3.4: Sample run of 'Resolution of Anaphora Procedure' [Lappin and Leass, 1994].

Step	Referent	Referring Expressions	Value
(1)	Sue	{Sue}	310
	unicorn	{a plastic unicorn}	280
	garden	{the garden}	230
(2)	Sue	{Sue}	155
	unicorn	{a plastic unicorn}	140
	garden	{the garden}	115
(3)	Sue	{Sue, she}	155+310=465
	unicorn	{a plastic unicorn, it}	140+280=420
	garden	{the garden}	115
	Jill	{Jill}	270
(4)	Sue	{Sue, she, she}	232.5
	unicorn	{a plastic unicorn, it, it}	210
	garden	{the garden}	57.5
	Jill	{Jill}	135

Table 3.4 shows a short sample run of the algorithm on the sentence sequence *Sue found a plastic unicorn in the garden. She handed it to Jill. She liked it very much.* At step (1), the referring expressions in the first sentence are found and initial salience scores are assigned (cf. Table 3.3); *Sue*, for example, receives 100 points for recency, 80 for subject, 50 for non-adverbial, and 80 for head noun. At step 2, all values are cut in half. No pronouns need to be resolved, so the next sentence is considered in step 3. Here, the pronoun *she* is resolved to the only candidate that morphologically agrees, *Sue*. The other pronoun has two possible antecedents, and the more salient referent needs

to be chosen. At this point, the syntactically-parallel *unicorn* receives additional 35 points and is determined as the antecedent. The referring expressions are entered in the table accordingly, and the new weights for this sentence are added to all the referents. At step 4, the scores are again cut in half, and the pronouns are resolved to the most salient ones that morphologically agree: *She* to *Sue*, and *it* to *unicorn*. Since this is the last sentence of the discourse, weight updating is not necessary.

An implementation of the algorithm, called JavaRAP, has been made available by Qiu et al. [2004].[6] It uses the Charniak parser for syntactic analysis and can be tested online on the web page. The authors report an accuracy of 58% obtained on the MUC-6 training data set. This "real life" evaluation contrasts with the result obtained by Lappin and Leass [1994], who executed the algorithm manually on "edited" output of a parser on a small, restricted-domain corpus and obtained an accuracy of 86%. Interestingly, Lappin and Leass found that in the ensemble of features, the hierarchy of grammatical roles is not very important: When leaving it aside, the accuracy is still 83%. The other factors thus seem to subsume this feature. Most important is 'recency', whose omission leads to merely 59% accuracy.

The difference between "real life" evaluation and simulations of resolution algorithms is emphasized by Mitkov et al. [2002], who point out that serious anaphora resolution requires a significant number of preprocessing steps (parsing, reliable NP identification, named-entity recognition, etc.) that all propagate their errors forward to the resolution module. Their system, MARS[7], uses a sequence of steps similar to RAP and also evaluates a range of features that lead to a ranking of antecedents on the basis of numerical scores. It is, however, embedded in an implemented text analysis system that handles the preprocessing tasks. Also, some of the features go beyond those considered by RAP. For instance, the most frequent referents in the text receive a bonus weight, as a way of accounting for topicality. Also, collocating verbs are tested as an approximation to semantic similarity: When a verb appearing close to the pronoun also occurs in the vicinity of an antecedent candidate, that candidate receives a bonus. And finally, the system includes a module for the classification of *animate entities*, which are generally viewed as more salient for anaphoric reference than inanimate ones. MARS was evaluated on a corpus of technical manuals, where it yielded an accuracy of 59%.

3.5.3   RESOLVING DEFINITE NOUN PHRASES

As mentioned earlier, pronouns play a specific role in linguistic processing and thus are "relatively easy" to resolve automatically; yet the performance of the algorithms discussed above is still far from perfect. With definite noun phrases, unfortunately, the situation is more complicated still, since their usage is much less governed by strong constraints and preferences. We assume at this point that a decision on the anaphoricity of a defNP has already been made (cf. Section 3.4), so that our task now is to find its most likely antecedent. This separation might in fact not be the most effective strategy for an implementation, but for our presentation purposes here we keep the subtasks distinct.

---

[6] `aye.comp.nus.edu.sg/~qiu/NLPTools/JavaRAP.html` (Jan 11, 2011)
[7] `clg.wlv.ac.uk/demos/MARS/` (Nov 22, 2010)

In our overview, we broadly distinguished between *direct* and *indirect* anaphoric relationships by defNPs. A directly-anaphoric defNP can simply express identity of referents (*We saw a unicorn ... The unicorn was ...*). As a variant of the (problematic) plural anaphora, reference can also be directly established to a member of a previously introduced set (*We saw a unicorn family. The father was ...*). But anaphoric NPs often add new information, such as a subjective evaluation (*We saw a unicorn. The poor creature was ...*). Here, besides filling in the adjectival premodifier, the noun has been replaced by a hyperonym (more general word), which in practice happens quite often, makes resolution more difficult, and is sometimes seen as already belonging to the realm of indirect anaphora, or 'bridging', as it was described at the end of Section 3.1.

A well-known approach to both direct and indirect anaphora by Vieira and Poesio [2001] implements defNP resolution on the basis of syntactic analyses for the sentences; in particular, they use data from the Penn Treebank. For the relatively straightforward cases of direct anaphora, the idea is to perform 'head matching': The lexical heads (that is, usually the rightmost word in an NP, before any possible postmodification begins) of the anaphoric defNP and its antecedent NP should be identical. Therefore, when defNP resolution is to be performed on a text, a preprocessing step consists in identifying all the NPs and their head nouns for the antecedent candidates.

Determining the set of antecedent candidates is in general quite difficult: One has to decide whether indefinite, definite, possessive, and other types of NPs should all be considered, and in principle, the topical structure of the text should be used to constrain the search space. Vieira and Poesio circumvent this problem and take a fixed-window approach, in which all NPs appearing within some maximum distance from the anaphor are taken to be antecedent candidates.

Neither is the head matching itself a trivial step, because modifiers can add complications. Thus, while in simple cases we would want to match the antecedent *a pretty, green unicorn* to the anaphor *the unicorn*, we do not want to match *the green unicorn* to *the blue unicorn*–despite their identical heads. Premodifiers and postmodifiers in the NPs therefore need to be considered. The heuristic rules employed by Vieira and Poesio are:

- An antecedent without a premodifier can match any anaphoric defNP with the same head. This covers cases where the anaphor adds more attributes: *a unicorn – the little unicorn*

- When both the defNP and the antecedent candidate are premodified, check whether those of the defNP are a subset of those of the antecedent. This covers cases where the anaphor has less information than the antecedent:

  - *a nice little unicorn – the unicorn:* match

  - *the unicorn community – the ecology-activist community:* no match

- When both the defNP and the antecedent candidate are postmodified, match only when the postmodification is the same:

  - *a unicorn with grey fur – the unicorn with grey fur:* match

   – *a unicorn with grey fur – the unicorn with black eyes and grey fur:* no match

Recall that these rules are merely heuristics—they yielded promising results for the corpus studied by Vieira and Poesio but in general obviously have their limitations.

As for bridging references, the authors devised heuristics for the first three cases from the list of Vieira and Teufel [1997], given above in Section 3.1 (page 44): lexical relations, bridges to proper names, and bridges to non-heads. Using a semantic link computation algorithm similar in functionality to the *WordNet Connect* tool that we introduced on page 25, the 'lexical relations' case is heuristically resolved with WordNet by checking whether the two nouns in question (defNP and antecedent candidate) are in the same synset, or in a hyponymy or hyperonymy relation, or they are co-hyponyms (have the same hyperonym), or they are in a meronymy relation. If any of these tests succeeds, an anaphoric relation is postulated.

Whether references to proper names can be resolved depends on the decision of a Named Entity Recognition module and a subsequent type check with WordNet, as in the first case. That is, for the pair *Intel – the corporation*, NER might find *company* as type, and the WordNet check would indicate synonymy between *company* and *corporation*, so that the antecedent is accepted. Finally, the non-head matching is handled by some additional matches:

- head of defNP with premodifiers of antecedent candidate:
  the stock market crash – the markets

- premodifiers of defNP with premodifiers of antecedents:
  his art business – the art gallery

- premodifiers of defNP with head of antecedent candidate:
  a 15-acre plot and main home – the home site

For solving the complete problem of classifying a defNP as nonanaphoric, directly anaphoric or indirectly anaphoric, and finding the antecedent, Vieira and Poesio use a decision tree that applies the heuristics discussed above (plus those for nonanaphoricity checking) in a fixed order and makes the decision. The authors also conducted experiments on learning the best sequence of decisions automatically. For the subtask of resolving direct anaphora, 62% recall and 83% precision are reported. For bridging, the results were not very good, but Vieira and Poesio point out that only few bridging references were encountered in their corpus (8% of all the defNPs).

3.5.4 WEB-ASSISTED RESOLUTION OF 'OTHER'-ANAPHORA

'Other'-anaphora, as in *crimes and other misdemeanors* is an interesting, specific case of nominal anaphora. Besides, it serves here to illustrate the idea of using web search as a possible replacement for lexical resources, which also applies to other (pardon the pun) kinds of nominal anaphora, in particular to bridging.

The fact that 'other'-anaphora (henceforth: *o-a*) involves neither proper coreference nor bridging might lead to the suspicion that it is not a form of anaphoricity at all. However, notice that the definition of anaphora ("its discourse referent can only be identified when its antecedent is interpreted") indeed subsumes *o-a*, since, in our example, the referent of *other misdemeanors* is a set of objects/concepts that does decidedly not contain *crimes*, i.e., the antecedent.

The first approach using the web for an anaphora resolution task is due to Markert et al. [2003], who tackled the problem that, unlike in *crimes and other misdemeanors*, the antecedent of the abstract 'X and other Y' configuration need not be adjacent. That is the case in the first of the two following examples from Markert et al., where the antecedent appears in italics and the anaphor in boldface:

Example 3.4   Koito has refused to grant Mr. Pickens seats on its board, asserting *he* is a greenmailer trying to pressure Koito's **other shareholders**.

Example 3.5   You either believe Seymour can do it again or you don't. Beside *the designer's age*, **other risk factors for Mr. Cray's company** include the Cray-3's […] chip technology.

The authors observe that while there is in general not a grammatical relation between antecedent and anaphor, there obviously is a semantic relation of type compatibility, because an 'other' linkage could otherwise not be established between the two. And the key idea is that this semantic relationship has a good chance of being structurally explicitly expressed in many other texts, where it can (to a large extent) be found automatically. Consider Example 3.5, where a hyponymy or similarity relation is stated between *risk factors* and the antecedent *age*. Other antecedent candidates to be considered in the resolution process are *Seymour* and *designer*. We wish to rule them out on the grounds of the hypothesis that both of these are less likely to be hyponyms or (quasi-)synonyms of *age*. Instead of consulting a lexical resource, however, we look for structural realizations of that relationship in other texts, and we try to find them using *prototypical patterns* of expressing that relation (following an idea of Hearst [1992]). For the relation considered here, NP$_1$ and other NP$_2$ is such a pattern that can be used to find instances of NP$_1$ and NP$_2$ standing in that relation. Then, we can use the results of such corpus searches for resolving our anaphor: When NP$_2$ is set to *risk factor*, an instantiation of NP$_1$ is established for each of the three antecedent candidates, resulting in three different query terms. The idea is that the query yielding the largest number of search hits will be the "real" antecedent–anaphor pair. Thus, for our example, we submit the queries (Seymour and other risk factors), (designer and other risk factors), and (age and other risk factors) to the corpus, and expect that the last one will have the most hits, indicating that *age* is indeed the antecedent for the *o-a* in the example text.

In principle, such an approach can be realized with any large raw corpus, but the authors found that, for instance, the 100M words British National Corpus (BNC) does not contain age and other risk factors at all. When submitting the queries to the web, using the Google API, however, this expression was found 400 times, whereas the other two queries resulted in 0 hits each, so that the disambiguation is rather clear.

In an extended experiment, Markert et al. collected 120 instances of *o-a* from the Wall Street Journal section of the Penn Treebank, where the antecedent was not structurally given, i.e., not adjacent to *and other* NP$_2$. As antecedent candidates, they took the NPs from the same and the preceding sentence, but excluding pronouns, since these would not work with the search query approach: (it and other risk factors) is not a helpful query. NP extraction is not trivial since complex NPs need to be broken into their parts (recall the discussion of pre- and post-modification above), as each of them is a separate antecedent candidate.

In the case of proper names, a standard NER module was used to determine the type, e.g., for *Seymour* the type *person*. The type was then used as antecedent candidate in the query, rather than the specific proper name, to overcome sparseness. To build the queries, both singular and plural forms of the antecedent candidates were formed, and the number of hits added up to yield the overall score for each candidate. Markert et al. found that this knowledge-poor technique resulted in the same range as those of their previous work with a WordNet-based resolution algorithm for *o-a*.

3.6   STATISTICAL APPROACHES TO COREFERENCE RESOLUTION

The last decade has seen a surge of interest in statistical and machine learning approaches to coreference resolution. While several researchers have also proposed unsupervised approaches, our discussion here will be restricted to supervised learning; this has been largely based on the coreference-annotated MUC and ACE corpora (see Section 3.2). Our goal is to introduce the most important techniques, whereas we will in general not describe quantitative results.[8] The reason is that results from work based on different data can often not be meaningfully compared; one important difference, for instance, is whether the approach performs *end-to-end* coreference resolution beginning from raw text, or starts with data where the referring expressions ('mentions') are already annotated, possibly with syntactic information such as heads.

The important role of such preprocessing was demonstrated by Soon et al. [2001] in their early and influential approach. They performed POS tagging, NP chunking, and NER, and merged the results of these steps, which lead to an overall set of mentions (where they allowed for embedding, or "nested NPs"; this is another point that systems diverge on). Soon et al. evaluated this step separately and found that on a test corpus of 100 texts from the annotated MUC-6 corpus, 85% of the NPs appearing in coreference chains are identified by their procedure. This means that a significant share of errors in end-to-end systems can be expected to be due to imperfect identification of mentions.

In contrast to the heuristic work on individual types of coreference described in the previous sections, the statistical approach takes a broader view and tackles the coreference problem at large: It seeks a partitioning of *all* mentions in a text into sets of coreferent ones. Pronouns, proper names, and full noun phrases are all being handled—but differences between these classes are used as features for classification, as we will see shortly.

---

[8]For an overview on supervised approaches that provides some more details and gives many more references to individual contributions, see Ng [2010].

One final delimitation of scope: In line with the majority of the research (and with the underlying corpora), in this section we consider only the *identity* relation between mentions (or, more precisely, between their discourse referents). Indirect anaphora is not being addressed.

3.6.1   FEATURES

Whatever the method of classification, the mentions first have to be represented as feature vectors. In the following, we provide an outline of the kinds of features that have been used for computing coreference. For features involving pairs of mentions, we call the second one *ana* (it here plays the role of an anaphor, but it might well be a proper name or other NP that according to our terminology is technically not 'anaphoric') and the antecedent candidate under investigation *ante*.

- **NP type:** The NP types of *ana* and *ante* are either read off a syntactic analysis, or, in shallow approaches, determined heuristically by looking at the surface expression. Thus, 'def-NP' can be guessed from the presence of *the*. Pronouns are further differentiated into reflexive, personal, demonstrative, and possessive pronoun. Another simple rule is that nouns starting with a capital letter can be assumed to be a proper name. Usually, specific pairings of *ana/ante* NP types are taken as features for classification.

- **Agreement:** While number agreement can usually be read off *ana* and *ante*, for gender agreement, one needs to supply an 'unknown' value. This holds when either *ana* or *ante* is an NP like *the president*, or a proper name whose gender cannot be determined from a (pre-stored) list of names. The system of Soon et al. [2001] tries to resolve unknown genders when later references to the same name disambiguate it, though, as in *Robin Smith – Mr. Smith*.

- **Shallow syntax:** Many systems use the grammatical roles of *ana* and *ante* as features; recall our discussion of 'transitions' in Centering and entity-based coherence. Another shallow syntactic feature is 'appositive', which tries to check whether *ana* is an apposition to *ante*; this is done by heuristics that, for instance, look at the punctuation, or determine whether a verb is present (which would vote against apposition). On the basis of this feature, rules can be employed such as: An indefinite NP that is not in apposition with a defNP is unlikely to be coreferent with any preceding defNP.

- **Deep syntax:** Several researchers have employed full parsing and then used either the parse trees or subtrees thereof as features, or computed useful extracts, such as dependency paths between root nodes and the nodes for *ana* and *ante*, respectively, (e.g., [Haghighi and Klein, 2009]). Another possibility is to calculate binding constraints within the same sentence, as mentioned earlier.

- **String matching:** For full NPs and names, simple string matching can be highly useful. In addition to exact and partial matching, some approaches use a robust version of the 'head identity' computed by Vieira and Poesio [2001] (as discussed above in Section 3.5.3): After removing articles and demonstrative pronouns, the strings of *ana* and *ante* can be checked for identity. Furthermore, it can be checked whether person names differ only in their prefixes (*Mr. Smith, Robin Smith*), and organization names can be reduced to each other (which might extend beyond matching when gazetteers are being used, leading to 'alias matching'). Other more elaborate techniques include computing minimum-edit distance, as done by Strube et al. [2002].

- **Lexical patterns:** Similar to the web-based method described in the previous section for 'other' anaphora, patterns can be used to guess whether two NPs are semantically related and thus likely to be coreferent. For instance, `ANA is a ANTE` can be instantiated and submitted as a web query, and the frequency be interpreted as indicator of coreference likelihood (see e.g., [Haghighi and Klein, 2009]).

- **Semantics:** A first step toward a deeper analysis is to check whether the semantic classes of *ana* and *ante* agree, for instance by looking up the head nouns in WordNet. The arising word-sense disambiguation problem has been tackled in very different ways, ranging from ignoring it (choosing always the first, most frequent word sense) to full-fledged WSD components. Next, semantic selectional restrictions/preferences have been used for pronouns: Determine the verb governing it and the pronoun's grammatical role, and check whether the antecedent candidate could occur in this role, too. This requires knowledge on semantic categories, which various researchers have mined for instance from Wikipedia.

- **Discourse:** As pronouns are known to have a strong preference for recent candidates, a distance feature is often used, which can be computed in various ways (e.g., number of intervening sentences). This is a simple discourse-based feature; a more interesting one is to compute referential accessibility in terms of text structure, as we will discuss it in the next chapter. Experiments on the role of text structure for pronoun resolution were done by Tetreault [2005].

The aforementioned early work by Soon et al. [2001], which is now often employed as a baseline, used only a small set of 12 such features, which can be computed with relatively lean knowledge on parts of speech and some morphology. The authors used NP type and structural position (but only in terms of POS sequences); number/gender agreement; string matching involving WordNet lookup for head nouns; and distance. In their evaluation, Soon et al. determined the utility of the different features and found that string matching, appositive-checking, and an 'alias' feature, which finds equivalence in date expressions and proper names, are by a wide margin most useful. (This result can be expected to be highly genre-specific for news stories, though.)

Later work, in contrast, often used several dozens of features; for example, Ng and Cardie [2002b] employed 34 grammatical features alone, and 53 in total. Their paper offers an in-depth discussion of the relative utility of different features.

3.6.2   MENTION-PAIR MODELS

In a widely-popular class of models, coreference resolution is formulated as a binary classification task: Given a pair of mentions, determine whether they are coreferent or not. The sum of these pairwise decisions is then to be transformed into a partitioning of the mentions. Unfortunately, this second step is not trivial, because the first can have lead to transitivity problems: It may have postulated coreference between NP_1 and NP_2, and between NP_2 and NP_3, but non-coreference between NP_1 and NP_3. Resolving such problems amounts to a clustering problem, and therefore, approaches to coreference resolution based on the mention-pair model typically implement a two-step process. Before looking at these steps, however, we have to briefly consider the methods of generating training instances, which is another defining characteristic of any instantiation of this model.

Training instances   The data for training a mention-pair classifier is obtained by mapping NPs in the annotated corpus to individual pairs of mentions, each represented as a feature vector and associated with a class label signifying coreference or non-coreference. It needs to be decided, however, *which* pairs of mentions are to be extracted from the corpus. The straightforward option is to take all mentions from a text and generate all possible pairs; however, this would lead to highly skewed data with a large majority of non-coreferent instances.

Soon et al. [2001] suggested a method that has later been adopted by many other approaches: They restrict the extraction to a local *ana/ante* pair and an associated set of negative instances that approximates the ambiguity encountered by the human reader when processing *ana*. Specifically, for any NP in a coreference chain in the text, a positive instance is created by taking the NP as *ana* and its closest preceding *ante*. Thus, a coreference chain of length n generates $n - 1$ positive instances for training. As for the negative instances, a reader's "resolution knowledge" is simulated by extracting all *intervening* NPs between *ana* and *ante*. Since the reader generally has no problem ignoring these when resolving *ana* to *ante*, the hypothesis is that intervening NPs are sufficiently different from the members of the coreference chain. Thus, all mentions that occur linearly between *ante* and *ana* are being combined with *ana* to form negative instances for the training set (regardless whether those mentions are part of any other chains or not). For example, if the subsequence of mentions in the text is $c_1 - e_3 - b_4 - g - c_2$, where g is an insular referring expression, and e_3 and b_4 are part of other chains, the negative instances are (e_3, c_2), (b_4, c_2), (g, c_2).

A slight modification was then added by Ng and Cardie [2002b] to this approach. In case *ana* is a full NP, the *ante* for the positive instance is chosen to be the closest *non-pronominal* antecedent (which might not be the immediate predecessor). The underlying assumption is that a pair [pronoun, full NP] is unlikely to yield productive learning results (neither for machines nor for humans). Other researchers have suggested to also filter the negative instances by removing pairs that violate gender/number agreement [Strube et al., 2002]; the assumption is that such obviously-wrong pairs do not constitute useful training material.

Classification of NP pairs Given the training data, the classifier can be built, and a variety of different techniques have been employed for that. Soon et al. [2001] used the C5 system (successor of C4.5) to learn a decision tree, and tested it on the MUC-6 and MUC-7 corpora. They reported F-measures of 62% and 60%, respectively. Later, their approach inspired an implementation that added a number of features and at the same time was designed in a modular fashion, so that it can serve as a research testbed for experiments [Versley et al., 2008]: The BART system[9] adds both syntactic (the syntactic relation between anaphor and antecedent) and semantic knowledge extracted from Wikipedia to the rather shallow features used by Soon et al. These additional features, as Versley et al. found, leave recall almost unaffected but significantly improve the precision.

As two examples for other classification techniques besides decision trees, we mention here the work of Luo et al. [2004], who used a maximum-entropy model, and Rahman and Ng [2009], who worked with support-vector machines.

Before invoking the classifier on a pair of NPs in a text, one can decide whether a preprocessing step of anaphoricity classification (as described in Section 3.4) should be performed for *ana*, so that determining an *ante* is limited to those NPs that are assumed to be indeed anaphoric. Some researchers found this to improve the resolution performance [Ng and Cardie, 2002a].

Partitioning the set of NPs With a trained classifier in place, it can be employed to make decisions on pairs of NPs in a text, which then have to be clustered into partitions corresponding to discourse referents (or *entities*). The ways of addressing the clustering step can be grouped into *local* approaches that consider only a small number of pairs, and *global* ones that aim to take as many pairings as possible into consideration.

The decidedly-local strategy by Soon et al. [2001] can be called *closest-first*. The text is processed from left to right, and for each NP, an antecedent is being sought by forming pairs that are submitted to the classifier. The candidate pairs are created in right-to-left order starting from the *ana* NP, and as soon as the classifier yields a positive result, that *ante* candidate is accepted. For illustration, we show here an abridged version of an example from Soon et al. The text with the identified NPs is given in Example 3.6; the boldfaced NPs form the chain to be built. Table 3.5 shows the decisions for *ana/ante* pairs in forming this chain, i.e., for the two *ana* NPs involved. The feature vector is: DIST, SEMCLASS, NUMBER, GENDER, PROPER-NAME, ALIAS, ANA-PRONOUN, DEF-NP, DEM-NP, STR-MATCH, APPOSITIVE, ANTE-PRONOUN.

Example 3.6 (**Ms. Washington**)$_{73}$'s candidacy is being championed by (several powerful lawmakers)$_{74}$ including ((**her**)$_{76}$ boss)$_{75}$), (Chairman John Dingell)$_{77}$ (D., (Mich.)$_{78}$) of (the House Energy and Commerce Committee)$_{79}$. (**She**)$_{80}$ currently is (a counsel)$_{81}$ to (the committee)$_{82}$.

Ng and Cardie [2002a] slightly modified the strategy by converting the classification decision to a confidence value and operating with a threshold: The first *ante* candidate (again searching right-to-left from *ana*) reaching the threshold is accepted; this is a *best-first strategy*. Notice that these local

[9]www.bart-coref.org (Jan 27, 2011)

Table 3.5: Classification of NP pairs in ex. 3.6 (after [Soon et al., 2001, p. 529]).

ante	ana	feature vector	class. decision
(several powerful lawmakers)$_{74}$	(her)$_{76}$	0, 1, −, 2, −, −, +, −, −, −, −, −	no
(Ms. Washington)$_{73}$	(her)$_{76}$	0, 1, +, 1, −, −, +, −, −, −, −, −	yes
(the House Energy and C. Committee)$_{79}$	(She)$_{80}$	1, 0, +, 0, −, −, +, −, −, −, −, −	no
(Mich.)$_{78}$	(She)$_{80}$	2, 0, +, 0, −, −, +, −, −, −, −, −	no
(Chairman J.D.)$_{77}$	(She)$_{80}$	3, 1, +, 0, −, −, +, −, −, −, −, −	no
(her)$_{76}$	(She)$_{80}$	3, 1, +, 1, −, −, +, −, −, −, −, +	yes

strategies circumvent the above-mentioned transitivity problem by not considering any more distant *ana/ante*-pairs at all. As Ng [2010] points out, such approaches tend to give too much weight to positive evidence: When NP_1 has been resolved to NP_2, and NP_2 to NP_3, these decisions will stay fixed even if it were easy to notice an incompatibility between NP_1 and NP_3. Furthermore, given the backward-search strategies described, the algorithms can only detect anaphoric reference, whereas cataphora is not accounted for.

One representative of a global search approach addressing these problems is the graph-based work by Nicolae and Nicolae [2006]. Their idea is to represent the overall coreference search space as an undirected, weighted graph with nodes corresponding to the NP mentions in the text, and edges to pairwise coreference relations, labeled with the confidence values returned by the classifier. Thus, a complete picture of pairwise coreference possibilities is taken as the starting point. The task then is to partition the graph into subgraphs that correspond to discourse entities, thereby optimizing over the weights. Nicolae and Nicolae devise a variant of the Minimum Cut algorithm (which we have already encountered in Section 2.2.4 when discussing the graph based text segmentation algorithm by Malioutov and Barzilay [2006]). In this algorithm, the weight of the cut of a graph is the sum of the weights of the edges crossing the cut, and the algorithm finds the partition that minimizes the cut weight. Nicolae and Nicolae suggest an adaptation of Minimum Cut, which involves training a separate model for deciding whether an existing subgraph should be subject to further cutting or whether the mentions assembled in the subgraph should be kept together. (For this purpose, separate training data with good and bad cut decisions was generated from the annotated corpus.)

Another possibility for considering the complete search space is the *Bell tree*, as suggested by Luo et al. [2004]. These authors return to the idea of processing the text incrementally, but unlike Soon et al. and Ng/Cardie, they allow all possible coreference assignments into their representation. When the first NP of a text is encountered, it starts a new entity chain. The second NP can either be placed in the same chain, or start a new one. Likewise, the third NP can be added to one of the chains built so far, or start a new one. And so forth. Consider Figure 3.2, which shows a tree representing this sequence of alternative decisions for a sequence of three NP mentions. Within the nodes, numbers denote mentions, and square brackets their grouping into entities. The *active* mention, which is to be integrated next, is marked with a ∗. Solid arrows indicate that the active mention is being integrated into a partial entity, dashed arrows signify the starting of a new entity (chain).

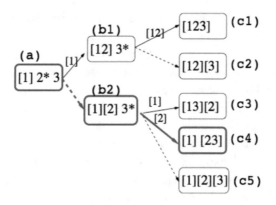

Figure 3.2: Bell tree representation for grouping three NPs into entities (from [Luo et al., 2004, p. 136]).

In such a tree, the number of leaf nodes equals the Bell number $B(n)$ (and hence the name of the tree), which is the number of ways the n objects can be partitioned into non-empty subsets. Our goal now is to find the leaf node that corresponds to the "best", or most probable, partitioning of mentions for a given text. Since the Bell number grows rapidly ($B(20) \approx 5.2 \times 10^{13}$), a full search is impossible; Luo et al. employ a *beam search* by pruning the tree in several ways (*inter alia*, a maximum number of paths to be followed, and a score threshold for nodes to be expanded further). The authors build two different models: One estimates the likelihood of pairing the active mention with the last mentions of the chains built so far; this is in line with the mention-pair model we have been considering so far in this section. Their second model, on the other hand, considers features of the complete candidate chains and compares the active mention to these; this is called an *entity-mention* model, which will be discussed further in the next subsection. However, Luo et al., on the basis of their data, found the mention-pair model to perform slightly better.

Notice that, while the Bell tree approach is certainly global in nature, due to the incremental decision-making it does not support detecting cataphoric reference, unlike the graph partitioning procedure of Nicolae and Nicolae.

3.6.3   ALTERNATIVE MODELS

A much-cited instantiation of the transitivity problem with three NPs (which we mentioned in abstract terms above) is a text containing this sequence of mentions: *Mr. Clinton – Clinton – she*. In a mention-pair model, the first two are very likely to be classified as coreferent on the basis of string matching, while the second and the third might also be judged as coreferent, e.g., due to recency. The conflict between the first and the third can be detected when features are propagated from individual mentions to entities, and when the active mention is indeed compared to the entities built so far, rather than to a few individual mentions only.

One way of addressing the transitivity problem is to employ *Integer Linear Programming (ILP)*. To this end, Finkel and Manning [2008] present an approach that extends earlier work by Denis and Baldridge [2007]. These authors had used ILP to construct a model that jointly accounts for anaphoricity classification and coreference resolution. As it had been shown with other NLP problems, ILP can be helpful when two subtasks "naturally" inform each other, and cascading them one way or the other does not lead to good results, because the first step does not have enough information. Denis and Baldridge observed that earlier attempts on cascading anaphoricity classification (see Section 3.4) and coreference resolution were largely unsuccessful. They demonstrate that their joint-ILP formulation, which combines the two tasks into a single objective function and adds constraints to ensure overall consistency, performs considerably better than an ILP formulation of coreference resolution alone and than baseline systems performing pairwise coreference classification and a cascade of anaphoricity and coreference modules. Thereafter, Finkel and Manning pointed out that the strengths of ILP (as also employed by Klenner [2007]) suggest using this technique for the transitivity problem: The objective function maximises the overall probabilities as given by pairwise classification, and when each variable encoding coreference between two mentions is made a binary variable, then constraints can be added to enforce transitivity. This can be seen as a step towards a more global view on resolving coreference in a text (even though still based on pairwise classification).

More generally, with *entity-mention* models, training and classification occur not on the basis of pair-of-mention features but on cluster-level features. These can be computed with the help of logical predicates such as ALL, MANY, or MOST, which abstract over the mentions that have been mapped to the entity and allow for enforcing, say, gender agreement between the active mention and ALL or just MOST mentions in the cluster. Luo et al. [2004], for instance, used ANY for computing cluster-level features in their entity-mention variant of the model described above.

While there had originally been little evidence that entity-mention models can outperform mention-pair models, recent work by Klenner and Tuggener [2011] suggests that they can yield good results. These authors exploit the fact that an entity-mention model lends itself quite naturally to incremental processing (though it can also be realized in non-incremental fashion), which then approximates the construction of referential chains in the human reading process. The active mention is being compared to all entities built so far and added to the one deemed most likely; there is no separation between classification and clustering steps. As a replacement for cluster-level features, Klenner and Tuggener represent a (partial) entity by a "prototype" that accumulates features from all mentions that have already been mapped to the entity, and that is used for comparison with the active mention. Their algorithm incorporates linguistic binding constraints and also utilizes a salience ranking inspired by RAP [Lappin and Leass, 1994] (as introduced in Section 3.5.2), but the weights are derived directly from annotated corpora. Having evaluated the approach on German and English data, the authors found the incremental procedure to perform better than a non-incremental variant.

Also sharing the concern for bringing back some linguistic knowledge into statistical approaches, in particular by restricting the accessibility of potential antecedents on theoretical grounds, Iida et al. [2009] propose a machine-learning-based operationalization of the *cache model* by Walker [1996], which was inspired by Centering Theory. The cache model tries to exploit the limited attention span of the human reader for anaphora resolution: Salient entities are kept in the cache, non-salient ones are moved to long-term memory, from which they may be recovered only under special circumstances. Antecedents are thus searched for in the cache first, and only if that fails, the larger set of candidates is considered. Iida et al. apply this idea to the problem of Japanese zero pronouns. The antecedent is first looked for within the current sentence: If a candidate is found with a high enough confidence, it is returned; otherwise, the search continues over the salient entities, as stored in the discourse cache. Here, too, a confidence threshold must be passed, because the zero-pronoun can also be non-referential, which is the outcome of the process if no weighty candidate is found.

A crucial problem here is the cache replacement policy: When do new entities enter the cache, and which others have to leave it? Iida et al. couch this as a *ranking* problem and use an SVM-ranker to learn a model from training data that gives the distribution of retained/discarded candidates per sentence. The features they employed are some syntactic and positional features as mentioned above, but in addition some properties of the current cache and discourse situation are being used.

Finally, another interesting recent approach by Cai and Strube [2010a], which also performs classification and clustering in a single step, is based on the idea of *hypergraph partitioning*. It is superficially similar to the work by Nicolae and Nicolae (discussed above), but recall that their procedure still separated a pairwise mention classification phase from the clustering (graph partitioning) phase. Besides, edges play different roles in the two representations. Cai and Strube represent the text as a hypergraph[10], where nodes correspond to mentions and edges correspond directly to relational features between several mentions. For illustration, see Figure 3.3, which shows the initial hypergraph built for the text in Example 3.7 below, but limited to the two entities *Obama* and *Sarkozy*. In the hypergraph, two edges denote the feature *partial string match*, one denotes *pronoun match*, and two denote the feature *all speak*, which is a (slightly idiosyncratic) feature that is true for mentions that appear close to a communication verb.

Example 3.7   [US President Barack Obama] came to Toronto today. [Obama] discussed the financial crisis with [President Sarkozy]. [He] talked to [him] about the recent downturn of the European markets. [Barack Obama] will leave Toronto tomorrow.

Training data is needed to determine the weights of the hyperedges (features); the weights are the percentages of the initial edges that are coreferent in the data. There are hyperedges with degree

---

[10]A hypergraph is a graph where an edge can connect more than two nodes.

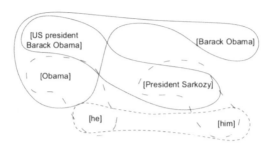

Figure 3.3: Hypergraph for NP analysis of Example 3.7 (from [Cai and Strube, 2010a, p. 145]).

> 2, which can be merged to form higher-degree edges, and hyperedges with degree = 2 for binary relations (such as apposition, substring), which are not to be merged.

Then, given a text that has been transformed to a hypergraph, the task is to find a cut that induces the strongest within-cluster and the weakest between-cluster relations. The authors use a spectral clustering method (2-way partitioning) with a stopping threshold, which is heuristically determined from development data. The algorithm follows the *Normalized Cut* strategy (rather than Minimal Cut), but since this algorithm does not produce singleton sets (which in our problem correspond to non-coreferential NPs and hence are important to allow for), a heuristic singleton creation detection step has to be added. As for results, the authors report that their approach outperforms the system of Soon et al. [2001] (when using the same feature set), as well as another baseline system.

3.7   EVALUATION

Over the past 10 years, the field of coreference resolution has seen a clear shift of attention from early symbolic methods, which involved rule-based linguistic analysis in various ways, to corpus-based machine-learning approaches that have been spurred by the development of annotated corpora and a series of shared tasks that allowed for systematic comparison of competing ideas. This comparison, however, bears another problem that we have not addressed yet: how to evaluate the quality of a coreference resolution system. It is by no means clear "how to count", since the kinds of errors that can occur are quite manifold. Applying straightforward precision and recall measures is problematic, because we need to distinguish three types of errors (which, moreover, might be argued to be not equally "bad"): wrong resolutions, missing resolutions (an anaphor is not resolved), and spurious resolutions (a non-anaphor is resolved). Intuitively, we want to reward a system that produces a partition that comes as close as possible to the true partition. To this end, an early influential approach was the MUC metric [Vilain et al., 1995]: For each cluster of mentions in the gold standard, compute the number of pairwise links that have to be added or deleted when mapping a system-computed cluster to it. Let S be the system-generated partition and T the gold-standard (true) partition:

$$Precision = \frac{\sum_{s \in S \cap t \in T \neq \emptyset} |s \cap t| - 1}{\sum_{s \in S} |s| - 1} \qquad Recall = \frac{\sum_{s \in S \cap t \in T \neq \emptyset} |s \cap t| - 1}{\sum_{t \in T} |t| - 1} \qquad (3.1)$$

One problem with this metric is that it unduly favors systems producing few, big clusters. Let us consider an example: $T = \{\{A, B, C\}, \{D, E, F, G\}\}$; $S = \{\{A, B\}, \{C, D\}, \{F, G\}\}$. The evaluation formulas produce the following:

$$Precision = \frac{(2-1) + (1-1) + (1-1) + (2-1)}{(2-1) + (2-1) + (2-1)} = 2/3 \qquad (3.2)$$

$$Recall = \frac{(2-1) + (1-1) + (1-1) + (2-1)}{(3-1) + (4-1)} = 2/5 \qquad (3.3)$$

However, if $S = \{\{A, B, C, D, E, F, G\}\}$, recall is a perfect 1.0, and precision $= 5/6$, which seems intuitively implausible.

A second problem is that the metric covers the information in "interesting" clusters but not in singleton sets, since a pairwise comparison is not possible. Thus, for data sets including singletons, the measure is not applicable. (This problem was inherited from the setup of the original MUC data, which had not contained singletons.) In response, the B^3 measure by Bagga and Baldwin [1998] computes precision and recall for all mentions m_i in the text individually:

$$Precision(m_i) = \frac{|S_{m_i} \cap T_{m_i}|}{|S_{m_i}|} \qquad Precision(m_i) = \frac{|S_{m_i} \cap T_{m_i}|}{|T_{m_i}|} \qquad (3.4)$$

Again, S_{m_i} is the system-computed cluster and T_{m_i} the gold-standard cluster. The results for all the mentions are combined (by averaging) into overall precision/recall figures for a text. Today, a few variants of B^3 as well as several other metrics are in use, and none is commonly regarded as superior. For this reason, e.g., Haghighi and Klein [2009] provide evaluation results for their coreference resolution with an array of four different metrics. Cai and Strube [2010b] present a thorough discussion of several contemporary metrics and argue that most of them (including the two mentioned above) are not suitable for end-to-end coreference resolution, which includes the automatic detection of mentions; in contrast, MUC and other measures assume that mentions are already given. Cai and Strube then suggest two variants of established metrics, which also account for mention detection.

3.8 SUMMARY

In this chapter, we introduced the notions of coreference and anaphora, and then discussed the variety of subproblems involved, along with some computational approaches towards solving them. An overall procedure for resolving coreference in a text T can be characterized as follows:

1. Identify the referring expressions RE_i (mentions) in T

2. Feature construction: For each RE_i, compute a set of features characterizing it

3. Anaphoricity classification: For each RE_i, decide whether it is anaphoric or not: reduce the search space by removing from RE_i the pleonastic pronouns, etc.

4. Candidate generation: For each RE_i, produce a set of potential antecedents $Ante_{RE_i}$

5. Filtering: Delete those members from each $Ante_{RE_i}$ that violate hard coreference constraints (e.g., agreement, binding)

6. Scoring: Order each $Ante_{RE_i}$ on the basis of soft constraints (preferences)

7. Clustering: Partition the set of all RE_i into clusters of mentions that refer to the same entity

Obviously, implementations may vary; for instance, it is controversial whether a step of anaphoricity classification should be included or not. Furthermore, as we pointed out, not all systems operate *end-to-end*: Often, mention identification is not included (because it is already present in the test data used for evaluation), so comparing different systems can at times be difficult.

Recent trends   While earlier research on coreference and anaphora has focused on individual sub-problems (recall, e.g., that Centering dealt just with pronouns, and that we saw a range of subproblem-specific solutions in Section 3.5), the more recent statistical approaches address the coreference problem at large. This is intuitively appealing, as the same entity can clearly be referred to within a text by rather different types of expressions.

For quite some time, the work on statistical methods centered on rich-feature models that tried to model the impact of very different factors, where the task is to learn appropriate weights. More recently, however, interesting (and successful) approaches have been proposed that instead solve coreference in a modular fashion, as a cascade of separate steps with one building on the results of the others.

In this vein, for example, Haghighi and Klein [2009] presented an unsupervised approach that according to the authors beat previous unsupervised systems and also approached the state of the art of supervised resolution. They employ three steps: First, syntactic analysis is performed and paths are constructed in the tree from an anaphor to potential antecedents (somewhat reminiscent of the pioneering tree walking algorithm of Hobbs [1978]), where the syntactic model is learned from a treebank. Second, candidate pairs are checked for semantic compatibility by inspecting head words and names; this compatibility is learned from unlabeled corpora, including web data. Finally, after these syntactic and semantic filters, the candidate that minimizes tree distance is selected.

Another example of a cascade of individual modules is realized in the system by Lee et al. [2011], which won the 2011 *CoNLL Shared Task* on coreference resolution: Tiers of deterministic models (*sieves*) are executed in the order from highest to lowest precision, with each tier refining the results of its predecessor. Some of the tasks performed by the modules have been introduced throughout this chapter, such as various methods of string matching, including head-word matching, or lexical-chain construction based on WordNet. Among the "new" tasks is a speaker-identification module that, *inter alia*, allows for handling 1st and 2nd person pronouns.

In such modular systems, "traditional" linguistic analysis is no longer mixed into large feature vectors but acts as distinct filtering steps, whereby many of the older ideas on coreference resolution appear to be revived, like in a few approaches we mentioned at the end of the previous section. Clearly, one reason for this development is that the knowledge needed for such linguistic filters has become increasingly available: Syntactic parsing has improved considerably in recent years, lexical knowledge (even if merely in the shape of huge sets of co-occurrence patterns) can be harvested from the web, etc.

Small Discourse Units and Coherence Relations

What is it that distinguishes a random sequence of sentences from a *text?* We have seen that a text (or a portion of it) addresses a common topic (Chapter 2), and that it keeps referring to the same entities (Chapter 3). In addition, however, the linear order of sentences is not arbitrary but reveals a certain inner logic: The meaning of a sentence usually relates to that of the previous sentences. In this chapter, we examine the notion of *coherence relation*, which seeks to capture this inner logic. Section 4.1 provides an introduction, and Section 4.2 looks at the task of finding the minimal units for such an analysis, i.e., the *segmentation* problem. At the linguistic surface, the most important signal for coherence relations are *connectives*, whose role will be examined in Section 4.3, followed by a discussion of certain other features that are amenable to automatic analysis. Then, in Section 4.4 we turn to the problem of building a text structure over coherence relations, and will discuss a number of approaches to parsing such structures. Technically, the interesting move here is from flat structures, as used for topic segmentation in Chapter 2, to hierarchical structures.

Why is it useful to analyse coherence relations and the structure they induce? Even when no "deep" understanding of a text is targeted, local information about relations between text spans enables more interesting information extraction; for example, we can try to identify when an author gives a *reason* for a statement of his—which might for instance be a personal opinion, leading to more elaborate versions of the sentiment analysis task. And on a higher level of text, i.e., beyond merely-local analyses, coherence structure has been shown to be relevant for text summarization, as it offers clues to the relative importance of particular text spans, which can be used to supplement standard statistical means for computing sentence weights.

4.1 COHERENCE RELATIONS

For grasping the intuitive idea, the phenomenon *coherence relation* is best illustrated with minimal pairs like the following from Hobbs [1979]:

Example 4.1   John took a train from Paris to Istanbul. He has family there.

Example 4.2   John took a train from Paris to Istanbul. He likes spinach.

While 4.1 is a natural discourse that poses no problem for understanding, most readers will stumble upon encountering 4.2 and either reject it as "incoherent", or take a bit of time to construct some involved explanation why, in some specific situation, the sentence pair might indeed make sense.

The difference points to a crucial feature of coherent discourse: the absence of what is called "non-sequiturs". In the linear flow of information, there ought to be no content-gap when connecting the segment currently under consideration to the meaning of the previous discourse as it has already been processed successfully. Reading usually proceeds so smoothly that we hardly notice the effort we make to establish those connections, to decide on what kind of "glue" is needed to link a new segment to the previous ones, and the established term for this glue is *coherence relation*.

While the term *coherence* (see the definition on page 1) refers to linking adjacent material on the level of semantic/pragmatic interpretation and thus "underneath the surface", the notion of *cohesion* (see the definition on page 20) characterizes the function of linguistic means for making connections explicit. This includes on the one hand lexical means such as pronouns or connectives: words whose interpretation requires the understanding of another text unit. But cohesion is also created on the syntactic level, for example by using comparatives, or by choosing parallel sentence structures for material that is to be interpreted in corresponding ways. Usually, coherence and cohesion coincide, but cohesion is not strictly necessary for coherence to arise; see Example 4.3, which does not contain overt signals yet poses no problem for interpretation. Vice versa, in Example 4.2 above we can find cohesion (the pronoun) but no coherence.

Example 4.3   John took a train from Paris to Istanbul. Turkey has become a popular tourist destination.

As for the coherence *relation*, we can view it as the formalization of the added value in comprehending a pair of discourse units; in other words, the information we construct in addition to that provided by the individual discourse segments themselves. The relation thus supplements the local coherence possibly arising from *entity mentions* in the two discourse units (recall our definition of entity-based local coherence on page 52). Sometimes, the coherence relation is explicitly marked in the text, as in this case:

Example 4.4   John took a train from Paris to Istanbul, because he has family there.

In contrast, Example 4.1 omitted the explicit marker, and it was understandable nonetheless, because the reader's world knowledge can be assumed to readily fill in the information that the second sentence quite probably gives the *reason* for the statement in the first sentence. Hence, when the coherence relation can be easily inferred, it is not necessary for the writer to signal it explicitly. Now, consider a slight extension of our short example discourse:

Example 4.5   [a] John took a train from Paris to Istanbul, departing from Montparnasse at noon. [b] He has family in Istanbul.

Still, John's having family in Istanbul is offered as an explanation for his going there, but sentence [b] does not connect quite as directly to the previous discourse as it did in 4.1 and in 4.4. Here in 4.5, the detail on his departure somehow intervenes—but it does not really disturb the information flow; the only difference is that the "point of attachment" for sentence [b] is not immediately preceding it but one segment shifted to the left, beyond the gerund clause. (After all, John's having family in Istanbul is not a reason for departing at some precise time from some particular train station, but for his general decision to make the trip.) We can say that the gerund clause, providing additional details, is *dominated* by the matrix clause, which thereby retains the job of serving as the anchor for the information coming in after the dominated clause is finished. Observing such effects leads many discourse researchers to stipulate a basic partitioning of coherence relations into (a) those that treat the related segments on a par, and (b) those that assign more weight to one of the two segments. In the pioneering work of Polanyi [1988] and later in SDRT [Asher and Lascarides, 2003], this distinction is labeled by the terms *coordinating* and *subordinating* coherence relations. The latter do not advance the discourse on the same level, but temporarily move one level down (or, using a different metaphor, provide some information "in parentheses"), before subsequent material then again attaches to the major segment. In this way, coherence relations serve not only as labels for the added informational value stemming from two discourse segments placed in adjacency, but also as *structure-building* devices for the discourse.

The distinction between the two types of relations obviously invites a comparison to syntactic sentence structure. In the RST framework, for example, Matthiessen and Thompson [1988] argued strongly in favor of a close conceptual correspondence between grammatical subordination and discourse subordination; this discussion is ongoing, see [Fabricius-Hansen and Ramm, 2008].

In the examples given so far, the content of one sentence provided the reason for the other. Clearly, there are certain other kinds of connections that can be made, such as:

Example 4.6   John took a train from Paris to Istanbul, but he never arrived.

Example 4.7   Although John took a fast train from Paris to Istanbul, he arrived late.

Example 4.8   John took a train from Paris to Istanbul. Afterwards, he called his mother.

Few scholars would dispute that coherence relations "exist" and are an important aspect of discourse processing. Unfortunately, though, the general agreement stops rather soon beyond this basic intuition. How *exactly* can 'coherence relation' be defined? How many are there? We believe that causes and reasons are an important case, but which others are to be accounted for? On what grounds do we justify the postulation of one particular set of coherence relations? And, is there *always* a coherence relation between adjacent sentences? Do they apply recursively to larger text spans as well? What is the relation [sic] between coherence relations and the *structure* of discourse? Basically, we can distinguish six different perspectives on studying coherence relations, which different researchers have adopted. (These perspectives are not completely disjoint, and so the following enumeration is a slight idealization, but keeping them separate serves to focus more clearly on the various viewpoints.)

Be skeptical and parsimonious.   One response to the question is to deny the possibility of a well-motivated and systematic set of coherence relations. There are so many reasonable ways of juxtaposing two spans of text, the argument goes, that there is no point in trying to enumerate and to differentiate them. This was, in essence, the view of Grosz and Sidner [1986] who emphasized the importance of distinguishing between coordinating and subordinating relations for capturing structural effects, but were not interested in any further differentiations. Their only two coherence relations thus are *satisfaction-precedence* (reader needs to understand the first message before the second makes sense to her) and *dominance* (one message supports the other and is structurally subordinated).

Resort to insights from philosophy.   If we do believe in the need to differentiate between semantic or pragmatic kinds of coherence relations, but we do not believe in merely stipulating them, we can check what influential philosophers had to say about the issue. Kehler [2002], in his account of coherence relations, cites the empiricist David Hume, who in the 18th century had posited that there are basically three ways of "connecting ideas": *contiguity* (temporal succession and other ways of being naturally adjacent), *cause-effect*, and *resemblance* (situations or entities are similar or dissimilar). Kehler then proposed 14 relations that are grouped in these three categories.

Be inspired by the lexicon of your language.   A different way of justifying relations is to inspect the linguistic means of signalling them. In the examples so far, the connectives *because, but, although, afterwards* have been used. Knott and Dale [1994] collected a large inventory of such connectives in English, undertook a replacement test to check for differences in meaning, and then set groups of similar connectives in correspondence to coherence relations. So, the idea is: When there is a meaningful way of connecting ideas, your language will have a way of marking it.[1] The same route was taken by Martin [1992], who thoroughly studied English connectives and associated syntactic means.

Be motivated by syntax and semantics.   An alternative linguistic approach is to view the matter from a semantic vantage point and to see discourse meaning as a natural extension of sentence meaning. An account of discourse structure then has to build on a formal account of sentence meaning and essentially use the same framework. A well-known theory is *Segmented Discourse Representation Theory* [Asher and Lascarides, 2003], which allows a coherence relation into its inventory when it can be clearly defined and differentiated from others, in syntactic and semantic terms.

Try to explain human cognition.   Human readers process text and build mental representations; psychologists have studied this extensively, for instance in the tradition of Kintsch [1988]. Researchers

---

[1]In later work, Knott and Sanders [1998] extended the approach to studying connectives in different languages.

investigating coherence relations (which readers can derive even when explicit connectives are absent; recall Example 4.1) emphasize that these relations must have a mental counterpart, and thus psycholinguistic methods can be employed to see what relations seem to be at work, and how. This is the primary motivation of research such as that of Sanders et al. [1992], who advocate defining coherence relations in terms of certain *primitives* that seem to play a role in cognition at large and can be used to compose a number of coherence relation definitions.

Be inspired by authentic texts. In some sense, the most "radically-empirical" approach is to collect a number of different texts and create analyses for them that on the one hand are intuitively plausible, and on the other hand wherever possible look for parallel situations that should be captured with the same relation. In this way, the inventors of *Rhetorical Structure Theory (RST)*, Mann and Thompson [1988], came up with about 25 different relations that proved useful in explaining the coherence of texts. The ensuing popularity of RST in discourse research strengthens this empirical argument—even though the underlying criterion for postulating a certain relation is still the subjective intuition of the developer of the theory (hopefully then shared by the analyst who applies it).

RST thus was the framework that from the beginning has been applied to significant amounts of authentic text, and it has gained considerable popularity in different branches of discourse research, and also in computational linguistics [Taboada and Mann, 2006a,b]. At first, it was widely used in text generation as a device for representing structural properties of the text to be produced; later, it was shown that the opposite direction is also possible, i.e., that RST can serve as a framework for parsing text. There are a number of aspects of RST that can be criticized, and we will mention some in Section 4.4, but due to its important role in discourse parsing work, we will take it as the primary tool for the purposes of this chapter.[2] This means that lines of research that are primarily inspired by linguistic grammar formalisms, and hence by the desire to extend sentence syntax and semantics "upward" to the discourse level will not be covered here in depth. To mention some work just briefly, Webber [2004] proposes an extension of lexicalized tree adjoining grammar (LTAG) to the discourse level, resulting in a formalism called D-LTAG; Danlos [2008] suggests discourse extensions to synchronized TAG; and a similar effort for Combinatory Categorial Grammar is made by Nakatsu and White [2010]. The work in Segmented Discourse Representation Theory [Asher and Lascarides, 2003] is mentioned in this chapter occasionally, but its main interest is on the side of linguistic semantics, targeting the question of computing text meaning systematically from sentence meanings. (For an insightful comparison of RST, SDRT, and a third framework—'conjunctive relations' as proposed by Martin [1992]—see [Bateman and Rondhuis, 1997].)

What, then, is a coherence relation in RST? The theory opts to make the *speaker intention* the central criterion for assigning a particular relation when analyzing a text. That is, when we read Example 4.5 above, RST predicts that we, more or less consciously, reconstruct the goals of the speaker/writer and find that she wanted to inform us about John's travelling action in [a], adding

---

[2]In fact, the term 'rhetorical structure', borrowed from RST, is often used for this level of text description in the literature. We consider this a somewhat skewed notion of 'rhetoric', though, and prefer the more neutral term 'coherence-relational structure'. After all, many of the relations involved are semantic or 'informational' in nature and have little or no connection to rhetorics.

Evidence

constraints on nucleus: reader might not believe nucleus to a degree satisfactory to writer

constraints on satellite: reader believes satellite or will find it credible

constraints on the N+S combination: reader's comprehending satellite increases reader's belief of nucleus

the effect: reader's belief of nucleus is increased

locus of the effect: nucleus

Figure 4.1: Definition of the coherence relation EVIDENCE, following Mann and Thompson [1988].

details about the departure, and then in [b] wanted to offer us an explanation for his decision. Let us contrast this with yet another variant of the example:

Example 4.9   [a] John took a train to Istanbul! [b] I saw him boarding it at platform two!

Here the situation appears to be slightly different. The utterance seems to make most sense when we reconstruct [a] as new and possibly surprising information that the author wants to convey to us; further, she reckons that we might not readily believe that statement, and therefore chose to add [b] as evidence that might strengthen our belief in the factuality of [a]. Under this interpretation, a discourse analyst would take 4.9 as an instance of the RST relation EVIDENCE. Its definition is shown in Figure 4.1, serving as an illustration of how Mann and Thompson [1988] chose to characterize their relations. We will not go into much detail here, but two aspects should be explained: (i) nuclearity and (ii) the semantics/pragmatics distinction.

Nuclearity   The terms *nucleus* and *satellite* in the definition indicate that RST takes EVIDENCE, and the vast majority of the other coherence relations, as giving different 'weight' to the elements being related. In Example 4.9, given the interpretation we described, [a] is the more central message, the one that the reader is to be convinced of; [b] on the other hand plays more of a supporting role, employed by the author in order to more reliably get message [a] across. Mann and Thompson therefore see the relation as composed of a nucleus and a satellite, and so the definitions provide characterizations of these two roles that have to be checked in a text when the analyst wants to apply a relation. There are a few relations that do not make this difference in weights, the so-called 'multinuclear' relations. One example is SEQUENCE, at work in 4.8 above, which applies when some events are stated to occur in temporal succession, with none being particularly more important for the author's purposes than the other. Another example is CONTRAST, where the message is that two situations are different (while being in principle comparable):

Example 4.10   John took a train to Istanbul, whereas Mary went to Moscow.

As a diagnosis, Mann and Thompson suggest a deletion test, which predicts that when removing all satellite units from a text, the main message is still recognizable (even though there will, obviously, be cohesion problems), whereas removal of nuclei from a text leads to incoherence.

'Semantic' versus 'pragmatic' relations   Looking once more at examples 4.1 and 4.9 above, we notice that in both cases the coherence relation (which, incidentally, is entirely implicit, i.e., not explicitly signalled) involves causality in a wide sense: In 4.1, the author uses the second sentence to explain the action reported in the first sentence. The 'causality' here is being reported: John did something, and he had a particular reason for it. In 4.9, we also find 'causality', but the relation is not merely being reported. The speaker having seen John boarding is not the cause or reason for John making the trip; rather, it is the reason for the speaker *making the statement* in [a]. The 'causal' relation thus holds not between two reported events out there in the world, but between two speech acts performed by the speaker. Similar to nuclearity, RST posits that this distinction generalizes to other relations, so that we speak of families of 'semantic' relations (between eventualities "in the world") and 'pragmatic' relations (between speech acts of the author). Mann and Thompson [1988] used the alternative terms 'subject-matter' versus 'presentational' relations for this phenomenon, meaning essentially the same.[3]

Another pair of terms, which was introduced by Moore and Pollack [1992], is 'informational' versus 'intentional' relations. This is essentially the same distinction, but Moore and Pollack in their study emphasized that text analysts often encounter ambiguity specifically along this dimension: Two discourse units may simultaneously be related on the informational (semantic) and on the intentional (pragmatic) level, and then the analyst has to make a more or less arbitrary choice. Moore and Pollack thus argued that two levels of analysis should be maintained in parallel; we will return to this viewpoint in Section 4.5.

Coherence relation: A specific relationship, holding on the semantic or the pragmatic level of description, between adjacent units of text. Definitions can be given in semantic terms, or in terms of speaker intentions (as in Rhetorical Structure Theory, RST). The granularity of a postulated relation set can differ widely, but relatively common are the groups *causality*, *similarity/contrast*, and *contiguity* (temporal or other). In the case of RST, most relations are said to hold between a unit that is more important for the purposes of the speaker (nucleus) and one unit that is less important, or supportive in nature (satellite). A similar distinction is made in Segmented Discourse Representation Theory (SDRT) between subordinating and coordinating relations, but here the structural consequences are being emphasized, instead of the intentional aspect.

The relation set of RST   Finally, we show in Figure 4.2 the full set of relations that Mann and Thompson had suggested. There is some variation between different publications (including the RST website[4]), but Figure 4.2 shows a core set, structured along the two dimensions we just introduced, with the original (and not uncontroversial) classification of the relations by Mann and Thompson.

---

[3]For an in-depth discussion of the semantic/pragmatic distinction, see, for instance, [Redeker, 1990] or [Sanders, 1997].
[4]www.sfu.ca/rst/ (Jan 5, 2011)

	Semantic	Pragmatic
Nucleus and Satellite	Elaboration	Motivation
	Circumstance	Antithesis
	Solutionhood	Background
	(Non-)Volitional Cause	Enablement
	(Non-)Volitional Result	Evidence
	Purpose	Justify
	Condition	Concession
	Otherwise	
	Interpretation	
	Evaluation	
	Restatement	
	Summary	
Multi-nuclear	Sequence	
	Contrast	
	Joint	

Figure 4.2: The set of coherence relations defined by Mann and Thompson [1988].

Their paper provides explanations, and a useful table with abridged definitions of all relations is provided on the RST website. We do not reproduce more definitions here, but an occasional relation will be discussed later in the chapter.

As for the nucleus/satellite distinction, Mann and Thompson's view of nuclearity as a central principle of discourse organization is not entirely unproblematic. As argued more extensively by Stede [2008a], annotators working with RST often report problems with making the decision on naming the more nuclear units. Further, when they are asked for the reason of a unit being nuclear, a fairly wide range of factors is being mentioned, including not only communicative purpose (intention) in the narrow sense but also 'newness' as opposed to 'givenness' (an information-structural notion), the structural role in the overall discourse, syntactic structure, or the sheer requirement of the relation definition. Regarding the last point, in the semantic relations CONDITION and PURPOSE, both units are obviously required for a complete message fulfilling this particular relation:

Example 4.11   If [the rain doesn't stop,]$_S$ [we will cancel the party]$_N$. (CONDITION)

Example 4.12   [John crossed the street]$_N$ so that [he could inspect the mural more closely]$_S$. (PURPOSE)

It is not clear that the satellites are of less importance in such cases, and it usually depends on the context which unit is actually more prominent for the overall message of the text. So the

N/S assignment by the relation definition seems to some extent arbitrary. Furthermore, at least with CONDITION, the instrument of the deletion test leads to unconvincing results, since the antecedent is clearly semantically necessary for the whole sentence to be understood properly.

Before we turn to the task of automatically segmenting a text and recognizing coherence relations, the reader is to be reminded that in RST and in similar theories, coherence relations hold not only between individual sentences (as in all our examples so far) but recursively between larger segments as well, resulting in a complete tree structure for a text (span), which we call a *coherence-relational structure*. This will be explored in Section 4.4.

4.2 SEGMENTATION: FINDING ELEMENTARY DISCOURSE UNITS

The goal of automatically finding coherence relations in text, and (optionally) building a recursive text structure over them implies a notion of an *elementary discourse unit*[5] (henceforth: EDU) that serves as the building block for such structures—similar to the role of words (or multiwords) as elementary units of sentences. EDUs then are the entities that are being related by coherence relations, thereby forming larger discourse units, which in turn may be linked by coherence relations. In this section, we consider the problem of identifying EDUs in text, that is, the *segmentation* problem. The underlying difficulty here, which renders the analogy to the word–sentence relation a little imprecise, becomes clear when we temporarily adopt a cognitive perspective: Readers, while processing a text, are assumed to mentally construct coherence relations, but this construction applies to their *interpretations* of spans of text. Similar to the anaphora resolution process, the entities being related are *abstract objects*[6], which might correspond nicely to a surface segment of the text, but not necessarily so.

With this complication kept in mind, we now discuss approaches to automatic segmentation, which in the absence of any interpretation has to simply assume that nice correspondence. Note that the segmentation task can be interesting for various applications independently of coherence-relational structure; it plays a role, for example, in sentence compression (for text summarization), and in textual alignment for machine translation.

4.2.1 DEFINING EDUS

For segmenting written text, it is basically taken for granted that sentence boundaries are also EDU boundaries, i.e., EDUs do not span across sentences. So the task boils down to deciding for a sentence whether it should be further segmented into smaller units. As hinted at, this is in principle a semantic and pragmatic issue. Thus, [Polanyi et al., 2004, p. 110] characterize elementary units as "the syntactic constructions that encode a minimum unit of *meaning* and/or discourse *function* interpretable relative to a set of contexts." A minimum unit of meaning, according to Polanyi et al., communicates information about no more than one 'event', 'event type' or 'state of affairs',

---

[5]Other terms to be found in the literature include *minimal discourse unit* and *discourse constituent unit*.
[6]See Asher [1993] for an extensive treatment of the role of abstract objects in discourse.

Table 4.1: Examples of minimal discourse units and their types [Polanyi et al., 2004].

Segment types	Realizations	Examples
Eventualities	clauses	[I heard the dog][that was barking.]
	predication	[California elected Schwarzenegger] [governor.]
	infinitival modif.	[They left] [to get the tickets.]
Interpolations	parentheticals	[The show [(and what a show it was)] lasted 4 hours.]
Fragments	section headings	[4. Discussion]
	list items	[e.g., [hydrogen,] [helium]]
Conj. operators	conjunction	[We arrived] [and] [got seats.]
Discourse operators	"scene setting" modifier	[On Tuesday,] [we will see the sites.]

whereas a minimal functional unit is one that encodes information about how it relates structurally, semantically, interactionally or rhetorically to other units in the discourse or to the extralinguistic context. With these criteria, the authors in a first step arrive at rather small units; Table 4.1 reproduces a few examples from [Polanyi et al., 2004, p. 111], where material in square brackets constitutes an individual EDU. In their second step, they add a discourse criterion to exclude a range of very small units: Proper discourse units are only those that can be "independently continued" in the subsequent discourse. Several grammatical realizations of events or event types thus lose their EDU status. In the following list, the underlined portions are by this criterion not separate segments: gerunds (*Singing is fun*), nominalizations (*Rationalization is useless*), auxiliaries and modal verbs (*I might have succeeded*), and clefts (*It was the tiger that we liked best*).

The task of defining the criteria for EDUs in a detailed manner is inevitable when guidelines for human annotators are to be produced (e.g., [Carlson and Marcu, 2001]). A central problem here is the treatment of various kinds of ellipsis. Another one concerns the status of relative clauses: There is a well-known semantic difference between restrictive and non-restrictive relative clauses in that the former serve "only" to identify a referent (which often can be paraphrased with an adjectival phrase), whereas the latter actually provide a new information unit and in this sense carry the discourse forward. In English, the two can often be distinguished by the choice of relative pronoun and comma.

Example 4.13   The red car narrowly won the race.

Example 4.14   The car that was red narrowly won the race.

Example 4.15   The red car, which my friend had bought last week, narrowly won the race.

Clearly, in 4.13 we would not want to attribute EDU status to the adjective *red*, and that is a good reason to also deny the relative clause in 4.14 that privilege. Whereas 4.15 indeed gives two different pieces of information, and, applying the 'continuation' criterion by Polanyi et al., both could be elaborated in the subsequent sentence. Therefore, the relative clause would be treated as an EDU. Granted, the distinction between non-/restrictive relative clauses is not always as clear-cut as here. Also, the suggestion to treat non-restrictive ones as separate EDUs is just one viewpoint (shared, for instance, by Lüngen et al. [2006], but not by Polanyi et al. [2004], as seen in Table 4.1). Existing annotation guidelines take different positions on this and on other questions; so far, it is by no means clear what an 'objective' definition of EDU ought to look like. Another example is the status of complement clauses:

Example 4.16   Tom said that the red car narrowly won the race.

While there are two verbs and hence two clauses, it seems reasonable to enforce the criterion that all EDUs of a sentence should by themselves be structurally complete. That holds for 4.15 above, where the demarcation of the relative clause yields two complete units of information: My friend bought the car last week, and the car won the race. On the other hand, separating the complement in 4.16 would yield *The red car narrowly won the race* and *Tom said*, and the latter is neither syntactically nor semantically complete. When a verb structurally takes a complement clause, we therefore would not assume an EDU boundary (in agreement with Tofiloski et al. [2009]; in disagreement with Carlson and Marcu [2001] and with Lüngen et al. [2006]).

   Prepositional phrases are also handled in different ways in the various approaches. For Tofiloski et al. [2009], any EDU must contain a verb, so that in *We stayed home because of the rain*, the underlined material will not be a separate EDU. Others, like Carlson and Marcu [2001] or Le Thanh et al. [2004], see two EDUs in such examples on the grounds of an overtly-signalled causal coherence relation.

   The case of relative clauses in 4.15 above also points to the issue of *embedded* EDUs: The friend-bought-car segment is not adjacent to but embedded in the car-won-race segment. Two other examples were already given in Table 4.1. From a descriptive viewpoint, when we apply the criteria developed above, the possibility of embedding seems to follow naturally. It is then an empirical question how many levels of embedding should be allowed.

Elementary discourse unit (EDU): A span of text, usually a clause, but in general ranging from minimally a (nominalization) NP to maximally a sentence. It denotes a single event or type of event, serving as a complete, distinct unit of information that the subsequent discourse may connect to. An EDU may be structurally embedded in another.

4.2.2   A SUBPROBLEM: ATTRIBUTION

An aspect of defining EDUs that clearly merits an extended discussion is the problem of *attribution*, which arises whenever a unit of information is presented not as simply stated by the author of the text, but is attributed to a third party. The clearest case is direct (quoted) speech:

Example 4.17   Then the CEO said: "The company has to be careful."

The issue is whether the colon marks an EDU boundary or not, and this decision needs to be synchronized with various others that immediately follow. From a semantic viewpoint, 4.17 is a paraphrase of

Example 4.18   Then the CEO said that the company has to be careful.

It seems a little unnatural to treat these two in different ways. Recall that above we argued that sentences involving complement clauses should not be split in two EDUs, as one EDU would be left incomplete; this argument would apply to the indirect speech reported in 4.18. By extension, 4.17 should then also be a single EDU.

A different view is held by Carlson and Marcu [2001], who in the RST Discourse Treebank (see Section 4.4) label two distinct segments in the cases of direct speech and attribution verbs. The EDUs are then connected by a coherence relation called ATTRIBUTION. This seems to be a sense extension of sorts to the notion of *coherence relation*, as there is not a regular semantic or pragmatic relationship between two events (such as SEQUENCE or EVIDENCE); instead, the link between the two segments is more a matter of textual presentation, which arguably does not warrant a separation into distinct EDUs. The segmentation algorithm of Tofiloski et al. [2009], mentioned above, also adopts this view and would thus treat examples like 4.17 and 4.18 as single EDUs (but that of Lüngen et al. [2006] would not).

Whatever the answer to the technical question of "how many EDUs", recognizing attribution is of great importance for basically any text analysis application. When some unit of information is extracted from a text, it usually matters whether that information represents the view of the author or of somebody else. In opinion mining, it should be worth distinguishing an author saying that Haiti's economic plan is "a sound basis for rebuilding" from that author quoting Bill Clinton saying this, as is the case in sentence 6.6 of SUFFERING. Likewise, in extractive text summarization, cutting a segment out of the middle of reported speech and adding it to a summary such that the source remains opaque can lead to incoherent or plain wrong summaries.

Recognizing reported speech and attributing it to its source can of course be considerably more difficult than the examples above indicate. The first two paragraphs of SUFFERING illustrate that direct speech can span over several sentences (1.14–1.17), and the source, along with a communication verb, can be given before (1.3, 1.6), after (2.6), or in the middle of the quotation (1.8, 1.13). Checking for quotation marks to identify direct speech will lead to near-perfect recall but possibly low precision, since, depending on the style conventions, the same quotation marks can also be used for elements

"Everything is going wrong," Guy LaRoche, a hospital manager, said.

```
Objective speech event:
        Text anchor: (the entire sentence)
        Source: <writer>
        Implicit: true

Direct subjective:
        Text anchor: said
        Source: <writer, Guy LaRoche>
        Target: 'Everything'
        Attitude type: negative
```

Figure 4.3: Partial representation of a sentence in the subjectivity annotation framework of Wiebe et al. [2005].

other than quotations. For identifying the source, patterns like '<source>: "<quote>"' need to be considered along with the many constructions involving communication verbs.

With indirect speech, the problem is harder. Sentences 5.2–5.4 of SUFFERING illustrate that direct and indirect speech can easily be mixed. Indirect speech spanning over more than one sentence can be very difficult to identify, especially in English where there might not be any overt signal (as opposed to, say, German, which would use subjunctive mood).

An elaborate annotation scheme for attribution (as part of the more general 'subjectivity' annotation task) was suggested by Wiebe et al. [2005]. It uses a frame-based approach where 'speech events' represent the action of a 'source' conveying a message. The events are said to be 'objective' when the author of the text is the implicit source, and 'subjective' when some portion of the text is attributed to somebody else. For illustration, Figure 4.3 shows a partial representation of SUFFERING sentence 2.6 in the framework of Wiebe et al. The 'objective speech event' frame is the author writing the complete sentence, while the 'direct subjective' frame stands for LaRoche's uttering a negative opinion (which in the framework would be further specified with intensity features, omitted here). Notice the nested source in the Direct subjective frame. A different sentence in SUFFERING, 5.2, gives an example for three levels of nesting: *Have we somehow been forsaken* is reportedly being asked by *some*, as reported by President Obama, as reported by the author of the text.

An implementation of a reported speech identification module (covering both direct and indirect speech) that uses pattern matching over chunked text is described by Krestel et al. [2008]. The patterns involve configurations of reporting verb, source and content, and are written in the JAPE language that comes with the GATE text analysis workbench[7]. The authors evaluated their program on seven *Wall Street Journal* articles (400 sentences with 133 reported speech constructs). Precision is generally very high (often 100%), whereas recall is on average 79% for detecting reporting verb and source, and 74% for finding the reported clause ('content').

---

[7]www.gate.ac.uk

For discourse analysis in general, the relevance of detecting reported speech can hardly be overestimated. For instance, when a topic segmentation module posits a boundary in the middle of a quotation (or indirect speech), this may lead to bad results, e.g., for summarization. Looking again at SUFFERING, this might very well happen between sentences 5.1 and 5.2, which have little overlap in content words, yet it is important to recognize 5.1 as a preparation for the quotation in 5.2. Further, boundaries of reported speech have effects on anaphora resolution: An anaphor within a quotation will usually not find its antecedent outside that quotation. Longer spans of indirect speech also have a tendency to create boundaries for anaphoric reference. And, of course, as mentioned at the beginning of this subsection, the handling of attribution strongly affects discourse segmentation and subsequent parsing of a coherence-relational structure.

4.2.3   AUTOMATIC EDU SEGMENTATION

Not surprisingly, implementations of discourse segmenters cannot draw many of the kinds of fine-grained distinctions we discussed above, and therefore they make use of simplifications. The majority of approaches, for example, do not allow embedded EDUs, in order to reduce the complexity of parsing. Also, features like the non-/restrictive relative clause difference cannot be computed for a language like German, which unlike English does not offer distinct relative pronouns. The presence of what Polanyi et al. called "scene-setting" PPs (see the last row in Table 4.1) can only be guessed— Lüngen et al. [2006], for example, do that by heuristically treating any PP that is separated by a comma as an EDU.

EDU segmentation has a strong influence on the results of a discourse parser building coherence-relational structure, as Soricut and Marcu [2003] determined: With perfect segments, the number of parser errors was reduced by 29%. Besides, independently of larger structures, the tasks of segmenting and assigning nuclearity status are important for text summarization, e.g., in conjunction with sentence compression [Sporleder and Lapata, 2005]. When we now describe recent approaches to segmentation, it should be borne in mind, though, that the results are somewhat difficult to compare, since the underlying notions of EDU can be quite different (as we have pointed out above).

In the early research of Marcu [2000], he operated strictly on the text surface and (manually) drew from a corpus a set of patterns for identifying EDUs, thereby extending ideas of Ejerhed [1996]. Marcu circumvented the problem of "defining" EDUs by taking a more top-down perspective: Looking for instances of coherence relations in the corpus, he marked a text span as an EDU whenever it took part in such a relation. His first implementation of a discourse parser then also performed segmentation as merely a byproduct of relation analysis, which was triggered by the presence of a *cue phrase* (essentially: connectives, see Section 4.3.1, and punctuation symbols) in the text. Upon encountering one, such as the word *although*, a number of search procedures were executed by the shallow analyzer in order to find the boundaries of the EDUs that are supposedly connected by the cue phrase. The procedures would draw boundaries, for example, at the end of the current sentence, at the position of a comma or a bracket, etc. The association between search instructions and cue phrases was done on the basis of the corpus analysis, which in the case of sentence-initial *Although* had revealed that the left boundary of the corresponding EDU is the word itself, and its right boundary is usually given by the first subsequent occurrence of a comma. Using such heuristic rules, Marcu achieved fairly impressive results, which initiated a lot of follow-up research on discourse parsing.

The subsequent work on segmentation more or less unanimously opted for taking the results of syntactic analysis into account, instead of operating on the text surface only. We can broadly distinguish two groups: Rule-based segmenters operating on syntax trees, and supervised machine learning approaches using an annotated corpus for training.

Rule-based approaches   Two quite similar segmentation approaches have been proposed by Le Thanh et al. [2004] (for English) and by Lüngen et al. [2006] (for German). Both use hand-crafted rules operating on sequences of syntactic categories and part-of-speech labels to guess potential EDU boundaries, and then add a filtering step to remove spurious candidates. In the case of Le Thanh et al., a further round of guessing boundaries on the basis of cue phrases, also followed by filtering, is executed.

Specifically, Lüngen et al. [2006] in the initial guessing phase postulate a boundary for every comma, quotation mark, or bracket in the sentence; the filter then utilizes syntactic features in trying to identify the spurious boundaries that mark enumerations, relative clauses, clausal subjects and complements, proportional clauses (*the more A, B*) and infinitival complements. For example, enumerations are identified by looking for identical POS sequences before and after a comma. The argument is that the overgenerate-and-filter approach reduces the number of feature checks that are needed overall.

Le Thanh et al. evaluated their segmenter against the boundaries in a hand-annotated corpus (RST Discourse Treebank, see Section 4.4.1) and report an F-measure of 86.9%. The results of Lüngen et al. are slightly worse, but an important difference is to be noted: Le Thanh et al. operated on the hand-crafted syntax trees of the Penn Treebank, whereas Lüngen et al. used a dependency parser and thus operated under "real life" conditions.

Recently, another segmenter based on syntactic rules was introduced by Tofiloski et al. [2009], called *SLSeg*. In a series of evaluations, the authors report results outperforming those of competing approaches (including a statistical one). They also measured the human inter-annotator agreement for their labeling task on the basis of annotation guidelines: with a kappa value of 0.85 it is quite good. *SLSeg* is available for download[8], and for illustration, Figure 4.4 shows the boundaries that the system computes for the penultimate paragraph of SUFFERING. EDUs are marked with C tags. Notice the M tag in the last sentence: The embedded non-restrictive relative clause was identified, and the sentence-initial NP copied to the second EDU so that two complete EDUs are placed in adjacency. (The M segment plays the role of a "trace".)

---

[8]www.sfu.ca/~mtaboada/research/SLSeg.html (Jan 15, 2011)

<C>Yet Haitian political culture has a long history of insularity, corruption, and violence,</C> <C>which partly explains why Port-au-Prince lies in ruins.</C> <C>If, after an earthquake that devastated rich and poor neighborhoods alike, Haiti's political and business élites resurrect the old way of fratricidal self-seeking,</C> <C>they will find nothing but debris for spoils.</C> <C>Disasters on this scale reveal something about the character of the societies in which they occur.</C> <C>The aftermath of the 2008 cyclone in Burma not only betrayed the callous indifference of the ruling junta</C> <C>but demonstrated the vibrancy of civil society there.</C> <C>Haiti's earthquake shows that, whatever the communal spirit of its people at the moment of crisis,</C> <C>the government was not functioning, unable even to bury the dead, much less rescue the living.</C> <C><M>This vacuum,</M> which had been temporarily filled by the U.N.,</C> <C>This vacuum now poses the threat of chaos.</C>

Figure 4.4: Segmentation result of SLSeg [Tofiloski et al., 2009] for sample paragraph.

Supervised learning   Work on learning-based segmentation is usually based on the RST Discourse Treebank (RST-DT, [Carlson et al., 2003]). This resource will be described in more detail in Section 4.4.1; the relevant information at this point is that it contains manually-annotated RST trees for 385 texts from the *Wall Street Journal*, most of which are linked to the Penn Treebank syntax trees. When ignoring the coherence relations, we thus find for each sentence a segmentation into EDUs in conjunction with their syntactic tree portions. Some of RST-DT was annotated simultaneously by two annotators, so that their agreement on the segmentation task can be measured; according to Soricut and Marcu [2003], it is very high (F-measure 98.3%).

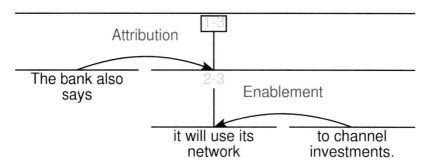

Figure 4.5: Sentence-level RST tree (after Soricut and Marcu, 2003, p. 153).

Soricut and Marcu presented a statistical segmentation step, as part of SPADE[9], their "sentence-level discourse parser". This phrase (which sounds a bit like a contradiction in terms) refers

[9]www.isi.edu/publications/licensed-sw/spade/ (Jan 16, 2011)

to a program that breaks sentences into EDUs and—as long as there is more than one EDU—builds a tree structure of coherence relations just for the sentence, irrespective of the surrounding context. The task has four aspects to it: segmenting the sentence into EDUs, deciding on bracketing (hierarchy), assigning the nucleus/satellite status, and assigning coherence relations. For illustration, Figure 4.5 shows a sample sentence from RST-DT with its RST annotation, adapted from [Soricut and Marcu, 2003, p. 150].

In SPADE, segmentation and parsing are realized as consecutive steps, and we concentrate here on the first. Soricut and Marcu argue that the word and its position in the syntax tree should be considered for making decisions on segments. To that end, they project the word to that phrase node in the tree where it plays the role of head constituent—see Figure 4.6. Features used for modeling the syntax are the node itself, its parent, and its siblings. That is, for deciding on the boundary between *says* and *it* in the example sentence, the term to be evaluated is [VP(says) [VBZ(says) * SBAR(will)]], with the asterisk denoting the potential boundary position. In this way, the corpus is used to estimate the probability of the presence of a boundary, given a word w and a syntactic tree t:

$$P(b|w, t) \simeq \frac{Count(N_p \rightarrow ... N_w * N_r ...)}{Count(N_p \rightarrow ... N_w N_r ...)} \tag{4.1}$$

Here, the numerator is the count of a particular syntactic rule where in the corpus a boundary has been inserted after w, and the denominator represents all the counts of that rule. However, as Soricut and Marcu consider the syntactic context alone too weak, the model makes use of fully lexicalized rules (using head projection, as indicated). After determining the probabilities from the corpus, the segmenter introduces a boundary whenever $P(b|w, t) > 0.5$. The authors evaluated their approach with two different syntax trees: Using the hand-crafted Penn Treebank trees, the F-measure is 84.7%; using trees from the Charniak parser, it is 83.1%. This was a promising result, since the difference between "perfect" trees versus state-of-the-art parser output is not very dramatic. Comparable results were achieved by Subba and Di Eugenio [2007], who used a neural-network (multi-layer perceptron) trained with POS tags, cue presence, and syntactic features from the surrounding words in the sentence.

Subsequent research centered on the question "how much syntax" one really needs to achieve good segmentation results. Sporleder and Lapata [2005] were interested in the two subtasks of segmentation and nuclearity assignment (since they consider these useful for various applications, independent of rhetorical relations) and specifically explored whether finite-state chunk parsing would be sufficient for these purposes. Their features were: the token preceding the potential boundary (no lemmatization or stemming was used), its part of speech, NP and VP chunks surrounding it, the linear position of the token in the sentence, the information whether it is clause-initial (as computed from the VP chunks), and the words with associated features from the surrounding context. Indeed, their results turned out to be comparable to those of Soricut and Marcu; for the segmentation step alone, they were in fact better.

Later, Fisher and Roark [2007] questioned the sufficiency of finite-state analysis. They first made various improvements to SPADE (notably by optimizing the role of the Charniak parser)

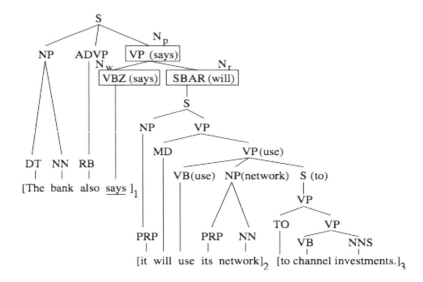

Figure 4.6: Lexicalized syntax tree [Soricut and Marcu, 2003, p. 150].

and achieved significantly better results, surpassing those of Sporleder and Lapata. Then, by adding more information from the parse trees than Soricut and Marcu had done, they trained a log-linear model and report a 34% error reduction over the original SPADE implementation. We hesitate to reproduce exact comparative figures here, since evaluation methods are not always easy to compare. For instance, Sporleder and Lapata had discarded all sentences from RST-DT that consisted of just a single EDU, on the grounds that no segmentation is to be done. Soricut and Marcu, as well as Fisher and Roark, opted for taking these sentences into account as well, the argument being that a non-segmentation is also a valid result for a sentence.

When the problem of embedded units is ignored, boundary detection can be cast as a binary classification task: At every token boundary there is either an EDU boundary or not. How much of a simplification is this, given the frequency of the problem? One indication is given by Afantenos et al. [2010], who work with a French corpus annotated in accordance with SDRT. They report that almost 10% of EDUs in that corpus are in fact part of an embedded structure. Notice that embedding does not only occur with relative clauses, as shown above. For example, sentence 7.2 of SUFFERING, repeated below for convenience, illustrates a temporal relation embedded in a conditional (here marked as suggested by RST).

Example 4.19 If, [after [an earthquake that devastated rich and poor neighborhoods alike,]$_{Seq_N}$ [Haiti's political and business élites resurrect the old way of fratricidal self-seeking,]$_{Seq_N}$]$_{Cond_S}$ [they will find nothing but debris for spoils.]$_{Cond_N}$

In order to account for embedding, Afantenos et al. perform a four-way classification of tokens as 'left,' 'right,' 'both,' or 'none,' where the first two indicate that the token constitutes the left or right boundary of an EDU, and 'both' means it is a single-token EDU. Any token in the middle of an EDU should be labeled 'none'.

Features used are partly lexical (connectives, reporting verbs) but largely syntactic; a full dependency parser is employed. The authors consider the lemma and POS tag of a token, its chunk tag and dependency path to the root node, inbound dependencies, and the linear position of the token in the sentence. These features are computed for the token in question as well as to the surrounding ones in a 7-token window. Finally, the outward chunk sequence (tags of the chunks that the token is embedded in), as well as token n-grams with n=1–6 are being added. Using a maximum entropy classifier, the resulting F-measure is 58%. This is significantly increased to 73% when adding a heuristic post-processing step that applies fairly simple rules for finding "stranded tokens".

4.3   RECOGNIZING COHERENCE RELATIONS

Having looked at elementary discourse units and their identification, we now take the next step and consider the problem of recognizing coherence relations and finding the segments being related. In the general case, not surprisingly, this requires *inference*, as in examples 4.1 and 4.9 above, where no overt linguistic signal is present but the reader can easily guess the REASON relationship. There is a line of research (which originated with [Hobbs, 1979]) trying to model these reasoning processes, and this also plays an important role in Segmented Discourse Representation Theory [Asher and Lascarides, 2003]. In this book, however, with the focus on knowledge-lean discourse processing, we look at robust and surface-oriented approaches to the automatic identification of coherence relations, which means that overt signals are the central source of information.

4.3.1   CONNECTIVES: AN INTRODUCTION

In our examples 4.4, 4.6, 4.7, 4.8, and 4.10, in Section 4.1 above, we noted that the words *because*, *but*, *although*, *afterwards*, and *whereas* serve to guide the reader's understanding in that they quite clearly convey the kind of coherence relation linking the two sentences involved. Their role is thus similar to that of the 'cue words' for topic segmentation introduced in Section 2.2.2. Our words here belong to the class of *connectives*, a group that is syntactically heterogeneous and hence needs to be characterized primarily on the levels of semantics and pragmatics. The key property is their *relational* meaning: They can only be interpreted successfully when two discourse segments are being set into correspondence with each other. From the semantic viewpoint, they therefore denote two-place relations.

The potentially very helpful role of connectives is illustrated by the following (authentic) text example, where the connectives and certain punctuation symbols working in tandem with them are underlined. For the purposes here, we assume a very fine-grained notion of EDU, so that conjunctions of NPs also serve as connectives.

Example 4.20   <u>Because</u> well-formed XML does not permit raw less-than signs <u>and</u> ampersands, <u>if</u> you use a character reference such as `&#60;` <u>or</u> the entity reference `&lt;` <u>to</u> insert the < character, the formatter will output `&lt;` <u>or</u> perhaps `&#60;`.[10]

The internal structure of this rather complex sentence becomes clear when we replace all EDUs by the _ character and add brackets:

Example 4.21   (Because (_ and _) , (if ((_ or _) to _), (_ or _)))

Besides the easily identifiable CAUSE and CONDITION, we have instances of DISJUNCTION and CONJUNCTION (relations not accounted for in "standard" RST), as well as a PURPOSE relation signalled by *to* (here in the sense of *in order to*).

Another favorable property of connectives is their belonging to the *closed-class* lexical items (or *function words*). In contrast to open-class words such as nouns, connectives are not easily invented but form a closed set, and moreover are never inflected. This renders them particularly convenient for the automatic analysis of coherence relations. It has to be kept in mind, however, that connectives are not the only lexical signals for relations: We also find the so-called *cue phrases*, which are much more open to lexical modification or extension. For example, in the pattern *A. Therefore, B.* the connective *therefore* could be replaced by the largely synonymous phrase *for this reason*, which might as well be extended to *for this important reason*, or to *for all these reasons*, etc. Furthermore, a relation such as CAUSE can also be conveyed by certain verbs, as in the pattern *A. This has lead to B*, which is considerably more difficult to identify than a "proper" connective.[11] Knott and Dale [1994] in their effort to build a catalogue of English cues for coherence relations, in fact adopted a fairly wide notion of 'relational phrase', which also includes items like *at the moment when* or *always assuming that*. Another term that is often being used for the larger class of lexical signals is 'discourse marker'. We think, however, that it is useful to distinguish the clearly closed-class items from the productive phrases, and in the remainder of this chapter, we limit our attention to connectives.

Even though we are ruling out the more lexically-productive cue phrases here, we have to account for connectives consisting of multiple tokens. *Even though* is an example that occurred not long ago in this text; *on the other hand* is another one. The problem of handling such "complex connectives" can be quite intricate, in some languages more than in others. Notice that a single coherence relation can be signalled by two, non-adjacent connectives:

Example 4.22   John decided to live in Istanbul, **but** he **nonetheless** refused to learn Turkish.

---

[10]Source: `www.cafeconleche.org/books/bible2/chapters/ch17.html` (Jan 9, 2010)
[11]For a study on discourse-relevant verbs, see [Danlos, 2006].

A discourse parser will identify both *but* and *nonetheless* as candidates for single connectives and then somehow needs to decide not to establish a separate relation for each of them. Looking especially at German, Stede and Irsig [2008] propose a classification of types of complex connectives and the various consequences for discourse parsing. In the following, though, we will not delve into this complication, and instead consider only the relatively simple case of connectives consisting of several consecutive tokens, like *as long as*. (In English, the more difficult cases do not seem to be very frequent.)

Connective: A closed-class, non-inflectable word or word group that semantically denotes a two-place relation, where the entities being related can in text be expressed as clauses. Syntactically, a connective can be a subordinating or coordinating conjunction, an adverbial, or (arguably) a preposition. The mapping between connectives and coherence relations depends on the granularity of the underlying set of relations; in general, however, it is an $m : n$ mapping.

Our definition raises two points that have not been settled yet. For one thing, the connectives we have seen in our examples relatively clearly signal a specific coherence relation, or a group of very similar ones. This is not always the case: There is *ambiguity* in interpreting connectives, which will be discussed shortly. Here, we just notice that some connectives are also syntactically ambiguous: The concessive *though*, for instance, can be used as a subordinating conjunction (as in Example 4.23 below), or as an adverbial that closes off a sentence, as in *John stayed home, though*.

The other point concerns the requirement that the related entities be expressible as clauses. This ensures that the connective indeed links eventualities, rather than, say, objects. The preposition *between*, for instance, semantically also corresponds to a two-place predicate, but its arguments will usually be locations or objects. Hence, in the sentence *The green book is between the laptop and the coffee maker* we would not want to recognize any coherence relation. The syntactic counterparts of the arguments of a coherence relation are typically clauses, or sometimes things that can "potentially be expressed as clauses", such as nominalizations. This leads to the view that prepositions can also act as connectives, and thus the following sentences are to be regarded as paraphrases, all expressing a CONCESSION relation:

Example 4.23   Though John had bought the ticket to Istanbul, he decided to stay home.

Example 4.24   Despite John's having bought the ticket to Istanbul, he decided to stay home.

Example 4.25   Despite his purchase of the ticket to Istanbul, John decided to stay home.

Beside minimal units, larger text segments (more precisely: their meaning) can also serve as arguments to a connective, provided that the syntactic behavior allows for it. Coordinating conjunctions and adverbials, especially in sentence-initial position, can link entire groups of sentences to each other. Therefore, we also find scope ambiguity—a word such as *therefore* at the beginning of this sentence clearly covers the immediately preceding sentence but its scope might include some more distant sentences as well.

How many connectives are there in a language? In a long-term effort dedicated to the syntactic and semantic description of German connectives, Pasch et al. [2003] documented roughly 350. Many of these are quite rarely to be found in actual language use, though. The (machine-readable) lexicon of frequent German connectives compiled by Stede and Umbach [1998] has 170 entries. Similarly, Knott and Dale [1994] had collected a list of about 200 English *relational phrases*, the majority of which would qualify as connectives according to our definition. They were gathered from a 221-page corpus of scientific papers written by 12 different authors, and thus can be assumed to be quite complete for relatively-formal English written language.

Now let us take at look at the connectives to be found in SUFFERING. In appendix A, following the text we show a "skeleton" of the text, which results from replacing all material between connectives with the '_' placeholder. Punctuation has been preserved to the extent that it either finishes a sentence or marks a subsentential discourse unit in tandem with a connective. A few simplifications have been made, e.g., quotation marks surrounding direct speech have been omitted. We will discuss some specific issues with this text later in the chapter. For now, notice two examples of "wide-scope" readings of connectives: Both paragraphs 7 and 8 start with contrastive connectives, and thereby the reader is invited to decide on the length of the discourse segments that the author intends to contrast here. Also, as a more global first observation, we find that both the density and the types of connectives change markedly, roughly in the middle of the text: At first we find only few connectives, and among them many vacuous instances of *and*; later, the text offers a lot of conditional and contrastive connectives. This is not accidental, as we will argue later in Chapter 5.

Penn Discourse Treebank   The largest available resource for English connectives and their arguments is the *Penn Discourse Treebank*[12] or *PDTB* [Prasad et al., 2008], which offers these annotations for the Wall Street Journal portion of the Penn Treebank. About 100 different connectives are covered, resulting in roughly 18,000 instances. Prepositions are not included, so the types of connectives are coordinating and subordinating conjunctions on the one hand, and adverbials on the other. The theory underlying the annotation distinguishes the two groups in that the former are seen as 'structural' connectives (the arguments are found through clausal syntax and/or adjacency in the text) and 'anaphoric' connectives, where one argument may be located somewhere in the prior discourse [Webber et al., 2003]. The two arguments of any connective are labeled ARG1 and ARG2, with the latter being the argument that is syntactically linked to the connective in the same sentence, and ARG1 is the "other" argument that may reside in a previous sentence. Here are two examples from the PDTB—the first is a relatively simple case of a structural connective, whereas the second illustrates the anaphoric case of ARG1 being non-adjacent:

---

[12]www.seas.upenn.edu/~pdtb/ (Dec 18, 2010)

Example 4.26   [Drug makers shouldn't be able to duck liability]$_{Arg1}$ [because]$_{Conn}$ [people couldn't identify precisely which identical drug was used.]$_{Arg2}$

Example 4.27   [France's second-largest government-owned insurance company, Assurances Generales de France, has been building its own Navigation Mixte stake]$_{Arg1}$ currently thought to be between 8% and 10%. Analysts said [they don't think it is contemplating a takeover]$_{Arg2}$, [however]$_{Conn}$, and its officials couldn't be reached.

In addition to marking the arguments, PDTB provides annotations of the coherence relation, taken from a three-level hierarchy. In contrast to RST, the relations are not meant to capture intentions; they are characterized decidedly on semantic grounds. The top level distinguishes between EXPANSION (one clause is elaborating information in the other), COMPARISON (information in the two clauses is compared or contrasted), CONTINGENCY (one clause expresses the cause of the other), and TEMPORAL (information in the two clauses is temporally related). Each group is then further subdivided, resulting in a total of roughly 40 different relations. The full hierarchy is shown below in Figure 4.7 on page 106.

The PDTB goes one step beyond connectives in that it also provides annotations of so-called 'implicit connectives': Within paragraphs, annotators have been asked to name a relation holding between adjacent sentences, by checking what connective *could* be inserted without changing the meaning of the discourse. This situation is being distinguished from cases where the relation is explicitly signalled not by a connective but by some phrasal expression (see our discussion above), which are separately annotated.

By concentrating strictly on local relationships, the PDTB does not make any a priori commitments to a type of larger discourse structure, and in this sense can be seen as 'pre-theoretical'. Accordingly, connectives are being annotated independently, and their arguments may occasionally overlap. (Which, in turn, might a posteriori be interpreted as evidence for the fact that simple trees are not sufficient to adequately represent the coherence-relational structure of a text—see Section 4.4.3)

According to Prasad et al. [2008], the overall agreement between annotators for identifying the arguments (both ARG1 and ARG2) was 90.2% for the explicit connectives and 85.1% for implicit connectives. When relaxing the matching criterion to merely partial overlap of arguments, these numbers rise to 94.5% and 92.6%, respectively. For the coherence relations, when counting at the top-level, agreement was 94%; somewhat lower figures apply when going to the second and third level of the hierarchy.

4.3.2   IDENTIFYING CONNECTIVES

We argued that, in principle, connectives are very useful signals for identifying coherence relations. Unfortunately, however, there is a problem of ambiguity: A word (or word sequence) that might be a connective can also have a different reading in which it does *not* signal any coherence relation.

Consider *for*, which can be an argumentative conjunction, or a preposition. A very similar ambiguity holds for *since*, which signals temporal SEQUENCE, or CAUSE, or REASON when a subordinating conjunction, but no such relation when used as preposition, as in *since 1992*. Many multi-word units have the same problem:

Example 4.28   As long as your essay is as long as my essay, the teacher will be pleased.

The two different readings of the candidate word or phrase are commonly called the 'discourse' reading (when signaling a coherence relation) and the 'sentential' reading (when instead contributing to the meaning of an individual clause or sentence).

How pervasive is this problem? In the corpus study of his pioneering discourse parsing work, Marcu [2000] looked not only at connectives but used a somewhat wider notion of 'cue phrase'. He reported that only 1,200 of 2,100 potential cue phrases in his corpus had in fact a discourse function. It thus seems that the problem should not be neglected. How many connectives, now in the narrow sense, are subject to this ambiguity? In a study on German, Dipper and Stede [2006] found that out of 170 frequent German connectives (from DiMLex, [Stede and Umbach, 1998]), 42 also have a sentential reading. And as additional evidence that sentential readings are indeed frequent (in English), Pitler and Nenkova [2009] determined that of the 100 connectives annotated in the PDTB, only 11 appear as a discourse connective more than 90% of the time, i.e., could be treated as "basically unambiguous": *although, in turn, afterward, consequently, additionally, alternatively, whereas, on the contrary, if, when, lest*, and *on the one hand...on the other hand*.

Next, in order to estimate the *difficulty* of the problem, it would be good to know to what extent it can be resolved by standard part-of-speech tagging. The above-mentioned cases of conjunction/preposition ambiguity, for instance, can be expected to be fairly unproblematic. We are not aware of quantitative results on this question, but the utility of POS tagging will clearly differ from language to language. In German, many connectives can also appear as *discourse particles* (a phenomenon that in German is much more frequent than in English), and as described by Dipper and Stede [2006], POS tagging is only of rather limited help there. Furthermore, for many adverbials the discourse/sentential ambiguity does not correspond to a POS ambiguity at all. Additional methods are therefore needed. However, the problem has not received a great deal of attention. Marcu [2000] at the time had used regular expressions for locating cue phrases and their scopes on the text surface (checking for the presence of punctuation symbols, etc.; see Section 4.2.3) and considered the general discourse/sentential problem too difficult to be tackled with surface-based methods. In his parser, he thus ignored those (potential) connectives that had many sentential readings in the corpus.

To find out whether syntactic trees would help with making the distinction, Pitler and Nenkova [2009] undertook a study with the PDTB, which is linked to the Penn Treebank sentence syntax. Since the discourse/sentential distinction in this data is reflected by the presence or absence of a connective annotation, they could train a maximum entropy classifier on several syntactic features to disambiguate the potential connectives. Features were the syntactic category of the candidate's node (i.e., a POS label or a phrase type), the category of the parent and of the left sibling in the tree, and three features for the right sibling: its category, and the presence or absence of a VP and of a trace within that subtree. In the experiment, the baseline was set by using only the string of the connective, which yielded an F-measure of 75.33% and an accuracy of 85.86%. Adding the syntactic features lead to a significant improvement: F-measure 92.28%, accuracy 95.04%. It is not clear what this means for practical discourse parsing, since perfect sentence parse trees are out of reach, but the result indicates that it could be fruitful to experiment with state-of-the-art syntax parsers for separating connectives from their sentential readings.

4.3.3   INTERPRETING CONNECTIVES

Since the early days of automatically detecting coherence relations in text, not surprisingly, connectives have been treated as the central source of information. Recall our 'XML parser' sentence (Example 4.20) that showed a nicely transparent underlying organisation as soon as all EDUs were omitted and only the connectives and some punctuation left intact (repeated from above):

Example 4.29   (Because (_ and _) , (if ((_ or _) to _), (_ or _)))

Connective configurations like this one inspired researchers in the early 1990s to experiment with straightforward pattern matching techniques for deriving the bracket structure automatically, and also assigning coherence relations to the connectives. For example, in their work on Japanese text, Sumita et al. [1992] used 18 coherence relations (among them *Reason, Parallel, Contrast, Exemplification, Repetition, Summarization, Topic shift*) and mapped connectives directly to one of them. (The authors note that their approach applies in particular to *argumentative* text, which is relatively rich in connectives.) For example, 4.29, a pattern-based approach would indeed work quite well. Assuming that our relation-parsing pattern set includes the following rules, a recursive pattern matcher could build the coherence-relational structure that corresponds to the bracketing shown above.

A and B	→	(CONJUNCTION A B)
A or B	→	(DISJUNCTION A B)
Because A, B	→	(CAUSE A B)
If A, B	→	(CONDITION A B)
A to B	→	(PURPOSE A B)

This is fine, but provokes the impression that some simplifications are being made for solving the general problem. Specifically, we find these four simplifications:

   (i) Each connective signals exactly one coherence relation.

   (ii) The "scope" of a connective can be detected with surface-based patterns.

   (iii) Each coherence relation in the text is signalled by a connective.

(iv) Recursive pattern matching indeed yields the right structure (related to ii).

While structure-building (iv) will concern us later in Section 4.4, we will now address the relationship between connectives and coherence relations (i) and the task of detecting their scope (ii). Thereafter (in Section 4.3.4), we look at the prospects of finding coherence relations in the *absence* of any connective, thus when simplification (iii) is removed.

The first parameter for the difficulty of the connective–relation mapping is, obviously, the size and granularity of the set of coherence relations to be used. As of today, there is no unanimously accepted set of that kind, so that for implementing a relation analyzer one has to either draw inspiration from one of the published theoretical accounts (such as RST, recall Figure 4.2, or SDRT) and possibly tailor that set to the particular application or text genre, or in case of corpus-based machine-learning work simply use the relations found in the training data.

Sense disambiguation   When the relation set is fixed, we are facing essentially a classical word-sense disambiguation problem: Each connective is associated with the set of relations that it can in principle express, and this set corresponds to the word senses. For a range of connectives, there is basically no ambiguity: For example, *if* and *in case* can only signal CONDITION; *although* and *nonetheless* map directly to CONCESSION. If we adopt the RST relation OTHERWISE from Mann/Thompson, it is hard to think of any connective other than *otherwise*. At the opposite end of the spectrum is the conjunction *and*, which can indicate a very wide range of relations, and it is very difficult to robustly disambiguate it.

In between the trivial and the very difficult cases, there are words like *since*, which can either signal a temporal or a causal relation, and certain features in the sentence can sometimes help to disambiguate (*Since last year you have been mean to me*) and sometimes not (*Since you have been mean to me, I have decided to move out*). We can distinguish this ambiguity (two clearly distinct senses) from *vagueness*, where the senses are not disjoint but overlapping, or possibly subsuming. Consider the conjunction *but*, which can signal a variety of contrastive relations. In the relation set of RST, three belong to this group, and *but* can mark all of them:

- **Multinuclear Contrast** (reader recognizes the contrast being stated)
  [I don't spend much money on clothes,]$_N$ but [lots of dollars go into books.]$_N$

- **Antithesis** (reader's positive regard for the nucleus increases)
  [Most books don't interest me,]$_S$ but [I'm really keen on historical novels.]$_N$

- **Concession** (reader's positive regard for the nucleus, which usually is incompatible with the satellite, increases)
  [I'm keen on historical novels,]$_S$ but [I never actually bought one myself.]$_N$

It seems that automatic disambiguation is hardly possible for such examples. For many practical purposes, however, it may very well be sufficient to just lump the three relations together, rather than differentiating between them. On the other hand, notice that certain connectives appear to be specific to one of the three relations: *Whereas* can replace *but* in the Contrast, but hardly in the Antithesis, nor in the Concession. For the latter, as indicated above, an *although* construction would be prototypical. In this way, we can see *but* as vague: It can appear in contexts where similar yet not quite identical coherence relations are being expressed, and its meaning overlaps with that of *whereas* and *although* (and that of several other contrastive connectives).

The idea of zooming in on the meaning of connectives by testing for substitutability in various contexts was systematically applied by Knott and Dale [1994] in their quest for semantic groups of similar connectives. This test is not unproblematic, as it has to abstract from syntactic features—connectives similar in meaning may have different structural properties, so that substitution can involve re-organizing the sentence. Thus, in the last example just discussed, we would need to transform the concessive sentence to *Although I'm keen on historical novels, I never actually bought one myself.* When the substitution is done, the question is whether the meaning of the text has changed notably; this is obviously a subjective decision, but Knott and Dale offer some hints on what counts as a shift in meaning and what does not. Besides finding similarities between different connectives, this test also serves to discover different senses of the same connective, as these will turn up in different substitution classes. In the end, they arrive at seven groups of connectives:

- Sequences (*first of all, next, in addition, ...*)

- Situating an event: temporally (*after, while, until, ...*), spatially (*where, wherever*)

- Cause/purpose (*because, if, given that, ...*)

- Similarity (*again, also, correspondingly, ...*)

- Contrast/violated expectation/choice (*though, but, naturally, ...*)

- Clarification (*that is, for instance, to conclude, ...*)

- Interruption (*incidentally, in any case, anyway, ...*)

Each group is internally structured into classes of usage situations that either subsume or overlap with each other, thus reflecting the substitutability of the connectives.

A different classification is the hierarchy of word senses/coherence relations used in the Penn Discourse Treebank [Prasad et al., 2008], shown in Figure 4.7. Notice the differences to the coherence relation set of RST (Figure 4.2 on page 86), which originated in a very different way—not by examining the connectives but by analyzing the relationships between adjacent text spans from a pragmatics viewpoint, in principle independent of the particular linguistic realization.

Now, to what extent can connectives be disambiguated automatically? So far, good results have been achieved for fairly coarse-grained classifications, with the assumption that the related segments are already given. In a pilot study with an earlier version of the PDTB, Miltsakaki et al. [2005] found that for three ambiguous connectives (*since* – temporal/causal; *while* – temporal/opposition/concessive; *when* – temporal/conditional) the sense can be computed with an accuracy of 89.5%, 71.9%, and 82.6%, respectively. This was done with a maximum-entropy classifier,

TEMPORAL
– Asynchronous
– Synchronous
—— precedence
—— succession

CONTINGENCY
– Cause
—— reason
—— result
– Pragmatic Cause
—— justification
– Condition
—— hypothetical
—— general
—— unreal present
—— unreal past
—— factual present
—— factual past
– Pragmatic Condition
—— relevance
—— implicit assertion

COMPARISON
– Contrast
—— juxtaposition
—— opposition
– Pragmatic Contrast
– Concession
—— expectation
—— contra-expectation
– Pragmatic Concession

EXPANSION
– Conjunction
– Instantiation
– Restatement
—— specification
—— equivalence
—— generalization
– Alternative
—— conjunctive
—— disjunctive
—— chosen alternative
– Exception
– List

Figure 4.7: Hierarchy of connective senses in the PDTB [Prasad et al., 2008].

considering the features 'form of auxiliary *have*' (has, have, had, not found), form of auxiliary *be*' (present, past, been, not found), 'form of the head' (part of speech tags indicating present, past, past participle, present participle), 'presence of a modal' (found, not found), and 'presence of temporal expression' (years, months, weekdays, etc).

Moving from these fairly superficial features to full syntax trees, Pitler and Nenkova [2009] experimented with the same features they used for non-/connective disambiguation (see above), i.e., the syntactic categories of the node containing the connective, parent, siblings, and some more information about the right sibling. They were interested in predicting the class (the highest level in the hierarchy) of all the connectives in the corpus. In the current version of PDTB, annotators are allowed to specify two different senses in case they were unable to make a decision; in these cases, Pitler and Nenkova thus counted either classified sense as correct. Because many connectives are unambiguous, and because the distribution of senses is highly skewed, it turns out that 93.7% accuracy can already be reached by considering just the connective as such; adding the syntactic features leads to a mild increase to 94.2%. Since the agreement among human annotators, as pointed out above, is 94% for the choice among the four groups, further improvement may in fact be out of reach.

Scope disambiguation   Identifying the type of relation signalled by a connective is only half of the overall job: We also need to find the boundaries of the segments that are being related (which were assumed as given in the work on sense disambiguation discussed above). When syntactic information is available, this is often relatively straightforward for two types of connectives. We use the PDTB terminology to refer to the segments as Arg1 and Arg2, and can describe the typical cases as follows.

- **Preposition**: Arg2 is the NP following the preposition, Arg1 is the governing clause.
  Despite [her bad mood,]$_{Arg2}$ [Susan decided to go to the party.]$_{Arg1}$

- **Subordinating conjunction:** Arg2 is the clause following the conjunction, Arg1 is the matrix clause.
  Because [Susan was in a bad mood,]$_{Arg2}$ [she did not go to the party.]$_{Arg1}$

- **Coordinating conjunction**: Arg2 is the sentence following the conjunction, Arg1 is some text segment preceding it.
  [Susan was in a bad mood,]$_{Arg1}$ but [she decided to go to the party.]$_{Arg2}$

- **Adverbial:** Arg2 is the clause containing the adverbial; Arg1 is some text segment preceding it.
  [Susan was in a bad mood.]$_{Arg1}$ [She nevertheless decided to go to the party.]$_{Arg2}$

With the first two, the linear order can vary, but this usually does not create complications. In fact, these cases are often easily identifiable with surface patterns, as they had already been used by Marcu [2000] or Sumita et al. [1992]. As an alternative, if syntax trees are given, the arguments of subordinating and sentence-medial coordinating conjunctions can be found with tree-walking algorithms that try to identify the appropriate syntactic constituents [Dinesh et al., 2005]. With sentence-initial coordinating conjunctions and adverbials, finding the scope can be more difficult, as the syntactic predictions are less helpful.

The general rule is that finding Arg2 is considerably easier than finding Arg1. This is confirmed, for instance, by the results of Elwell and Baldridge [2008], where the accuracy for Arg2 with various models is 92% to 94%, while for Arg1 it is 78% to 82%. With adverbials, a good heuristic is to assume that Arg1 corresponds to the preceding sentence, but it might also be further away. Sometimes, we find ambiguity even in the case of subordinating conjunctions, when scoping is unclear. A much-cited example from the PDTB:

Example 4.30   [Drug makers shouldn't be able [to duck liability]] because [people couldn't identify precisely which identical drug was used.]$_{Arg2}$

Two different bracketings indicate candidates for Arg1, depending on whether the predicate *be able* is read as having scope over the rest of the sentence or only over the following infinitive clause. The overall distribution of Arg1's in the PDTB, according to Prasad et al. [2008], is: 65% are in the same sentence as the connective; 30% are in the sentence immediately preceding that of the connective; and 9% are in some non-adjacent sentence.

Wellner and Pustejovsky [2007] and Elwell and Baldridge [2008] (henceforth WP, EB) use very similar approaches to PDTB-based argument identification. Due to the potential non-adjacency of Arg1, the problem of finding it is very similar to anaphora resolution, which reminds us that what we are "really" looking for in connective argument search is an *abstract object*, as mentioned at the beginning of this section. Therefore, these authors argue, finding the exact text span of an argument can be very difficult, and a somewhat easier task—which for many practical purposes may very well be sufficient—is to identify just the lexical *head* of the argument constituent. To this end, using the syntactic annotations of the Penn Treebank and a head projection technique, the PDTB is mapped to a format where arguments of connectives are represented by their lexical heads.

Then, for the task of argument head finding, the search space needs to be limited. For one thing, only verbs, common nouns and adjectives are considered as candidates, and furthermore, a maximum distance of 10 syntactic "dependency steps" is imposed. From the technical perspective, WP and EB argue that the problem should be tackled with a maximum-entropy ranker rather than with a classifier, as there is a relative large search space still, and it is clear that only one candidate word can "win": The ranker can account for these inter-dependencies, whereas a series of individual classification decisions cannot. Their model for ranking a candidate head α_i as an argument head $\hat{\alpha}$ given a connective π and a document x is:

$$P_{\hat{\alpha}}(\alpha_i | \pi, x) = \frac{exp(\Sigma_k \ \lambda_k f_k(\alpha_i, \pi, x))}{\Sigma_{\alpha_j \in C_{\hat{\alpha}}(\pi, x)} \ exp(\Sigma_k \ \lambda_k(\alpha_j, \pi, x))} \tag{4.2}$$

Here, f_k are feature functions, λ_k are their respective weights, and $C_{\hat{\alpha}}(\pi, x)$ is the set of candidate arguments for connective π in document x. For reasons of space, we do not completely reproduce the rich feature sets used by WP and EB, which comprise 'baseline features' (connective and argument words, position of connective in the sentence, relative ordering of connective and argument, inclusion of argument in the connective sentence), constituent path features, dependency path features, connective type (coordinating, subordinating, adverbial), and some lexico-semantic features for capturing the presence of attribution (cf. Section 4.2.1). EB use a somewhat larger feature set than WP, but their primary innovation is to use (4.2) for training not just one model but a range of separate models: (i) one model for each connective, and (ii) one model for each connective type. The idea is to capture the similarities in behavior of syntactically-equivalent connectives as well as the idiosyncratic behavior of individual connectives. To protect against data sparseness, these models are then interpolated into various versions of combined models. In the end, a combination of the general model (as used by WP), the connective type model, and the specific-connective model indeed yields the best result, a 77.8% accuracy for identifying both argument heads of the connective. The results differ widely between connective types, though: 81% to 84% for subordinating conjunctions, 74% to 78% for coordinating conjunctions, and 59% to 68% for adverbs (using perfect syntax trees; the figures for automatic parses are somewhat lower).

Recently, Prasad et al. [2010] concentrated on finding the "difficult" argument Arg1 and proposed a somewhat different approach. First, rather than identifying the lexical head of the argument, they argue that it is of more practical value to look for the sentences *containing* the argument. Next, while they agree with EB that scope classification should pay attention to the different properties of connective classes, they doubt that the *syntactic category* is indeed the crucial feature for creating these classes. Instead, they suggest to classify connectives in terms of whether the connective and its Arg1 are collocated in the same sentence or not, and further, whether the connective and its Arg1 are collocated in the same paragraph or not. The underlying hypothesis is that discourse relations are structured differently on the levels of sentence, paragraph, and text, and that connective behavior varies accordingly.

For the sentence level, Prasad et al. observe that the arguments of both subordinating conjunctions and sentence-medial coordinating conjunctions will both be found in the same sentence as the connective, whereas the Arg1 of sentence-initial coordinating conjunctions is located in a different sentence. The Arg1s of discourse adverbials are located mostly in different sentences, but sometimes also in the same sentence as the connective. This leads to a grouping into the two classes of 'intra-sentential' versus 'inter-sentential connectives', which cuts across the standard syntactic classes (as they were used by EB). In experiments with a binary classifier, Prasad et al. used as features the connective head, connective position and syntactic path from the connective to the root of the sentence. Their preliminary results show that the difficult class of discourse adverbials can be classified for their two types of Arg1 location with an accuracy of 93%. In comparison, a straightforward baseline approach assuming that Arg1 is located in a different sentence achieves 86%.

Finally, Prasad et al. argue that a similar distinction should be made on the paragraph level, when it is assumed to represent a thematically-coherent unit of the text. Thus, 'ParaInit' connectives are those that appear in a paragraph-initial sentence, while 'ParaNonInit' connectives appear elsewhere in the paragraph. The hypothesis that ParaNonInit connectives and their Arg1s are more likely collocated in the same paragraph (while the Arg1 of a ParaInit connective can only occur in a previous paragraph) is confirmed in the PDTB, where for 98% of the ParaNonInit connectives, the Arg1 appears within the same paragraph.

A second hypothesis on the role of paragraphs is that the scope of ParaInit connectives is more difficult to find than that of ParaNonInit connectives, since new paragraphs are often motivated by a new topic, which may be linked to some topic or entity mentioned *anywhere* in the prior text—and not just in the preceding sentence. This hypothesis is also confirmed in the PDTB: While 91% of the time, the Arg1 of ParaNonInit connectives is the previous sentence, this is true only 49% of the time for the Arg1 of ParaInit connectives.

In summary, the scope of many conjunctions can be detected quite reliably on the basis of syntactic information. For the more difficult cases (including foremost the adverbials), certain aspects of higher-level text structure, viz. paragraph breaks, have been shown to be helpful.

4.3.4   DETECTING IMPLICIT COHERENCE RELATIONS

Connectives, as we have now discussed at length, are obviously the most important source of information for classifying coherence relations. But, it is equally obvious that not every sentence in a text contains a connective, and yet the text can be perfectly coherent. So, what can be done in the *absence* of connectives? Is there a chance to find a relation anyway, and without resorting to reasoning and inference?

Let us first consider the magnitude of the problem. According to Redeker [1990], about half of the coherence relations in text are not explicitly signalled. Other researchers give somewhat higher figures: In the studies of Soria and Ferrari [1998] , Schauer and Hahn [2001], Stede [2004], Taboada [2006], and Subba and Di Eugenio [2009], the number of signalled relations is given as slightly more or less than 40%. Sporleder and Lascarides [2008] report that in the British National Corpus, half of the sentences lack a connective; since sentences often have more than one EDU, the "segment connectivity" will probably also be around 40%. SUFFERING is an example of a relatively 'explicit' text, as shown in Appendix A, with almost half of the segment boundaries being marked by a connective (including several instances of the vacuous *and*, though).

As can be expected, the proportion of overt signals is not the same for the different coherence relations. CONCESSION, for example, is a relatively complex relation that the reader cannot simply infer—it must be marked by a connective. CONDITION similarly needs an overt signal, but here it may be just syntactic rather than lexical, as in *Had he read the book thoroughly, he would have passed the exam*. On the other hand, considering the relation set of RST (Figure 4.2 on page 86), certain relations are usually not signalled; there is, for example, no typical connective for BACKGROUND. Finally, there is a large middle ground of relations that may be signalled or not, because the reader often can easily infer their presence; this is the case for the various causal and temporal relations.

The observation of occasional optionality raises an interesting question: How important is the presence of a connective for these "middle ground" relations anyway? Could the reader understand the connection in the same way if the connective were omitted? Soria and Ferrari [1998] tested this with (Italian) texts that were prepared in two variants (with or without connective) and found that removing the connective leads to difficulties for subjects identifying the coherence relation—but to different degrees for the three groups of relations used: With ADDITIVE relations, 73% of the original marked instances were correctly identified; when removing the connective, the rate is 64%. For CAUSE relations, the corresponding figures are 89% and 60%; for CONTRAST relations, 83% and 43%.[13]

So, the recognition rate clearly decreases when the connective is removed, but still: A fairly impressive number of instances is still correctly identified by readers. This means that the context must somehow provide enough information, or in other words: There is redundancy between the connective and other information in the text segments being related. This observation leads to

---

[13]As for the latter, it is a bit unfortunate that no finer-grained results are given, as a huge difference between CONCESSION and general CONTRAST is to be expected. For example, Marcu and Echihabi [2002] report that only 61 of the 238 CONTRAST relations in the RST Discourse Treebank (see Section 4.4.1) are explicitly signalled; whereas CONCESSION, as indicated, basically always needs an overt signal.

the idea that automatic identification of unsignaled relations could be accomplished by exploiting features present in the signalled cases, i.e., to use the signalled instances as training data for classifying unsignaled instances.

Marcu and Echihabi [2002] (henceforth ME) explored a 'radical' version of this idea by using only the surface word forms as features. For this bold move, they reduced the space of coherence relations to just four: CONTRAST; a cluster of CAUSE, EXPLANATION, and EVIDENCE (CEV); CONDITION; and ELABORATION. The idea is that this coarse set should lead to relatively noise-free training data. In a 1-billion word corpus, without any annotations, ME used surface patterns to identify connectives and (approximations of) their arguments; for example, the pattern [BOS Although Arg2, Arg1 EOS] would find *Although* at the beginning of a sentence (BOS), look for the next comma and take all intervening material as Arg2; and all material between that comma and the end of the sentence (EOS) is taken as Arg1. The Arg1/2 pairs are grouped according to the four relations, and the connectives removed, as we are interested in learning precisely the *non*-connective features. In this way, between 900,000 and 4 million examples are created per relation. The hypothesis now is that the word pairs formed from Arg1 and Arg2 can serve as useful features. Using a Bayesian framework, the authors compute the most likely relation r as $argmax_r P(r|Arg1, Arg2)$ by considering all the word pairs of the arguments:

$$\Pi_{(w_i, w_j) \in Arg1 \times Arg2} P((w_i, w_j)|r) \tag{4.3}$$

where the probabilities of word pairs given relations are computed with maximum likelihood estimation from the extracted pairs. To study the contrast between the "related" segments and arbitrary unrelated ones, ME also extracted non-adjacent segments, once from the same text, and once from different texts. In the experiment, for each pair of relations (including the two no-relation variants) a separate classifier was trained so that binary decisions were made. Classification was done on the original examples, with connectives removed. This led to accuracies ranging from 64% (CONTRAST versus NO-RELATION) up to 93% (CEV versus ELABORATION), with a 50% baseline, as equal numbers of relation samples were taken as the basis. The authors then also trained a six-way classifier for the full problem, which achieved almost 50% accuracy.

The less radical option for finding unsignaled relations, obviously, is not to trust the effects of massive training data but to take linguistic features into account. Sporleder and Lascarides [2005] (henceforth SL05) worked with positional features (intra- versus inter-sentential relation; position at beginning or end of paragraph); length of arguments; lemmas and stems of the words in the arguments; parts of speech; WordNet classes; temporal and aspectual features as heuristically computed from the verb complex; number of various types of syntactic phrases in an argument (as a measure of complexity); and the presence of pronouns and ellipses. Using a slightly different set than ME, SL05 worked with a five-way classifier for distinguishing between CONTRAST, EXPLANATION, RESULT, SUMMARY, and CONTINUATION, and achieved an accuracy of 57.6% when classifying the original instances, with connectives removed. They also determined which features are the most useful and found that stems and words, POS tags, and the intra/inter distinction are among those yielding best results.

This type of approach to classifying unsignaled coherence relations by training on signalled ones is not entirely unproblematic. In later work, Sporleder and Lascarides [2008] provide an extensive discussion and point out that in addition to the presupposed redundancy between connective and "surrounding features" there is in fact a second assumption being made: The "real" signalled and unsignaled instances of relations have to be sufficiently similar so that training on the former can yield acceptable results on the latter. If both assumptions were true, however, authors deciding whether to use a connective or not would basically make an arbitrary choice. This seems odd, and Sporleder/Lascarides argue that in fact the second assumption does not seem to be empirically valid. Notice that the results obtained by ME as well as those of SL05 come from classifying the instances of originally-signalled relations—it is not clear how well the procedure performs on originally-unsignaled instances. Sporleder and Lascarides [2008] designed experiments to test this. They used two different classification methods and found that, for the better one, the performance of classification drops significantly to an accuracy of around 25%, which, in their setting, is only 5% above random guessing. So, the models learn quite well from originally-signalled instances, but they do not generalize well to unsignaled examples, that is, to a major part of the real application scenario.

4.3.5   FINDING RELATIONS: THE PROBLEM AT LARGE

In our presentation so far, the division between the two tasks of identifying 'implicit' and 'explicit' relations is to some extent artificial: When given a text, a procedure is needed that finds the most likely relation between two segments, regardless of the presence of one particular type of cue, namely a connective. Therefore, at the end of this section, we briefly consider the problem from a somewhat broader perspective.

In his early work on identifying coherence relations, Corston-Oliver [1998] divided the realm of features into *constraints* and *preferences*: The former have to be present for a relation to be considered at all, and the latter then try to find the most likely one from the remaining candidates. Illustrating the idea with the SEQUENCE relation potentially applying to two adjacent clauses, Corston-Oliver posited constraints such as the absence of progressive aspect and of attributive predicates in the two clauses, and a matching of tense and aspect among the two. Furthermore, no clause may be subordinate, as SEQUENCE is seen as a coordinating (in the sense of Polanyi [1988] and SDRT, Asher and Lascarides [2003]) or multi-nuclear (in the sense of RST) relation. When the 11 necessary criteria are met, a base score of 20 is granted to SEQUENCE; this can be increased in the second phase where preferences are evaluated: the presence of a temporal conjunction adds 10 points, for instance.

Today, manually assigning such scores seems problematic, but the type of approach has since inspired a lot of subsequent research that more systematically, or in a data-driven manner, used rich-feature models (that include connectives among many others). For instance, Reitter [2003], working on both English and German text, was the first to use support vector machines (SVM) for classifying coherence relations. His features included connectives and their position in the segment, punctuation, types of noun phrases, lexical similarity (in the sense of Hearst [1997], see Section 2.2.4) and span length. Reiter's multi-class classifier for 12 relations yielded an accuracy of 62% on English data (RST Discourse Treebank, to be introduced in Section 4.4.1 below), where almost 8000 instances were available for training; for German, the training set was much smaller (less than 2000), and accuracy was 39%.

In a recent study, Hernault et al. [2010] also used SVM-based classification and obtained the interesting result that using connectives (from a fixed list of 300 instances) as features is less successful than taking 3-grams over tokens, punctuation, and paragraph boundaries. From their training corpus, they acquired a list of 12,000 such 3-grams in their relation configurations, and relation classification performance was better than with the connective list. Working with both the 3-grams and the connectives was also slightly worse than the 3-gram-only variant.

Using a different learning technique (inductive logic programming, ILP), Subba and Di Eugenio [2009] employed a large set of features (in addition to those mentioned above, they used modals, tense, comparatives, superlatives, negation, and others) and also a compositional-semantic analysis coming from a parser augmented with verb class information (which can be expected to be quite relevant for coherence relations). With the ILP framework, first-order rules can be learned from an annotated corpus; a sample verbalization of one such rule is: "IF segment A contains a cause and a *theme*, the same object that is the *theme* in A is also the *theme* in segment B, and B contains the discourse cue *and* at the front THEN the relation between A and B is PREPARATION-ACT." (Some of the coherence relations used are specific to the text genre, which is instructions.) Notice that these rules are quite similar in nature to the sets of constraints that Corston-Oliver [1998] had assembled manually at the time. When the relation classifier is applied on the level of individual sentences, its F-measure (for 26 different relations) is 63%, but it drops sharply when moving on to the level of the text; we will return to this work in the next section.

4.4   COHERENCE-RELATIONAL TEXT STRUCTURE

So far in this chapter, we have looked at the notions of coherence relation, elementary discourse unit, and connective, and at the task of recognizing coherence relations automatically. Doing this on an individual basis for a text loosely corresponds to 'chunk parsing' on the sentence level, where a series of individual, non-recursive syntactic segments is being sought. Nonetheless, we have already alluded to the fact that quite naturally there is *embedding* among coherence relations, as in our example sentence 4.20 on page 98, which showed this nested structure within a single sentence: (Because (_ and _), (if ((_ or _) to _), (_ or _))). Likewise, beyond the sentence boundary, a connective can have scope over several sentences. Consider the last paragraph of SUFFERING, which starts with *but*: The possibility of change in Haiti here is most likely contrasted with the *long history of insularity, corruption, and violence*, i.e., the topic of the complete paragraph 7, as it is introduced in 7.1. Accordingly, there is for many purposes a need to do more than chunking, that is, to apply full parsing, which results in a structure induced by coherence relations.

It is, however, much less clear where this basic observation should lead us to. Are there any constraints on the possibilities of such embedding? What is the level of description for the coherence-relational structure: A sequence of sentences, a paragraph, or even a complete text? Do we assume a full coverage, or can material be left out in such a structural description? What are the formal properties of this structure—are trees sufficient, or do we need more general graphs?

We take the last question as a guideline for structuring this section and first look at models assuming tree structures, notably RST, and present approaches to parsing such structures automatically. (The other questions posed above will be taken up along the way.) Afterwards, we review arguments for the need for more complex structures and, again, discuss work on deriving them automatically.

4.4.1   TREES

Rhetorical Structure Theory   In Section 4.1, we presented the list of coherence relations assumed in RST and explained the distinction between semantic and pragmatic relations, as well as the idea of nuclearity. Now, we add the structural hypotheses that were advanced by Mann and Thompson [1988] and later made more precise by Marcu [1996].

The overall aim of Mann and Thompson was to provide an explanation for the phenomenon of *coherence*—recall our definition given on page 1. 'Hanging together' for RST means that coherence relations[14] are at work throughout the text, they are recursively embedded in one another, and they cover the text completely; no portion may be left behind, because then the text would be not coherent. Next, RST posits that relations always hold between *adjacent* text segments (EDUs or larger spans). The intuition is that there are no 'non-sequiturs' in the text: There must not be a segment that is not meaningfully connected to its left or to its right neighbor. Finally, Mann and Thompson argue that a text segment should always fulfill a single function or "play a single role" within its context. This amounts to the constraint that a node in the coherence-relational structure have exactly one parent.

RST Tree: A text is segmented into a sequence of EDUs. Coherence relations hold between adjacent EDUs, thus forming a node in the structure, and recursively between adjacent larger segments. Every node has exactly one parent (except for the root node), and all EDUs of the text take part in the tree structure, which does not have any crossing branches. Most relations assign different status (nucleus, satellite) to the segments. Almost all relations span over exactly two segments (exceptions are JOINT, LIST, SEQUENCE).

For illustration, see Figure 4.8, which shows an RST analysis of the last sentences of SUFFERING (repeated from the Chapter 1). The notation follows the suggestions of Mann and Thompson, as they are implemented in RSTTool[15], a program for manually building analyses. This notation which slightly obscures the underlying tree properties. Horizontal lines indicate text segments, vertical lines denote nuclearity status; satellites are connected to their nuclei by curved arrows.

---

[14]A full list of RST relations with definitions is given at the RST website: `www.sfu.ca/~rst` (Dec 12, 2010)
[15]`www.wagsoft.com/RSTTool` (Jan 20, 2011)

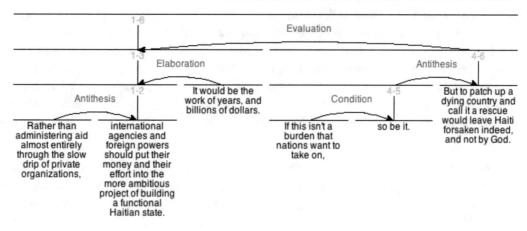

Figure 4.8: RST analysis of the last sentences of SUFFERING.

In his analysis of RST, Marcu [1996] noted a vagueness in the process of devising an analysis, namely when it comes to relating larger text spans to one another. Assuming that a specific relation definition seems to be applicable, what exactly is the criterion for the decision? Does the relation have to hold between the two segments in their entirety, or between any material *within* these segments? Marcu suggested to remove the vagueness by adhering to a rather strict interpretation of nuclearity. According to Mann and Thompson, the nucleus is "more central to the writer's purposes", and there is a deletion test according to which the satellite EDUs of a text can be omitted and the main message of the text can still be understood; this is not the case when nuclei are removed.[16] But when nuclei are being carefully selected at *any* level of analysis, i.e., for EDUs and larger segments alike, then we can differentiate EDUs according to "how nuclear" they are on the various levels; i.e., we can define a salience ranking over EDUs that reflects the number of nucleus and satellite segments that the EDUs participate in. In particular, the most salient EDU(s) of any segment can be found by starting at the node corresponding to that segment and descending toward the EDUs, always following the nuclear links. This will lead to a single EDU if only mononuclear relations are being passed, or to several ones if multinuclear relations are encountered on the path. In Figure 4.8, we start at node 1-6 and follow the nuclear links downward (which here incidentally form a straight line) to the segment beginning with *international agencies*.

Marcu's idea was to apply this procedure whenever the relation between larger text segments has to be decided. He called this the *strong compositionality criterion* for RST: A relation holding between two segments must also hold between the most nuclear EDUs in these two segments. Consider once more Figure 4.8: According to compositionality, the EVALUATION relation between nodes 1-3 and 4-6 holds specifically between the EDUs *international agencies...* and *But to patch*

[16]Recall, however, our critical remarks on the notion of nuclearity in Section 4.1.

up...—which indeed makes sense, as the main message here is that a functional Haitian state should be built, and merely patching up a dying country cannot accomplish that goal.

Extending the binary feature "most nuclear" to a partial ordering of all EDUs can be done in several different ways. Whatever precise algorithm is chosen, the result is a salience ranking of EDUs that can for instance be exploited for the task of extractive text summarization: When looking for the most "relevant" sentences in a text, the nuclearity-induced salience ranking can be taken as a crucial feature [Marcu, 2000]—provided that RST trees can be constructed reliably and robustly, of course.

RST Discourse Treebank   The first large discourse-annotated corpus for English was constructed by Carlson et al. [2003] on Wall Street Journal articles from the Penn Treebank. In total, 385 articles with 176,000 words were segmented into roughly 22,000 EDUs and tagged with coherence relations. The texts cover different domains and genres (news, editorials, letters), and they differ widely in length; on average, a text contains 57 EDUs.

The annotation follows the principles of RST but uses a significantly larger set of relations. As for the EDUs, the approach follows Mann and Thompson in basically assuming clauses as the units of analysis. However, clauses that are subjects, objects, or complements of a main verb are not treated as EDUs in this corpus; further, a number of phrasal EDUs are accounted for when the connective is a preposition or phrasal expression that strongly suggests a coherence relation (e.g., *because of, in spite of, according to*).

While Mann and Thompson had suggested about 25 coherence relations (shown in Figure 4.2 above), the RST Discourse Treebank (henceforth: RST-DT) uses 53 mononuclear and 25 multinuclear relations. The set was formed in a data-driven manner, by extensively analyzing the corpus in a preparatory stage. The relations are grouped into 16 categories; many of the fine-grained variants result from just switching the nuclearity assignment between the segments. The groups are: Attribution, Background, Cause, Comparison, Condition, Contrast, Elaboration, Enablement, Evaluation, Explanation, Joint, Manner-Means, Topic-Comment, Summary, Temporal, Topic Change. This set does not merely extend the "classical" groupings of coherence relations (see Section 4.1) but includes labels for phenomena that rather operate on a level of textual presentation—notice that Attribution (discussed in Section 4.2.1) is here treated as coherence relation, as well as the information-structural notions of Topic-Comment and Topic Change. (We will comment on these decisions later in Chapter 5.) In addition, two "pseudo-relations" are used. Textual-Organization relates pairs like heading and text, and thus covers phenomena we had analyzed as 'logical document structure' in Chapter 2. And to represent embedding, the pseudo-relation Same-Unit connects the two discontinuous parts that are split by the embedded segment.

The tagging was done by extensively trained annotators on the basis of a detailed manual[17], which provides fairly specific guidelines for EDU segmentation, but leaves some room for subjective judgement in assigning relations. At some point, a pre-segmentation of the text was performed and authorized by the authors of the manual, in order to ensure higher quality. Inter-annotator-

---

[17]See www.isi.edu/~marcu/discourse (Jan 22, 2011)

agreement was tracked during the whole process, 53 of the documents (13.8%) were double-tagged. When considering just the 16 relation groups rather than the 78 specific relations, pairwise agreement reaches up to kappa = .82. Carlson et al. [2003] report that the annotation of a single document could take anywhere from 30 minutes to several hours, depending on the length and topic of the article.

4.4.2 PARSING COHERENCE-RELATIONAL TREES

The automatic derivation of RST-style trees subsumes the subtasks we discussed in the previous section, viz. segmentation and relation identification. For building trees effectively, a common assumption is that they are *binary* trees. That is, all multinuclear relations (SEQUENCE, LIST, JOINT) involving more than two segments are mapped to a hierarchical version—see Figure 4.4.2. From a descriptive viewpoint, this is not unproblematic, because on the one hand, it adds (unwarranted) information to the discourse representation (the flat list is turned into a right-branching tree), and on the other hand, information can be lost when, for instance, two LISTs are meaningfully embedded into another. This is rare, however, so for practical purposes the compromise seems appropriate. Therefore, supervised learning approaches that use the RST-DT commonly perform a pre-processing step of transforming the data to binary trees.

Then, a notation is needed to represent trees in a practical manner. For example, Soricut and Marcu [2003] encode an RST tree as a set of tuples $[R, i, m, j]$, where R is a coherence relation holding between the span ranging from EDUs i to m and the span of EDUs $m + 1$ to j. The tree of our sample analysis in Figure 4.8 would in this notation be written as: {[ANTITHESIS,1,1,2], [ELABORATION,1,2,3], [CONDITION,4,4,5], [ANTITHESIS,4,5,6], [EVALUATION,1,3,6]}.

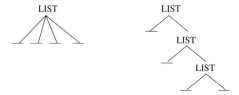

Figure 4.9: Converting a multinuclear tree to a right-branching binary tree.

As another simplification, in comparison to manual annotation, parsers usually do not employ the full set of relations that are distinguished in the underlying theory. Work that is based on the RST-DT uses the 18 coarse relations that we mentioned above; other researchers have worked with different sets of the same or a somewhat smaller size.

The majority of RST-style parsers perform EDU segmentation as a first step that is independent of the remaining work; that is, EDUs are determined by separate criteria (cf. our discussion in Section 4.2). The remaining tasks for the "proper" parsing step are choosing coherence relations, assigning spans to them (which we will keep calling 'arguments' in line with our discussion of connectives above), and deciding which argument(s) obtain the status of nucleus. For choosing relations, we have already discussed relevant features in the previous sections, but when it comes to building trees, certain structural features can also be taken into account, which will be discussed below.

For the parsing task, the 'sequentiality principle', which we stated in the definition of the RST tree, makes life much easier: The sequence of the EDUs in the text is identical to the left-to-right reading of the terminal frontier of the corresponding discourse tree. Only adjacent segments can be related, which reduces the overall search space enormously. Basically, this induces a context-free structure on the segments, and the task becomes comparable to the standard syntactic constituent parsing of sentences, with no long-distance dependency complications, apart from EDU embedding, if that is to be accounted for.

Exploring the analogy further, we notice that it is hardly possible to make good predictions on coherence relation configurations, based on constraints on what kind of coherence-relational structure would *not* be allowed for texts in general. Accordingly, top-down parsing is difficult, and RST-style trees are instead built with bottom-up techniques. We split the discussion into two groups: variants of shift-reduce parsing (where the sequence of decisions can be learned) and "other" bottom-up techniques.

Decision-based shift-reduce parsing   From a decision-based viewpoint, the tree-building task is a sequence of individual operations that incrementally construct the tree by successively adding EDUs. Such a greedy search can lead to linear-time algorithms, which is important when longer stretches of discourse are to be analyzed, and other standard parsing algorithms running in cubic time would be prohibitive. An early implementation of a shift-reduce parser for RST trees was presented by Marcu [1999], who demonstrated that the sequence of parsing operations can be learned from an annotated corpus.

The basic idea of shift-reduce parsing is to operate with a stack holding partial trees and a sequence of input units (here: EDUs). Parsing proceeds by either moving an EDU from the input sequence onto the stack (SHIFT) or merging the two trees that are currently on top of the stack (REDUCE). Reducing means (i) assigning nucleus/satellite status to the two segments and (ii) assigning a coherence relation. Marcu worked with 17 relations and combined these with the three nuclearity assignments nuc-sat, sat-nuc, and nuc-nuc, yielding a total of 102 different Reduce operations, plus the Shift operation, that the parser needs to choose from.[18]

We illustrate the procedure with the excerpt from SUFFERING shown in Figure 4.8 above. Assuming both a perfect segmentation and a perfect parser here, the start configuration is an empty stack and the sequence of EDUs that is shown in the figure. The first two operations are Shifts, since the stack has to be filled before Reduce can be considered. Step 3 would be, in Marcu's notation, a Reduce-Antithesis-SN operation, building the tree (ANTITHESIS (Rather .. organizations,)$_S$ (international .. state.)$_N$) which is now the only item on the stack. Next, EDU 3 is shifted onto the stack, and then combined with the other tree, using the rule Reduce-Elaboration-NS. Once again, we have only one tree on the stack. Then, EDUs (If .. on,) and (so be it.) are shifted to the stack and afterwards are combined by the Reduce-

---

[18]Hence, in contrast to standard RST, Marcu allowed all relations in both a nucleus/satellite and a multinuclear configuration.

Condition-SN rule. Now, two trees reside on the stack, but the parser decides to first shift the final EDU onto it and apply the rule Reduce-Antithesis-SN. Finally, the two trees on the stack are merged by the rule Reduce-Evaluation-NS.

Marcu manually annotated a corpus of texts with RST trees and then automatically converted them to the sequence of parsing operations that would construct them. This was the training data for his machine learning experiment, for which he used the C4.5 decision tree inducer. The features were restricted to evaluate the top three items on the stack and the first item in the input sequence. In addition to relation-specific features as discussed in the previous section, Marcu used the last five parsing operations as well as a few structural features (number of trees on the stack; types of textual units in those trees, i.e., paragraph, sentence, or headline; number of immediate children of root nodes; relations linking those children to the root; etc.) The parse-action classifier in isolation achieved an accuracy of 61%. When adding the segmentation task and thus building complete trees automatically, the performance of Marcu's system ranged about 15-20% below the performance of humans on three different datasets.

Several variants of the reduction scheme have been explored since that early work, e.g., by Sagae [2009] (based on the RST-DT) and by Subba and Di Eugenio [2009]. The latter do not learn the Shift operation but use it as default when no Reduce rule can be applied with a high enough confidence. Reduce rules are implemented as relation classifiers that are being tested at all valid attachment points of the tree built so far, and the highest-scoring combination of relation and attachment point is selected. The rules also evaluate some structural features such as the hierarchical representation of the segments built. An interesting aspect of the approach is the use of semantic representations, as mentioned in Section 4.3.5. The accuracy of the trees, using a relatively large set of 26 coherence relations, is around 35%.

Other bottom-up techniques   The decision-based shift-reduce parsing approaches treat the sequence of EDUs as essentially unstructured: Even though sentence boundaries can serve as a features for the classifiers, the attachment problem is seen as basically the same for each incoming EDU. A different strategy is to assume that a coherence relation will never relate a *part* of a sentence to an adjacent sentence (or a part of it), or in other words: Sentence boundaries are crossed only when full discourse trees have been built for the sentences already. This leads to the idea of first performing only *sentence-level discourse parsing* (including segmentation into EDUs) and then combining the sentence-level trees into discourse trees.[19]

Sentence-level parsing, not surprisingly, is much easier. Subba and Di Eugenio [2009], for example, found that their parser (mentioned above) performs almost twice as well on the sentence level, viz. with an accuracy of 63%. Also, one can argue that sentence-level parsing is a useful task in its own right, e.g., for information extraction, quite similar to the arguments in favor of single-relation analysis, which we covered in the previous section. To this end, Soricut and Marcu [2003]

---

[19]The assumption that sentence boundaries are not to be crossed may be disputed; in the (German) Potsdam Commentary Corpus [Stede, 2004], there are several examples of non-restrictive relative clauses that rhetorically prepare the reader for the next sentence and thus are first attached across the sentence boundary to their right.

developed the sentence-level discourse parser SPADE, which was the first RST-style parser to be made publicly available.[20] SPADE first performs syntactic analysis using the Charniak parser, and then employs a standard bottom-up chart-parsing algorithm to build a coherence-relational tree for the sentence. The probabilistic model that estimates the goodness of such a tree DT separates the likelihood of a structural configuration of two segments from that of a relation holding between these segments, and takes the product of these individual probabilities over all the segment combinations in the tree:

$$P(DT|\Theta) = \prod_{c \in DT} P_s(ds(c)|\Theta) \times P_r(rel(c)|\Theta) \qquad (4.4)$$

Here, c is an individual tuple representing a relation and its spans (the tuple notation was introduced at the beginning of this section), rel is a function returning the relation from a tuple, and ds correspondingly returns the EDU numbers representing the spans. Θ is the conditioning parameter for computing the two probabilities P_s and P_r, and it is constructed from the lexicalized syntactic parse tree of the sentence, to which the EDU boundaries have been added. In order to generalize over the syntax trees (and to learn the features from a corpus), Soricut and Marcu assume that those nodes in the syntax tree that are adjacent to the EDU boundaries are the most informative ones for the sentence-level discourse parsing task. Consider Figure 4.10, where these 'boundary nodes' appear in boxes, and notice that each EDU except one must have a 'head node' that is attached to an 'attachment' node residing in a separate EDU; only the EDU containing the root of the tree has just an attachment node and not a boundary-head of its own. The set of dominance relations between lexicalized head nodes and attachment nodes serves as the abstract representation of the syntactic configuration of the sentence that is to be discourse-parsed. In the figure, this *dominance set* is written as D; in short, it says that EDU 2 is dominated by EDU 1 ($2 < 1$) and EDU 3 is dominated by EDU 2 ($3 < 2$).

The dominance set is now taken as the Θ parameter in equation 4.4, and the estimates of P_s and P_r consider different parts of that information: For P_s, the lexical heads are ignored, so that the mere syntactic labels are used to estimate the presence of a structural relationship within an EDU pair (in addition, those elements of D that do not have at least one EDU in the span being considered, c, are filtered out). For P_r, the EDU identifiers are filtered out, since the relation is expected not to be influenced by the linear position of spans.

The model was trained by maximum-likelihood estimation, using the sentence-level discourse trees from RST-DT and syntactic analyses provided by the Charniak parser. With the set of 18 coherence relations, Soricut and Marcu report an F-measure of 49%, as compared to 37% obtained by the decision-based parser introduced above. Human annotation agreement is at F-measure 77%, so the gap is still quite significant, even for this sentence-level version of the overall task. The authors proceeded to calculate the effects of using perfect syntax trees, which yielded an error reduction of 14%, whereas the positive effect of using perfect segments is twice as large. In combination, thus with perfect input, the difference between the parser and human performance is given as only 1.5%.

[20]`www.isi.edu/publications/licensed-sw/spade/` (Jan 16, 2011)

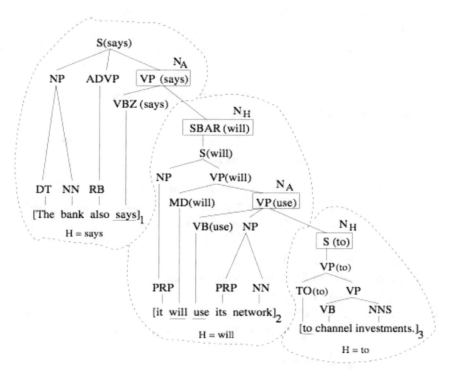

$$D = \{ (2, SBAR(will)) < (1, VP(says)) , (3, S(to)) < (2, VP(use)) \}$$

Figure 4.10: Lexicalized syntactic tree with EDU boundaries (from Soricut and Marcu [2003, p. 150]).

The route of staging discourse-level parsing on top of sentence-level parsing was taken in the rule-based (i.e., with no machine learning involved) approach of Le Thanh et al. [2004]. First, segmentation and sentence-level discourse parsing are interleaved, and then discourse-level trees are built from the sentence trees. The hand-coded rules assign heuristic scores to each pair of adjacent trees, indicating which coherence relation is most expected. The scores are computed using standard relation-indicating features as discussed in Section 4.3, and also take the textual organization into account: A separate score is given to prefer building subtrees in the same paragraph, as opposed to joining segments that are parts of different paragraphs. To solve the problem of approximating the overall optimal solution, i.e., to find the best tree, Le Thanh et al. maintain a hypothesis store and employ a beam search algorithm: A limited depth-first search is executed at the most promising hypothesis involving adjacent spans, then the overall current hypothesis situation is reconsidered and the point for further search may shift. The authors evaluated their system with RST-DT on a variety of subtasks; the F-measure reported for full RST tree construction, using a set of 14 relations, is 40%.

A similar but less computationally-expensive bottom-up search strategy was recently proposed by Hernault et al. [2010]. These authors base their data-driven work on the RST-DT and employ two different classifiers, echoing the distinction employed by Soricut and Marcu [2003] in their two-tiered model:

- A binary classifier STRUCT that yields a score for the decision whether *any* coherence relation holds between a pair of adjacent segments,

- A multi-class classifier LABEL that decides on the relation label (using the 18 relations from RST-DT) and nuclearity assignment for a pair of adjacent segments.

Both classifiers are implemented by means of support vector machines (SVM). Given the sequence of EDUs, the algorithm runs STRUCT on each pair of adjacent EDUs, selects the highest-ranking pair, applies LABEL to it, and builds the corresponding partial tree. This tree is then twice given to STRUCT (once for each neighbor), and again LABEL is applied to the highest-scoring pair of adjacent segments overall, resulting in the next tree combination, and so forth. The pseudocode is shown in Figure 4.11. In contrast to the shift-reduce approaches, and to the beam search of Le Thanh et al. [2004], the strategy of Hernault et al. can be called a radically-greedy one, since the entire sequence of EDUs and partial trees is subject to choosing the maximally-likely next combination, which is then fixed (instead of taken as a hypothesis that may later be overwritten).

input: $L \leftarrow < e_1, e_2, ..., e_n >$ (list of EDUs)
for all (l_i, l_{i+1}) in L **do**
  $Scores[i] \leftarrow \text{STRUCT}(l_i, l_{i+1})$
end for
while $|L| > 1$ **do**
  $i \leftarrow max(Scores)$
  $NewLabel \leftarrow \text{LABEL}(l_i, l_{i+1})$
  $NewSubTree \leftarrow \text{CreateTree}(l_i, l_{i+1}, NewLabel)$
  $Scores[i-1] \leftarrow \text{STRUCT}(l_{i-1}, NewSubTree)$
  $Scores[i+2] \leftarrow \text{STRUCT}(NewSubTree, l_{i+2})$
  $delete(Scores[i])$
  $delete(Scores[i+1])$
  $L \leftarrow [l_0, ..., l_{i-1}, NewSubTree, l_{i+2}, ...]$
end while
return l_0

Figure 4.11: Bottom-up RST-parsing algorithm by Hernault et al. [2010, p. 9] (abridged).

Some details about the LABEL classifier have already been provided in Section 4.3.5; in the context of full text parsing, it also uses as feature of a segment the tree of coherence relation labels that have so far been assigned to that segment, the hypothesis being that there are certain tendencies of relation embedding.

As for the STRUCT classifier, it takes sentence and paragraph boundaries into consideration, as well as various measures for the size of segments (tokens, EDUs) and for the distance to the beginning and end of the text. (It has been hypothesized that for several relations, there are significant length differences between nucleus and satellite, and that relations are distributed in different ways across the text.) When looking at EDUs within a sentence, STRUCT also uses several features that are similar to the dominance sets introduced by Soricut and Marcu [2003]. Also, to approximate the compositionality criterion for embedded nuclei (see Section 4.4.1), the lexical and syntactic features of the central nucleus within a segment are copied to the feature set of that segment.

4.4.3   GRAPHS

While RST-style trees are convenient to process, their descriptive adequacy is not undisputed. Do the constraints on structural descriptions indeed reflect the level of complexity that is found in texts? There are two issues in particular that have prompted some researchers to opt for more general representational devices, i.e., different types of graphs: crossing branches in the descriptions, and nodes with multiple parents.

One central source of dispute is the purported role of anaphora (see Chapter 3). Undoubtedly, an anaphoric NP can find its antecedent quite "far away" in the previous discourse, even though the intervening material has meanwhile carried the discourse forward. Text understanding by humans thus requires a store of discourse referents that can be searched when an anaphor is encountered. Much less clear is whether this should have consequences for coherence-relational structure, i.e., whether we need a store for propositions or macro-propositions as well. In other words, can a coherence relation be established between a discourse segment and a non-adjacent one? Consider this example from Webber et al. [1999]:

Example 4.31   (a) On the one hand, John loves Barolo. (b) So he ordered three cases of the '97. (c) On the other hand, because he's broke, (d) he *then* had to cancel the order.

Within the contrastive relation between (a-b) and (c-d), there are two individual causal relations (a,b) and (c,d). But furthermore there is an italicized *then* in (d), which invites establishing a temporal-sequence relation between this clause and a suitable antecedent. The most likely candidate for the antecedent, however, is (b), since the canceling event naturally follows the ordering-event. But when all these relations are established, we end up with crossing links: The (d-b) relation cuts across the overall contrast.

Webber et al. [1999] trace the problem to a class distinction between connectives that supposedly follows from their syntactic properties: While conjunctions (both subordinating and coordinating) can only relate adjacent material, on structural grounds, adverbials are much less constrained and may pick up their "antecedents" anywhere in the previous discourse. The authors therefore speak of 'structural' versus 'anaphoric' connectives and suggest seeing discourse structure as induced only by the former, whereas the behavior of the latter should be regarded on a par with standard anaphoric relations. (And hence, from the cognitive viewpoint, yes indeed we need a store also for propositional material.)

The Barolo example at the time was constructed by Webber et al., but the subsequent work on the PDTB resulted in authentic instances of phenomena that seem to question the sufficiency of tree structures [Lee et al., 2008], such as this one:

Example 4.32   (a) The London index finished 2.4% under its close of 2233.9 the previous Friday, (b) although it recouped some of the sharp losses staged early last week on the back of Wall Street's fall. (c) London was weak throughout Friday's trading, however, ...

In the PDTB, the subordinate clause (b) is related to both (a) and (c), on the grounds of the connectives *although* and *however*. When looking at the example in isolation, this seems convincing, but, as Egg and Redeker [2010] point out, this might be too narrow a perspective. The goal of the PDTB annotation is to explicitly capture *local* connections only: Each connective is scrutinized as to what minimal units it relates. By definition, then, considerations of higher-level discourse structure do not play a role. A local instance of a node with multiple parents does not entail that on the discourse level, there is not a possibility to account for the additional dependency by relating larger segments and exploiting Marcu's compositionality principle, according to which a relation between larger segments also (or, in particular) holds between the central nuclei of these segments. And this is in fact at the center of the debate: Is it sufficient to delegate non-local dependencies to the compositionality principle, or do we have to reckon with further dependencies that do not involve central nuclei? Once more stated from the cognitive viewpoint: Granted, we need to store propositional material for future backward links, but can we reduce this need to central nuclei? If so, then the tree structure might still be sufficient for describing coherence-relational structure.

Among the proponents of the need for graphs are Wolf and Gibson [2005], who claim that trees are too weak, and advocate the use of so-called *chain graphs* instead. They built an annotated corpus of Wall Street Journal texts (see below) and explicitly contrast their analyses with those of the RST-DT. We cite one example here:

Example 4.33   (a) Mr. Baker's assistant for inter-American affairs, Bernard Aronson, (b) while maintaining (c) that the Sandinistas had also broken the cease-fire, (d) acknowledged: (e) "It's never very clear who starts what."

The graph representation of Wolf and Gibson is shown in Figure 4.12. The abbreviations are: *expv* - VIOLATED EXPECTATION; *elab* - ELABORATION; and *attr* - ATTRIBUTION. Notice that an equivalent RST-style tree cannot be built right away because of the SAME relation between (d) and (a). According to Wolf and Gibson, a SAME relation holds if a subject NP is separated from its predicate by an intervening discourse segment; recall the SAME-UNIT 'pseudo-relation' used in the RST-DT for such envelope structures. In fact, the analysis provided

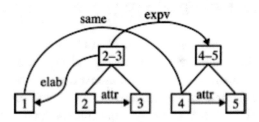

Figure 4.12: Graph representation of Example 4.33 (from Wolf and Gibson [2005, p. 267]).

by Carlson et al. [2003] for this example uses a SAME-UNIT between segments (a-c) and (d), and an ELABORATION between (a) and (b-c). Since (a) is the nucleus of that ELABORATION, it is qua compositionality the element to participate in the SAME-UNIT relation. In this way, many examples of crossing branches given by Wolf and Gibson boil down to the aforementioned question whether the compositionality principle should act as a replacement for an explicit link or not. Egg and Redeker [2010] discuss a few other cases of this kind and conclude that trees plus compositionality are sufficient.

The opposite view is advanced by Baldridge et al. [2007], who work in the framework of SDRT [Asher and Lascarides, 2003]. They give some arguments for the thesis that the representative power of RST-style trees is too weak, and they explicitly claim that factoring in the strong compositionality principle does not solve the problem. (Many of their examples are from analyzing spoken dialogue, though, where the direct interaction might well lead to different structural properties than in text.) SDRT instead uses directed acyclic graphs (DAGs), and the authors propose a head-driven dependency parsing approach to automatically build up such structures.

Discourse Graph Bank   This resource built by Wolf and Gibson, which is distributed via the Linguistic Data Consortium (LDC), consists of 135 texts from AP Newswire and the Wall Street Journal, annotated with coherence relations that can violate the tree constraints enforced in the RST-DT. The set of relations distinguishes between *directed* and *undirected* relations: In a CONDITION, for example, there is clearly a semantic difference between the status of the two arguments. Unlike RST, however, the notion of direction is not equated with a notion of *weight*; there is no nucleus/satellite distinction on pragmatic grounds in the Graph Bank relations. The annotation proceeded in three steps: Segmentation into EDUs was followed by a grouping of adjacent segments that are topically related; in the third step, coherence relations were added to establish links to segments that remain disconnected. Similar to the PDTB coding procedure, annotators were encouraged to use a connective insertion test in order to find out whether a particular relation holds. The authors measured the inter-annotator agreement, which was in the same range as that of the RST-DT.

4.5   SUMMARY: GUESSING OR UNDERSPECIFYING?

We started this chapter on relatively solid ground: The existence of coherence relations as a device for creating under-the-surface connectivity in text, is beyond dispute. Soon, however, we noted, that there is as of today no agreed-upon set of such relations that would be necessary, or useful, to describe the relational aspects in text. Different approaches use somewhat different sets, which to some extent is due to people working with different genres (see, e.g., the specific informational relations needed for handling instructional text by Subba and Di Eugenio [2009]). The other source of disagreement is the theoretical perspective: Do we want to explain coherence from the viewpoint of, e.g., formal semantics, psycholinguistics, or language technology?

Nonetheless, there are clear similarities and overlaps between different sets, and for many practical purposes it is sufficient to assume some ensemble that has proved empirically useful. In other words, discourse parsing research need not wait for the grand solution of the "what relations exist" problem. We proceeded to show that often, coherence relations can be automatically found in text (notwithstanding another source of disagreement: the precise definition of EDUs), and we argued that doing so is indeed relevant for many applications. This is one reason why the Penn Discourse Treebank (PDTB), with its somewhat modest annotations ("just" connectives and their arguments) is enjoying much attention and has inspired similar efforts for other languages.

Regarding the next step, it is also clear that recursive embedding among coherence relations is to be found in texts, and again, for many purposes it is interesting and valuable to find such local configurations of coherence relations automatically; for instance, in order to reconstruct the reasons that are given by an author for some particular opinion of his. Thereafter, however, things become a little messy. When annotators are asked to build RST trees, many studies (including that of Carlson et al. [2003], and our own with the Potsdam Commentary Corpus, [Stede, 2004]) have found that agreement is high on the level of EDUs and just above, but decreases when it comes to relating larger spans of text to one another. There are very many subjective choices to be made, and often the same annotator feels ready to defend a number of competing analyses as equally plausible.

In addition, as we briefly noted just above, different discourse researchers make conflicting proposals as to what expressivity and complexity is needed to adequately describe the phenomenon of coherence-relational structure.

Two issues result from this situation: (i) What level of description, in a text, is the right one for assigning coherence-relational structure? (ii) In what way should coherence be annotated, and represented in corpora, in order to be maximally useful for different research purposes?

As for (i), experience with annotation experiments points to the recommendation of confining coherence-relational structure to relatively small units of text, roughly paragraphs, rather than forcing annotators to glue large trees together on a level of description that might be more adequately described by content zone or topic structure, as discussed in Chapter 2. We will return to this point in the final chapter, and here merely add the question what the "cognitive counterpart" of huge RST trees would supposedly be: Are readers likely to mentally construct complex configuration of relations spanning large stretches of text, and actually keep them in mind for a while?

As for (ii), one way to proceed with the research is to "take the data and run": Work with discourse structure corpora that have been built and distributed, and perform all sorts of machine learning experiments on them, as has been done foremost with the RST-DT (and the PDTB on the individual-relation level). This is understandable as an engineering strategy, but does not help much to make progress with the underlying issues. One reason why a relatively high inter-annotator agreement has been found with the RST-DT is that the annotation guidelines at various points give quite specific directions on how to behave when in doubt, in the way of preferring relation X to relation Y, etc. This leads to more consistent annotation but makes the resulting corpus hardly useful for purposes of advancing the theory, because this would require precisely the *cases of doubt* to be explicitly represented, for these are the phenomena that need clarification. Annotators stumbling upon difficult pieces of authentic text are an extremely valuable resource for making progress with the theory. When "forcing" them into a decision, though, the information on the difficulty is lost.

The alternative to enforcing decisions is, of course, to encode the ambiguity, i.e., to have annotators label multiple alternatives (as we discussed briefly for the problem of coreference annotation in Section 3.2). If that is done, more theoretically-oriented research can explore the interesting cases, and at the same time, more practically-oriented work can convert the data to a non-ambiguous version (if needed) by retroactively enforcing some "arbitrary" choices, which in the other approach had been encoded in the annotation manual.

Several proposals for underspecification in discourse structure have been made. For example, Schilder [2002] suggested a formalism that borrows from and extends Discourse Representation Theory (DRT, Kamp and Reyle, 1993). Reitter and Stede [2003] described an XML format for RST-style trees that allowed for representing both alternative relation assignments and different decisions on the related segments, leading to the notion of a parse forest on the discourse level [Hanneforth et al., 2003]. Egg and Redeker [2008] discuss how the syntactic structure of sentences can be projected upward to the discourse level, systematically taking ambiguity into account and giving a formal representation language for underspecified structures. Such efforts have so far not lead to larger corpora annotated with "ambiguity preserved", though, which thus is a desideratum for future work.

CHAPTER 5

Summary: Text Structure on Multiple Interacting Levels

Discourse processing, in the view advanced here, is the process of analyzing text documents and assigning structure to them on different levels of description. That is, we are not looking for *the* one and only text structure, but acknowledge that different perspectives (of application or theoretical investigation) place different aspects in the foreground and others in the background. In a nutshell, the levels we have discussed are these:

- **Logical document structure:** The layout signals the rough structure of the document.

- **Content zone structure:** Different texts need different kinds of functional units to achieve their purpose.

- **Topic structure:** Lexical signals and word distribution indicate topic shifts.

- **Referential structure:** Coreference links create local coherence and signal topic continuity.

- **Coherence-relational structure:** Additional meaning can arise when two clauses are put together, with or without a connective.

Even though one or another level might yield a boring description for some texts (e.g., the first three structures might be rather trivial for short news reports), in principle the descriptions on these levels apply to the vast majority of texts, irrespective of their genre. The only one that needs adaptation is the content zones, as they are specifically tailored to the genre in question. Apart from that, the levels are rather genre-neutral.

This is in contrast to certain "deeper" levels of description that are not equally applicable to all kinds of text. For instance, there is a lot of interesting work on uncovering *temporal event structure*: What are the individual events reported in the text, and in what temporal relations do they stand to each other?[1] For such a description to make sense, the text must contain enough events in recognizable temporal relationships. This is typically the case for *narratives*, but not for *expository* texts such as encyclopedia articles that explain how a certain device works. Similarly, a deep, and useful, representation of an *argumentative* text would reflect the claims made by the author, the arguments given in support of the claims, possibly some potential counter-arguments along with their dismissals. Again, such a description would be pointless for the expository text, or for the narrative.

---

[1] See, for instance, www.timeml.org (Jan 27, 2011)

Genre and text type   We discussed the notion of *genre* in Chapter 2 and pointed out that it is largely characterized by conventions in structuring the text and possibly in linguistic formulation. This does not quite correspond to the terms we used just above, though: *Narrative, expository, argumentative*, as well as *instructive* and *descriptive* are not individual genres. Instead, these terms describe what we can *do* with language: tell a story, explain something, argue for or against something, instruct someone to do something, or describe something. This functional classification is orthogonal to that of genres and much more coarse-grained: The number of genres has been estimated at 1500 [Dimter, 1981], while the number of our new categories is five. What is interesting about them is their being correlated with linguistic features such as verb class, tense, aspect, or clause structure. Smith [2003] used the term *discourse mode* for her inventory of such categories and provided a detailed study of how these modes are reflected in the way a text progresses forward, and how that in turn can be read off the surface-linguistic features. Some earlier research called such categories *text type* (e.g., Werlich [1975]). In contrast to genre, the discourse mode or text type need not be stable across an entire text. Instead, as Smith emphasized, it is a feature of a local span of text. For instance, a news report may narrate an event that happened yesterday and then switch to a description of a person that was involved. The sequence of tense, the aspect and Aktionsart of the verbs will change accordingly. Our example text, SUFFERING, does in fact demonstrate such changes in text type. It begins with narration and description, and toward the end markedly shifts to argumentation: The author builds up an argument for his position why the countries trying to help Haiti should do so in certain ways and not in others. To notice this, it is sufficient to take a look at the distribution of connectives, as shown following the text in the appendix. From the fifth paragraph onward, we find a clear increase in causal and contrastive connectives, which is a typical feature of argumentation. Whereas in the first half of the text, connectives are less frequent overall, and the prevalent one is the semantically rather empty *and*.

Discourse processing, in order to compute useful information about a text, should be aware of both genre and text type: We should be clear about what steps of analysis apply across different genres and which do not. Similarly, it would be helpful to notice changes in text type, because it can give clues to content zones, or indicate where some particular information might be found and where not.

Interactions between levels   The fact that we introduced the levels one by one does not mean that in practice they also have to be analyzed one by one. Neither are they independent from a descriptive viewpoint (a number of interactions between them have been pointed out already), nor should implementations necessarily treat all tasks in isolation. On the contrary, some recent work suggests that joint models for, e.g., coreference and coherence-relational structure may be more effective than individual ones. Here are just a handful of other examples for interactions: Coreference chains could be very helpful for topic segmentation and presumably lead to better results than lexical chains, but, as we noted, the full coreference problem is still difficult to solve. As a first step, Kauchak and Chen [2005] supplemented lexical chains with named-entity chains, i.e., a partial solution to coreference. The task of resolving coreference itself can profit from higher-level segmentation or structuring decisions, since antecedents are less likely to cross higher-level borders. To this end, Göcke and Witt [2006] exploit logical document structure for anaphora resolution. Other discourse-level constraints on pronoun resolution have been recognized since the early work of Hobbs [1979] and Hirst [1981]. A study focusing on RST, arguing for antecedents to be more likely in nuclear segments than in satellites, was presented by Cristea et al. [1998]. As a final example, the relation between RST-style parsing and higher-level document structure was investigated by Bärenfänger et al. [2006].

Multi-level corpora   For exploring such interactions thoroughly, and exploiting them for higher-quality analysis modules, corpora are needed that are annotated on different levels in parallel (cf. [Stede, 2008b]). We mentioned several issues with corpus annotation in Section 3.2, and similar remarks would apply to corpora offering coherence-relational structure. Leaving certain problems with annotation guidelines and issues of ambiguity and underspecification aside, what is still rare today is data that offers multiple annotations of the same texts, in such a way that levels can be systematically related to each other. The multiple annotations that originated for the Penn Treebank over the years are a step into that direction, as is the Ontonotes corpus[2], which focuses on adding semantic and coreference annotations to syntax trees, and doing this decidedly for a mix of different text genres. The Open American National Corpus[3] (OANC) follows similar goals. For studying discourse phenomena, having more levels "beyond the sentence", such as topics, connectives, and coherence relations at one's disposal, along with a comfortable software infrastructure, would be highly desirable for furthering our understanding of coherence, cohesion, and other aspects of texts.

---

[2]www.bbn.com/ontonotes (Jan 27, 2011)
[3]americannationalcorpus.org/OANC/ (Jan 27, 2011)

APPENDIX A

Sample text

COMMENT

SUFFERING
by George Packer

[1.1] The night after the earthquake, Haitians who had lost their homes, or who feared that their houses might collapse, slept outdoors, in the streets and parks of Port-au-Prince. [1.2] In Place Saint-Pierre, across the street from the Kinam Hotel, in the suburb of Pétionville, hundreds of people lay under the sky, and many of them sang hymns: [1.3] "God, you are the one who gave me life. [1.4] Why are we suffering?" [1.5] In Jacmel, a coastal town south of the capital, where the destruction was also great, a woman who had already seen the body of one of her children removed from a building learned that her second child was dead, too, and wailed, [1.6] "God! I can't take this anymore!" [1.7] A man named Lionel Gaedi went to the Port-au-Prince morgue in search of his brother, Josef, but was unable to find his body among the piles of corpses that had been left there. [1.8] "I don't see him—it's a catastrophe," Gaedi said. [1.9] "God gives, God takes." [1.10] Chris Rolling, an American missionary and aid worker, tried to extricate a girl named Jacqueline from a collapsed school using nothing more than a hammer. [1.11] He urged her to be calm and pray, and as night fell he promised that he would return with help. [1.12] When he came back the next morning, Jacqueline was dead. [1.13] "The bodies stopped bothering me after a while, but I think what I will always carry with me is the conversation I had with Jacqueline before I left her," Rolling wrote afterward on his blog. [1.14] "How could I leave someone who was dying, trapped in a building! …[1.15] She seemed so brave when I left! [1.16] I told her I was going to get help, but I didn't tell her I would be gone until morning. [1.17] I think this is going to trouble me for a long time." [1.18] Dozens of readers wrote to comfort Rolling with the view that his story was evidence of divine wisdom and mercy.

[2.1] The earthquake seemed to follow a malignant design. [2.2] It struck the metropolitan area where almost a third of Haiti's nine million people live. [2.3] It flattened the headquarters of the United Nations mission, which would have taken the lead in coördinating relief, and killed dozens of U.N. employees, including, reportedly, the mission chief, Hédi Annabi. [2.4] In a country without a building code, it wiped out whole neighborhoods of shoddy concrete structures, took down hospitals, wrecked the port, put the airport's control tower out of action, damaged key institutions from the Presidential Palace to the National Cathedral, killed the archbishop and senior politicians, cut off power and phone service, and blocked passage through the streets. [2.5] There was almost no heavy equipment in the capital that could be used to move debris off trapped survivors, or even to dig mass graves. [2.6]"Everything is going wrong," Guy LaRoche, a hospital manager, said.

[3.1] Haitian history is a chronicle of suffering so Job-like that it inevitably inspires arguments with God, and about God. [3.2] Slavery, revolt, oppression, color caste, despoliation, American occupation alternating with American neglect, extreme poverty, political violence, coups, gangs, hurricanes, floods—and now an earthquake that exploits all the weaknesses created by this legacy to kill tens of thousands of people. [3.3]"If God exists, he's really got it in for Haiti," Pooja Bhatia, a journalist who lives in Haiti, wrote in the *Times.* [3.4] "Haitians think so, too. Zed, a housekeeper in my apartment complex, said God was angry at sinners around the world, but especially in Haiti. [3.5] Zed said the quake had fortified her faith, and that she understood it as divine retribution."

[4.1] This was also Pat Robertson's view. [4.2] The conservative televangelist appeared on "The 700 Club" and blamed Haitians for a pact they supposedly signed with the Devil two hundred years ago ("true story"), advising people in one of the most intensely religious countries on earth to turn to God. [4.3] (Similarly, he had laid the blame for the September 11th attacks and Hurricane Katrina on Americans' wickedness.) [4.4] In Robertsonian theodicy—the justification of the ways of God in the face of evil—there's no such thing as undeserved suffering: [4.5] people struck by disaster always had it coming.

[5.1] At the White House, President Obama, too, was thinking about divine motivation, and he asked the same question implied in the hymn sung by Haitian survivors under the night sky: [5.2]"After suffering so much for so long, to face this new horror must cause some to look up and ask, Have we somehow been forsaken?" [5.3] But Obama's answer was the opposite of Zed's and Robertson's: [5.4] rather than claiming to know the mind of God, he vowed that America would not forsake Haiti, because its tragedy reminds us of "our common humanity."

[6.1] Choosing the humanistic approach to other people's misery brings certain obligations. [6.2] The first is humanitarian: [6.3] the generous response of ordinary Americans, along with the quick dispatch of troops and supplies by the U.S. government, met this responsibility, though it couldn't answer the overwhelming needs of people in Haiti. [6.4] But beyond rescue and relief lies the harder task of figuring out what the United States and other countries can and ought to do for Haiti over the long term, and what Haiti is capable of doing for itself. [6.5] Before the earthquake, Hédi Annabi declared that the U.N. had stabilized Haiti to the point where its future was beginning to look a little less bleak. [6.6] Bill Clinton, the U.N. special envoy to Haiti, has sounded even more optimistic about investment and growth, and after the earthquake he pointed to Haiti's new national economic plan as a sound basis for rebuilding.

[7.1] Yet Haitian political culture has a long history of insularity, corruption, and violence, which partly explains why Port-au-Prince lies in ruins. [7.2] If, after an earthquake that devastated rich and poor neighborhoods alike, Haiti's political and business élites resurrect the old way of fratricidal self-seeking, they will find nothing but debris for spoils. [7.3] Disasters on this scale reveal something about the character of the societies in which they occur. [7.4] The aftermath of the 2008 cyclone in Burma not only betrayed the callous indifference of the ruling junta but demonstrated the vibrancy of civil society there. [7.5] Haiti's earthquake shows that, whatever the communal spirit of its people at the moment of crisis, the government was not functioning, unable even to bury the dead, much less rescue the living. [7.6] This vacuum, which had been temporarily filled by the U.N., now poses the threat of chaos.

[8.1] But if Haiti is to change, the involvement of outside countries must also change. [8.2] Rather than administering aid almost entirely through the slow drip of private organizations, international agencies and foreign powers should put their money and their effort into the more ambitious project of building a functional Haitian state. [8.3] It would be the work of years, and billions of dollars. [8.4] If this isn't a burden that nations want to take on, so be it. [8.5] But to patch up a dying country and call it a rescue would leave Haiti forsaken indeed, and not by God.

(Sentence numbers inserted by MS.)

CONNECTIVES IN SAMPLE TEXT

[1.1] _ .
[1.2] _ and _ :
[1.3] _ .
[1.4] _ ?
[1.5] _ and _
[1.6] _ !
[1.7] _ but _ .
[1.8] _ .
[1.9] _ .
[1.10] _ .
[1.11] _ , and as _ _ .
[1.12] When _ , _ .
[1.13] _ , but _ before _ afterward _ .
[1.14] _ !
[1.15] _ when _ !
[1.16] _ , but _ .
[1.17] _ .
[1.18] _ .

[2.1] _ .
[2.2] _ .
[2.3] _ and _ .
[2.4] _ and _ .
[2.5] _ or even _ .
[2.6] _ .

[3.1] _ .
[3.2] _ and _ to _
[3.3] If _ , _ .
[3.4] _ , but _ .
[3.5] _ , and _ .

[4.1] _ .
[4.2] _ and _ .
[4.3] _ .
[4.4] _ .
[4.5] _ .

[5.1] _ and _ .
[5.2] After _ , _ and _ ?
[5.3] But _ :
[5.4] rather than _ , _ , because _ .

[6.1] _ .
[6.2] _ :
[6.3] _ , though _ .
[6.4] But _ , and _ .
[6.5] Before _ , _ .
[6.6] _ , and after _ _ .

[7.1] Yet _ .
[7.2] If _ , after _ , _ .
[7.3] _ .
[7.4] _ not only _ but _ .
[7.5] _ , whatever _ , _ , much less _ .
[7.6] _ .

[8.1] But if _ , _ .
[8.2] Rather than _ , _ .
[8.3] _ .
[8.4] If _ , _ .
[8.5] But _ and _ and _ .

Bibliography

Stergos Afantenos, Pascal Denis, Philippe Muller, and Laurence Danlos. Learning recursive segments for discourse parsing. In *Proc. of the 7th International Conference on Language Resources and Evaluation (LREC)*, Malta, 2010. Cited on page(s) 96

Mira Ariel. Accessibility theory: an overview. In Ted Sanders and Wilbert Spooren, editors, *Text Representation: Linguistic and Psycholinguistic Aspects*, pages 29–88. John Benjamins, Amsterdam, 2001. Cited on page(s) 54

Nicholas Asher. *Reference to Abstract Objects in Discourse*. Kluwer, Dordrecht, 1993. Cited on page(s) 87

Nicholas Asher and Alex Lascarides. *Logics of Conversation*. Cambridge University Press, Cambridge, 2003. Cited on page(s) 81, 82, 83, 97, 112, 125

Amit Bagga and Breck Baldwin. Algorithms for scoring coreference chains. In *Proc. of the 1st International Conference on Language Resources and Evaluation (LREC)*, pages 563–566, Granada/Spain, 1998. Cited on page(s) 75

Jason Baldridge, Nicholas Asher, and Julie Hunter. Annotation for and robust parsing of discourse structure on unrestricted texts. *Zeitschrift für Sprachwissenschaft*, 26:213–239, 2007. Cited on page(s) 125

Maja Bärenfänger, Mirco Hilbert, Henning Lobin, Harald Lüngen, and Csilla Puskás. Cues and constraints for the relational discourse analysis of complex text types – the role of logical and generic document structure. In *Proc. of the 2nd Workshop on Constraints in Discourse (CID)*, Maynooth, Ireland, 2006. Cited on page(s) 11, 13, 131

Regina Barzilay and Michael Elhadad. Using lexical chains for text summarization. In *Proc. of the Intelligent Scalable Text Summarization Workshop (ISTS '97)*. Association for Computational Linguistics, 1997. Cited on page(s) 19, 25

Regina Barzilay and Mirella Lapata. Modeling local coherence: An entity-based approach. *Computational Linguistics*, 34(1):1–34, 2008. DOI: 10.1162/coli.2008.34.1.1 Cited on page(s) 52, 53

John Bateman and Klaas Jan Rondhuis. "Coherence relations": towards a general specification. *Discourse Processes*, 24(1):3–50, 1997. DOI: 10.1080/01638539709545006 Cited on page(s) 83

David L. Bean and Ellen Riloff. Corpus-based identification of non-anaphoric noun phrases. In *Proc. of the 37th Annual Meeting of the Association for Computational Linguistics*, pages 373–380, College Park/MD, 1999. Association for Computational Linguistics. DOI: 10.3115/1034678.1034737 Cited on page(s) 55, 56

Doug Beeferman, Adam Berger, and John Lafferty. Statistical models for text segmentation. *Machine Learning*, 34(1-3):177–210, 1999. DOI: 10.1023/A:1007506220214 Cited on page(s) 18, 19, 36

Douglas Biber. A typology of English texts. *Linguistics*, 27:3–43, 1989. DOI: 10.1515/ling.1989.27.1.3 Cited on page(s) 7

Heike Bieler, Stefanie Dipper, and Manfred Stede. Identifying formal and functional zones in film reviews. In *Proc. of the 8th SIGDIAL Workshop*, Antwerp, 2007. Cited on page(s) 15

David Blei. Introduction to probabilistic topic models. *Communications of the ACM*. To appear. Cited on page(s) 35, 36

David Blei, Andrew Ng, and Michael Jordan. Latent Dirichlet allocation. *Journal of Machine Learning Research*, 3:993–1022, 2003. Cited on page(s) 36

Kalina Bontcheva, M. Dimitrov, D. Maynard, V. Tablan, and H. Cunningham. Shallow methods for named entity coreference resolution. In *Proc. of the Workshop sur les Chaines de référence et résolveurs d'anaphores, TALN*, Nancy, France, 2002. Cited on page(s) 57

Susan Brennan, M. Friedman, and Carl Pollard. A centering approach to pronouns. In *Proc. of the 25th Annual Meeting of the Assoc. for Computational Linguistics*, pages 155–162. Assoc. for Computational Linguistics, 1987. DOI: 10.3115/981175.981197 Cited on page(s) 51, 52

Alexander Budanitksy and Graeme Hirst. Evaluating WordNet-based measures of semantic distance. *Computational Linguistics*, 32(1):13–47, 2006. DOI: 10.1162/coli.2006.32.1.13 Cited on page(s) 27

Jie Cai and Michael Strube. End-to-end coreference resolution via hypergraph partitioning. In *Proc. of the 23rd International Conference on Computational Linguistics (COLING)*, pages 143–151, Beijing, China, 2010a. Cited on page(s) 73, 74

Jie Cai and Michael Strube. Evaluation metrics for end-to-end coreference resolution systems. In *Proc. of SIGDIAL 2010: the 11th Annual Meeting of the Special Interest Group in Discourse and Dialogue*, pages 28–36, Tokyo, 2010b. Cited on page(s) 75

Lynn Carlson and Daniel Marcu. Discourse tagging reference manual. Technical report, Univ. of Southern California/ISI, 2001. Cited on page(s) 88, 89, 90

Lynn Carlson, Daniel Marcu, and Mary Ellen Okurowski. Building a discourse-tagged corpus in the framework of Rhetorical Structure Theory. In Jan van Kuppevelt and Ronnie Smith, editors, *Current Directions in Discourse and Dialogue*. Kluwer, Dordrecht, 2003. Cited on page(s) 94, 116, 117, 125, 126

Freddy Choi. Advances in domain independent linear text segmentation. In *Proc. of the 1st Meeting of the North American Chapter of the Association for Computational Linguistics (NAACL)*, pages 26–33, Seattle/WA, 2000. Association for Computational Linguistics. Cited on page(s) 29, 31, 32, 33, 38

Herbert Clark. Inferences in comprehension. In D. Laberge and S. J. Samuels, editors, *Basic Processes in Reading: Perception and Comprehension*, pages 243–263. Lawrence Erlbaum, Hillsdale/NJ, 1977. Cited on page(s) 44

Simon Corston-Oliver. Identifying the linguistic correlates of rhetorical relations. In *Proc. of the COLING/ACL Workshop on Discourse Relations and Discourse Markers*, pages 8–15, Montréal, 1998. Cited on page(s) 112, 113

Dan Cristea, Nancy Ide, and Laurent Romary. Veins theory: A model of global discourse cohesion and coherence. In *Proc. of the 17th International Conference on Computational Linguistics and 36th Annual Meeting of the Association for Computational Linguistics (COLING/ACL'98)*, pages 281–285, Montreal, Canada, 1998. DOI: 10.3115/980451.980891 Cited on page(s) 131

Laurence Danlos. 'Discourse verbs' and discourse periphrastic links. In *Proc. of the 2nd Workshop on Constraints in Discourse (CID)*, pages 59–65, Maynooth/Ireland, 2006. Cited on page(s) 98

Laurence Danlos. A discourse formalism using synchronous TAG. In M. Aunargue, K. Korta, and J. Lazzarabal, editors, *Language, Representation and Reasoning*. University of Basque Country Press, 2008. Cited on page(s) 83

Pascal Denis and Jason Baldridge. Joint determination of anaphoricity and coreference resolution using integer programming. In *Proceedings of Human Language Technologies 2007: The Conference of the North American Chapter of the Association for Computational Linguistics*, pages 236–243, Rochester/NY, 2007. Association for Computational Linguistics. Cited on page(s) 72

Gaël Dias, Elsa Alves, and José Gabriel Pereira Lopes. Topic segmentation algorithms for text summarization and passage retrieval: An exhaustive evaluation. In *Proc. of the 22nd national conference on Artificial intelligence (AAAI)*, pages 1334–1339, 2007. Cited on page(s) 31, 32, 38

Mathias Dimter. *Textklassenkonzepte heutiger Alltagssprache*. Niemeyer, Tübingen, 1981. Cited on page(s) 130

Nikhil Dinesh, Alan Lee, Eleni Miltsakaki, Rashmi Prasad, Aravind Joshi, and Bonnie Webber. Attribution and the (non)-alignment of syntactic and discourse arguments of connectives. In

Proc. of the ACL Workshop on Frontiers in Corpus Annotation II: Pie in the Sky, Ann Arbor/MI, 2005. DOI: 10.3115/1608829.1608834 Cited on page(s) 107

Stefanie Dipper and Manfred Stede. Disambiguating potential connectives. In Miriam Butt, editor, *Proc. of KONVENS '06*, pages 167–173, Konstanz, 2006. Cited on page(s) 102

Markus Egg and Gisela Redeker. Underspecified discourse representation. In Anton Benz and Peter Kühnlein, editors, *Constraints in Discourse*, pages 117–138. John Benjamins, Amsterdam, 2008. Cited on page(s) 127

Markus Egg and Gisela Redeker. How complex is discourse structure? In *Proc. of the 7th Conference on International Language Resources and Evaluation (LREC)*, Malta, 2010. Cited on page(s) 124, 125

Jacob Eisenstein. Hierarchical text segmentation from multi-scale lexical cohesion. In *Proceedings of Human Language Technologies: The 2009 Annual Conference of the North American Chapter of the Association for Computational Linguistics*, pages 353–361, Boulder, Colorado, 2009. Association for Computational Linguistics. DOI: 10.3115/1620754.1620806 Cited on page(s) 36

Jacob Eisenstein and Regina Barzilay. Bayesian unsupervised topic segmentation. In *Proc. of the Conference on Empirical Methods in Natural Language Processing*, Waikiki/HW, 2008. DOI: 10.3115/1613715.1613760 Cited on page(s) 37

Eva Ejerhed. Finite state segmentation of discourse into clauses. In *Proc. of the ECAI '96 Workshop on Extended Finite State Models of Language*, Budapest, 1996. DOI: 10.1017/S1351324997001629 Cited on page(s) 92

Robert Elwell and Jason Baldridge. Discourse connective argument identification with connective specific rankers. In *Proc. of the IEEE Conference on Semantic Computing (ICSC)*, Santa Clara/CA, 2008. DOI: 10.1109/ICSC.2008.50 Cited on page(s) 107, 108

Richard Evans. Applying machine learning toward an automatic classification of *it*. *Literary and Linguistic Computing*, 16(1):45–57, 2001. DOI: 10.1093/llc/16.1.45 Cited on page(s) 55

Cathrine Fabricius-Hansen and Wiebke Ramm, editors. *'Subordination' versus 'coordination' in sentence and text – from a cross-linguistic perspective.* John Benjamins, Amsterdam, 2008. Cited on page(s) 81

Atefeh Farzindar and Guy Lapalme. Legal text summarization by exploration of the thematic structures and argumentative roles. In *Proc. of the Text Summarization Branches Out Workshop*, pages 27–34. Association for Computational Linguistics, 2004. Cited on page(s) 19

Jenny Rose Finkel and Christopher D. Manning. Enforcing transitivity in coreference resolution. In *Proc. of the 46th Annual Meeting of the ACL: Human Language Technologies Short Papers*, pages

45–48, Columbus/OH, 2008. Association for Computational Linguistics. DOI: 10.3115/1557690.1557703 Cited on page(s) 72

Seeger Fisher and Brian Roark. The utility of parse-derived features for automatic discourse segmentation. In *Proc. of the 45th Annual Meeting of the Association of Computational Linguistics*, pages 488–495, Prague, Czech Republic, 2007. Association for Computational Linguistics. Cited on page(s) 95

Michel Galley, Kathleen R. McKeown, Eric Fosler-Lussier, and Hongyan Jing. Discourse segmentation of multi-party conversation. In *Proc. of the 41st Annual Meeting of the Association for Computational Linguistics*, pages 562–569, Sapporo, Japan, 2003. Association for Computational Linguistics. DOI: 10.3115/1075096.1075167 Cited on page(s) 29, 37

Rüdiger Gleim, Ulli Waltinger, Alexandra Ernst, Alexander Mehler, Dietmar Esch, and Tobias Feith. The eHumanities Desktop — an online system for corpus management and analysis in support of computing in the humanities. In *Proc. of the Demonstrations Session of the 12th Conference of the European Chapter of the Association for Computational Linguistics (EACL)*, Athens, 2009. Cited on page(s) 26

Daniela Göcke and Andreas Witt. Exploiting logical document structure for anaphora resolution. In *Proc. of the 5th International Conference on Language Resources and Evaluation (LREC)*, Genoa, Italy, 2006. Cited on page(s) 11, 131

Barbara Grosz and Candace Sidner. Attention, intentions, and the structure of discourse. *Computational Linguistics*, 12(3):175–204, 1986. Cited on page(s) 82

Barbara Grosz, Aravind Joshi, and Scott Weinstein. Centering: A framework for modelling the local coherence of discourse. *Computational Linguistics*, 21(2):203–226, 1995. Cited on page(s) 51, 52

Aria Haghighi and Dan Klein. Simple coreference resolution with rich syntactic and semantic features. In *Proceedings of the Conference on Empirical Methods in Natural Language Processing*, pages 1152–1161, Singapore, 2009. Association for Computational Linguistics. Cited on page(s) 66, 67, 75, 76

M.A.K. Halliday and R. Hasan. *Cohesion in English*. Longman, London, 1976. Cited on page(s) 19

Thomas Hanneforth, Silvan Heintze, and Manfred Stede. Rhetorical parsing with underspecification and forests. In *Proc. of the HLT-NAACL Conference Short Papers*, pages 31–33, Edmonton/Canada, 2003. DOI: 10.3115/1073483.1073494 Cited on page(s) 127

John Hawkins. *Definiteness and Indefiniteness*. Croom Helm, London, 1978. Cited on page(s) 56

Marti A. Hearst. Automatic acquistion of hyponyms from large text corpora. In *Proc. of the 14th International Conference on Computational Linguistics (COLING)*, Nancy/France, 1992. DOI: 10.3115/992133.992154 Cited on page(s) 64

Marti A. Hearst. TextTiling: Segmenting text into multi-paragraph subtopic passages. *Computational Linguistics*, 23(1):33–64, 1997. Cited on page(s) 18, 29, 30, 31, 113

Hugo Hernault, Hemut Prendinger, David duVerle, and Mitsuru Ishizuka. Hilda: A discourse parser using support vector machine classification. *Dialogue and Discourse*, 1(3):1–33, 2010. URL `http://elanguage.net/journals/index.php/dad/article/view/591`. Cited on page(s) 113, 122

Julia Hirschberg and Diane J. Litman. Empirical studies on the disambiguation of cue phrases. *Computational Linguistics*, 19(3):501–530, 1993. Cited on page(s) 21

Lynette Hirschman and Nancy Chincor. MUC-7 coreference task definition version 3.0. Technical report, NIST, 1997. URL `http://www-nlpir.nist.gov/related_projects/muc/proceedings/co_task.html`. Cited on page(s) 46

Graeme Hirst. *Anaphora in Natural Language Understanding*. Springer, Berlin/Heidelberg, 1981. Cited on page(s) 131

Graeme Hirst and David St-Onge. Lexical chains as representations of context for the detection and correction of malapropisms. In Christiane Fellbaum, editor, *WordNet: An electronic lexical database*. MIT Press, 1998. Cited on page(s) 25

Jerry Hobbs. Resolving pronoun references. *Lingua*, 44:311–338, 1978. DOI: 10.1016/0024-3841(78)90006-2 Cited on page(s) 58, 76

Jerry Hobbs. Coherence and coreference. *Cognitive Science*, 3:67–90, 1979. DOI: 10.1207/s15516709cog0301_4 Cited on page(s) 79, 97, 131

Eduard Hovy, Mitchell Marcus, Martha Palmer, Lance Ramshaw, and Ralph Weischedel. Ontonotes: The 90% solution. In *Proceedings of the Human Language Technology Conference of the NAACL, Companion Volume: Short Papers*, pages 57–60, New York/NY, June 2006. Association for Computational Linguistics. Cited on page(s) 51

Susan Hudson, Michael Tanenhaus, and Gary Dell. The effect of the discourse center on the local coherence of a discourse. In *Proc. of the 8th Annual Conference of the Cognitive Science Society*, pages 96–101. Lawrence Erlbaum, 1986. Cited on page(s) 51

Ryu Iida, Kentaro Inui, and Yuji Matsumoto. Capturing salience with a trainable cache model for zero-anaphora resolution. In *Proceedings of the Joint Conference of the 47th Annual Meeting of the ACL and the 4th International Joint Conference on Natural Language Processing of the AFNLP*, pages 647–655, Suntec, Singapore, 2009. Association for Computational Linguistics. Cited on page(s) 73

Hans Kamp and Uwe Reyle. *From Discourse to Logic*. Kluwer, Dordrecht, 1993. Cited on page(s) 127

Min-Yen Kan, Judith L. Klavans, and Kathleen R. McKeown. Linear segmentation and segment relevance. In *Proc. of the 6th International Workshop on Very Large Corpora (WVLC-6)*, pages 197–205, Montrèal, 1998. Association for Computational Linguistics. Cited on page(s) 18, 29

David Kauchak and Francine Chen. Feature-based segmentation of narrative documents. In *Proc. of the ACL Workshop on Feature Engineering for Machine Learning in Natural Language Processing*, pages 32–39, Ann Arbor, Michigan, June 2005. Association for Computational Linguistics. DOI: 10.3115/1610230.1610237 Cited on page(s) 20, 37, 38, 130

Andrew Kehler. *Coherence, Reference, and the Theory of Grammar*. CSLI Publications, Stanford, 2002. Cited on page(s) 82

Walter Kintsch. The use of knowledge in discourse processing: A construction-integration model. *Psychological Review*, 95:163–182, 1988. DOI: 10.1037/0033-295X.95.2.163 Cited on page(s) 82

Manfred Klenner. Enforcing consistency on coreference sets. In *Proc. of the Conference on Recent Advances in Natural Language Processing (RANLP)*, pages 323–328. Borovets, Bulgaria, 2007. Cited on page(s) 72

Manfred Klenner and David Tuggener. An incremental entity-mention model for coreference resolution with restrictive antecedent accessibility. In *Proc. of the Conference on Recent Advances in Natural Language Processing (RANLP)*, pages 178–185. Hissar, Bulgaria, 2011. Cited on page(s) 72

Alistair Knott and Robert Dale. Using linguistic phenomena to motivate a set of coherence relations. *Discourse Processes*, 18(1):35–62, 1994. DOI: 10.1080/01638539409544883 Cited on page(s) 82, 98, 100, 105

Alistair Knott and Ted Sanders. The classification of coherence relations and their linguistic markers: An exploration of two languages. *Journal of Pragmatics*, 30:135–175, 1998. DOI: 10.1016/S0378-2166(98)00023-X Cited on page(s) 82

Olga Krasavina and Christian Chiarcos. Pocos: The Potsdam Coreference Scheme. In *Proc. of the Linguistic Annotation Workshop (LAW) at ACL-07*, Prague, 2007. DOI: 10.3115/1642059.1642084 Cited on page(s) 50

Ralf Krestel, Sabine Bergler, and René Witte. Minding the source: automatic tagging of reported speech in newspaper articles. In *Proc. of the 6th International Language Resources and Evaluation Conference (LREC)*, pages 2823–2828, 2008. Cited on page(s) 91

Shalom Lappin and Herbert J. Leass. An algorithm for pronominal anaphora resolution. *Computational Linguistics*, 20(4):535–561, 1994. Cited on page(s) 55, 59, 60, 61, 72

Huong Le Thanh, Geetha Abeysinghe, and Christian Huyck. Generating discourse structures for written text. In *Proc. of the 20th International Conference on Computational Linguistics (COLING)*, pages 329–335, Geneva/Switzerland, 2004. DOI: 10.3115/1220355.1220403 Cited on page(s) 89, 93, 121, 122

Alan Lee, Rashmi Prasad, Aravind Joshi, and Bonnie Webber. Departures from tree structures in discourse: Shared arguments in the penn discourse treebank. In *Proc. of the 3rd Workshop on Constraints in Discourse (CID)*, Potsdam/Germany, 2008. Cited on page(s) 124

Heeyoung Lee, Yves Peirsmann, Angel Chang, Nathanael Chambers, Mihai Surdeanu, and Dan Jurafsky. Stanford's multi-pass sieve coreference resolution system at the conll-2011 shared task. In *Proc. of the 15th Conference on Computational Natural Language Learning: Shared Task*, pages 28–34, Portland/OR, 2011. Cited on page(s) 76

Yifan Li, Petr Musilek, Marek Reformat, and Loren Wyard-Scott. Identification of pleonastic *it* using the web. *Journal of Artificial Intelligence Research*, 34:339–389, 2009. DOI: 10.1613/jair.2622 Cited on page(s) 54

Diane Litman and Rebecca Passonneau. Combining multiple knowledge sources for discourse segmentation. In *Proc. of the 33rd Meeting of the ACL*, pages 108–115. Association for Computational Linguistics, 1995. DOI: 10.3115/981658.981673 Cited on page(s) 18

Harald Lüngen, Henning Lobin, Maja Bärenfänger, Mirco Hilbert, and Csilla Puskas. Text parsing of a complex genre. In Bob Martens and Milena Dobreva, editors, *Proc. of the Conference on Electronic Publishing (ELPUB 2006)*, Bansko, Bulgaria, 2006. Cited on page(s) 89, 90, 92, 93

Xiaoqiang Luo, Abe Ittycheriah, Hongyan Jing, Nanda Kambhatla, and Salim Roukos. A mention-synchronous coreference resolution algorithm based on the bell tree. In *Proceedings of the 42nd Meeting of the Association for Computational Linguistics (ACL'04)*, pages 135–142, Barcelona, Spain, 2004. DOI: 10.3115/1218955.1218973 Cited on page(s) 69, 70, 71, 72

Susan LuperFoy. *Discourse pegs: A computational analysis of context-dependent referring expressions.* PhD thesis, University of Texas at Austin, 1991. Cited on page(s) 43

Igor Malioutov and Regina Barzilay. Minimum cut model for spoken lecture segmentation. In *Proc. of the 21st International Conference on Computational Linguistics and 44th Annual Meeting of the Association for Computational Linguistics (COLING/ACL)*, pages 25–32, Sydney, 2006. Association for Computational Linguistics. DOI: 10.3115/1220175.1220179 Cited on page(s) 32, 33, 70

William Mann and Sandra Thompson. Rhetorical structure theory: Towards a functional theory of text organization. *TEXT*, 8:243–281, 1988. DOI: 10.1515/text.1.1988.8.3.243 Cited on page(s) 3, 83, 84, 85, 86, 114

Christopher Manning. Rethinking text segmentation models: an information extraction case study. Technical Report SULTRY-98-07-01, University of Sydney, 1998. Cited on page(s) 17, 28, 36

Daniel Marcu. The rhetorical parsing of unrestricted texts: A surface-based approach. *Computational Linguistics*, 26(3):395–448, 2000. DOI: 10.1162/089120100561755 Cited on page(s) 92, 102, 107, 116

Daniel Marcu. Building up rhetorical structure trees. In *Proc. of the Thirteenth National Conference on Artificial Intelligence*, Portland/OR, 1996. AAAI. Cited on page(s) 114, 115

Daniel Marcu. A decision-based approach to rhetorical parsing. In *Proc. of the 37th Annual Meeting of the Association for Computational Linguistics*, pages 365–372, College Park/MD, 1999. Association for Computational Linguistics. DOI: 10.3115/1034678.1034736 Cited on page(s) 118

Daniel Marcu and Abdessamad Echihabi. An unsupervised approach to recognizing discourse relations. In *Proc. of the 40th Anniversary Meeting of the Association for Computational Linguistics*, 2002. DOI: 10.3115/1073083.1073145 Cited on page(s) 110, 111

Katja Markert, Malvina Nissim, and Natalia Modjeska. Using the web for anaphora resolution. In *Proc. of the EACL Workshop on the Computational Treatment of Anaphora*, Budapest, 2003. Cited on page(s) 64

James R. Martin. Language, register and genre. In *Children writing: Reader*. Deakin University Press, Geelong, Victoria, 1984. Cited on page(s) 7, 13

James R. Martin. *English text: system and structure*. John Benjamins, Philadelphia/Amsterdam, 1992. Cited on page(s) 82, 83

Christian Matthiessen and Sandra Thompson. The structure of discourse and 'subordination'. In J. Haiman and S. Thompson, editors, *Clause combining in grammar and discourse*, pages 275–329. John Benjamins, Amsterdam, 1988. Cited on page(s) 81

Alexander Mehler, Sergei Sharoff, and Marina Santini, editors. *Genres on the web: Computational models and empirical studies*. Text, Speech and Language Technology. Springer, Berlin/Heidelberg/New York, 2010. Cited on page(s) 7

Eleni Miltsakaki, Nikhil Dinesh, Rashmi Prasad, Aravind Joshi, and Bonnie Webber. Experiments on sense annotations and sense disambiguation of discourse connectives. In *Proc. of the 4th Workshop on Treebanks and Linguistic Theories (TLT)*, Barcelona, 2005. Cited on page(s) 105

Hemant Misra, Francois Yvon, Joemon Jose, and Olivier Cappe. Text segmentation via topic modeling: an analytical study. In *Proc. of the 18th ACM Conference on Information and Knowledge Management*, Hong Kong, 2009. DOI: 10.1145/1645953.1646170 Cited on page(s) 34

Ruslan Mitkov. *Anaphora Resolution*. Longman, London, 2002. Cited on page(s) 40

Ruslan Mitkov, Richard Evans, and Constantin Orasan. A new, fully automatic version of Mitkov's knowledge-poor pronoun resolution method. In *Proc. of the 3rd International Conference on Intelligent Text Processing and Computational Linguistics (CICLing*, 2002. Cited on page(s) 61

Natalia N. Modjeska. *Resolving Other-Anaphora*. PhD thesis, School of Informatics, University of Edinburgh, 2003. Cited on page(s) 43

Johanna Moore and Martha Pollack. A problem for RST: The need for multi-level discourse analysis. *Computational Linguistics*, 18(4):537–544, 1992. Cited on page(s) 85

Jane Morris and Graeme Hirst. Lexical cohesion computed by thesaural relations as an indicator of the structure of text. *Computational Linguistics*, 17(1):21–48, 1991. Cited on page(s) 23, 24, 26

Crystal Nakatsu and Michael White. Generating with Discourse Combinatory Categorial Grammar. *Linguistic Issues in Language Technology*, 4(1):1–62, 2010. Cited on page(s) 83

Vincent Ng. Supervised noun phrase coreference research: The first fifteen years. In *Proceedings of the 48th Annual Meeting of the Association for Computational Linguistics*, pages 1396–1411, Uppsala, Sweden, 2010. Association for Computational Linguistics. Cited on page(s) 65, 70

Vincent Ng and Claire Cardie. Identifying anaphoric and non-anaphoric noun phrases to improve coreference resolution. In *Proc. of the 19th International Conference on Computational Linguistics (COLING)*, Taipei/Taiwan, 2002a. DOI: 10.3115/1072228.1072367 Cited on page(s) 56, 69

Vincent Ng and Claire Cardie. Improving machine learning approaches to coreference resolution. In *Proceedings of 40th Annual Meeting of the Association for Computational Linguistics*, pages 104–111, Philadelphia/PA, 2002b. Association for Computational Linguistics. DOI: 10.3115/1073083.1073102 Cited on page(s) 67, 68

Cristina Nicolae and Gabriel Nicolae. Bestcut: A graph algorithm for coreference resolution. In *Proceedings of the 2006 Conference on Empirical Methods in Natural Language Processing*, pages 275–283, Sydney, Australia, 2006. Association for Computational Linguistics. DOI: 10.3115/1610075.1610115 Cited on page(s) 70

Malvina Nissim. Learning information status of discourse entities. In *Proc. of the 2006 Conference on Empirical Methods in Natural Language Processing*, pages 94–102, Sydney, Australia, 2006. Association for Computational Linguistics. DOI: 10.3115/1610075.1610090 Cited on page(s) 57

Malvina Nissim, Shipra Dingare, Jean Carletta, and Mark Steedman. An annotation scheme for information status in dialogue. In *Proc. of the 4th International Language Resources and Evaluation Conference (LREC)*, 2004. Cited on page(s) 56

Tadashi Nomoto and Yoshihiko Nitta. A grammatico-statistical approach to discourse partitioning. In *Proc. of the 15th International Conference on Computational Linguistics (COLING)*, pages 1145–1150, Kyoto, 1994. DOI: 10.3115/991250.991338 Cited on page(s) 29

Manabu Okumura and Takeo Honda. Word sense disambiguation and text segmentation based on lexical cohesion. In *Proc. of the 15th International Conference on Computational Linguistics (COLING)*, pages 755–761, Kyoto, 1994. DOI: 10.3115/991250.991268 Cited on page(s) 26, 28

Renate Pasch, Ursula Brauße, Eva Breindl, and Ulrich Herrmann Waßner. *Handbuch der deutschen Konnektoren*. Walter de Gruyter, Berlin/New York, 2003. Cited on page(s) 100

Rebecca Passonneau and Diane Litman. Discourse segmentation by human and automated means. *Computational Linguistics*, 23(1):103–139, 1997. Cited on page(s) 18, 20, 22, 36, 37

Ted Pedersen, Serguei Pakhomov, Siddarth Patwardhan, and Christopher Chute. Measures of semantic similarity and relatedness in the biomedical domain. *Journal of Biomedical Informatics*, 40(3):288–299, 2007. DOI: 10.1016/j.jbi.2006.06.004 Cited on page(s) 27

Lev Pevzner and Marti A. Hearst. A critique and improvement of an evaluation metric for text segmentation. *Computational Linguistics*, 28(1):19–36, 2002. DOI: 10.1162/089120102317341756 Cited on page(s) 19

Emily Pitler and Ani Nenkova. Using syntax to disambiguate explicit discourse connectives in text. In *Proc. of the ACL-IJCNLP 2009 Conference Short Papers*, pages 13–16, Suntec, Singapore, 2009. Association for Computational Linguistics. DOI: 10.3115/1667583.1667589 Cited on page(s) 102, 106

Massimo Poesio and Ron Artstein. Anaphoric annotation in the ARRAU corpus. In *Proc. of the 6th International Language Resources and Evaluation Conference (LREC)*, 2008. Cited on page(s) 49

Massimo Poesio, Rosemary Stevenson, Barbara di Eugenio, and Janet Hitzeman. Centering: a parametric theory and its instantiations. *Computational Linguistics*, 30(3):309–363, 2004. DOI: 10.1162/0891201041850911 Cited on page(s) 51

Livia Polanyi. A formal model of the structure of discourse. *Journal of Pragmatics*, 12:601–638, 1988. DOI: 10.1016/0378-2166(88)90050-1 Cited on page(s) 81, 112

Livia Polanyi, Chris Culy, Martin van den Berg, Gian Lorenzo Thione, and David Ahn. A rule based approach to discourse parsing. In *Proc. of the SIGDIAL '04 Workshop*, pages 108–117, Cambridge/MA, 2004. Assoc. for Computational Linguistics. Cited on page(s) 87, 88, 89

R. Prasad, N. Dinesh, A. Lee, E. Miltsakaki, L. Robaldo, A. Joshi, and B. Webber. The Penn Discourse Treebank 2.0. In *Proc. of the 6th International Conference on Language Resources and Evaluation (LREC)*, Marrakech, Morocco, 2008. Cited on page(s) 100, 101, 105, 106, 107

R. Prasad, A. Joshi, and B. Webber. Exploiting scope for shallow discourse parsing. In *Proc. of the 7th International Conference on Language Resources and Evaluation (LREC)*, Malta, 2010. Cited on page(s) 109

Ellen F. Prince. The ZPG letter: Subjects, definiteness, and information status. In W. Mann and S. Thompson, editors, *Discourse description: Diverse linguistic analyses of a fund-raising text*, pages 223–255. John Benjamins, Amsterdam, 1992. Cited on page(s) 42, 54, 56

Long Qiu, Min-Yen Kan, and Tat-Seng Chua. A public reference implementation of the RAP anaphora resolution algorithm. In *Proc. of the 4th International Language Resources and Evaluation Conference (LREC)*, pages 291–294, 2004. Cited on page(s) 61

John R. Quinlan. *C4.5: Programs for Machine Learning*. Morgan Kaufmann, San Francisco/CA, 1993. Cited on page(s) 36

Altaf Rahman and Vincent Ng. Supervised models for coreference resolution. In *Proceedings of the Conference on Empirical Natural Language Processing*, pages 968–977, 2009. DOI: 10.3115/1699571.1699639 Cited on page(s) 69

Marta Recasens, Eduard Hovy, and M. Antònia Martí. A typology of near-identity relations for coreference (nident). In *Proc. of the 7th International Conference on Language Resources and Evaluation (LREC)*, Malta, 2010. Cited on page(s) 50

Gisela Redeker. Ideational and pragmatic markers of discourse structure. *Journal of Pragmatics*, 14: 367–381, 1990. DOI: 10.1016/0378-2166(90)90095-U Cited on page(s) 85, 110

Tanya Reinhart. Coreference and bound anaphora: A restatement of the anaphora questions. *Linguistics and Philosophy*, 6:47–88, 1983. DOI: 10.1007/BF00868090 Cited on page(s) 44

David Reitter. Simple signals for complex rhetorics: On rhetorical analysis with rich-feature support vector models. *LDV Forum*, 18(1/2):38–52, 2003. Cited on page(s) 112

David Reitter and Manfred Stede. Step by step: underspecified markup in incremental rhetorical analysis. In *Proc. of the 4th International Workshop on Linguistically Interpreted Corpora (LINC)*, Budapest, 2003. Cited on page(s) 127

Jeffrey C. Reynar. An automatic method of finding topic boundaries. In *Proc. of the 32nd Annual Meeting of the Association for Computational Linguistics*, pages 331–333, Las Cruces/NM, June 1994. Association for Computational Linguistics. DOI: 10.3115/981732.981783 Cited on page(s) 28, 32

Jeffrey C. Reynar. Statistical models for topic segmentation. In *Proc. of the 37th Annual Meeting of the Association for Computational Linguistics*, College Park/MD, 1997. DOI: 10.3115/1034678.1034735 Cited on page(s) 19, 20, 22, 37

Julia Ritz, Stefanie Dipper, and Michael Götze. Annotation of information structure: An evaluation across different types of text. In *Proc. of the 6th International Language Resources and Evaluation Conference (LREC)*, pages 2137–2142, 2008. Cited on page(s) 56

John Rotondo. Clustering analysis of subject partitions of text. *Discourse Processes*, 7:69–88, 1984. DOI: 10.1080/01638538409544582 Cited on page(s) 17, 18

Kenji Sagae. Analysis of discourse structure with syntactic dependencies and data-driven shift-reduce parsing. In *Proc. of the 11th International Conference on Parsing Technologies (IWPT'09)*, pages 81–84, Paris, 2009. Association for Computational Linguistics. DOI: 10.3115/1697236.1697253 Cited on page(s) 119

Ted Sanders. Semantic and pragmatic sources of coherence: On the categorization of coherence relations in context. *Discourse Processes*, 24(1):119–147, 1997. DOI: 10.1080/01638539709545009 Cited on page(s) 85

Ted Sanders, Wilbert Spooren, and Leo Noordman. Toward a taxonomy of coherence relations. *Discourse Processes*, 15:1–35, 1992. DOI: 10.1080/01638539209544800 Cited on page(s) 83

Holger Schauer and Udo Hahn. Anaphoric cues for coherence relations. In Galia Angelova, editor, *Proc. of the Conference on Recent Advances in Natural Language Processing (RANLP)*, pages 228–234. 2001. Cited on page(s) 110

Frank Schilder. Robust discourse parsing via discourse markers, topicality and position. *Natural Language Engineering*, 8(2-3):235–255, 2002. DOI: 10.1017/S1351324902002905 Cited on page(s) 127

Mahdi Shafiei and Evangelos Milios. A statistical model for topic segmentation and clustering. In *21st Canadian Conference on Artificial Intelligence*. Windsor, Ontario, 2008. Cited on page(s) 36

H. Gregory Silber and Kathleen F. McCoy. Efficiently computed lexical chains as an intermediate representation for automatic text summarization. *Computational Linguistics*, 28(4):488–496, 2002. DOI: 10.1162/089120102762671954 Cited on page(s) 25

E.F. Skorochod'ko. Adaptive method of automatic abstracting and indexing. In *Information processing 71: Proceesings of the IFIP Congress*, pages 1179–1182. North Holland, 1972. Cited on page(s) 29

Carlota Smith. *Modes of discourse. The local structure of texts*. Cambridge University Press, Cambridge, 2003. Cited on page(s) 130

Wee Meng Soon, Hwee Tou Ng, and Daniel Chung Yong Lim. A machine learning approach to coreference resolution of noun phrases. *Computational Linguistics*, 27(4):521–544, 2001. DOI: 10.1162/089120101753342653 Cited on page(s) 65, 66, 67, 68, 69, 70, 74

Claudia Soria and Giacomo Ferrari. Lexical marking of discourse relations — some experimental findings. In *Proc. of the COLING/ACL Workshop on Discourse Relations and Discourse Markers*, Montréal, 1998. Cited on page(s) 110

Radu Soricut and Daniel Marcu. Sentence-level discourse parsing using syntactic and lexical information. In *Proc. of the Human Language Technology Conference of the North American Chapter of the ACL*, pages 149–156, Edmonton/Canada, 2003. DOI: 10.3115/1073445.1073475 Cited on page(s) 92, 94, 95, 96, 117, 119, 121, 122, 123

Caroline Sporleder and Mirella Lapata. Discourse chunking and its application to sentence compression. In *Proc. of the HLT/EMNLP Conference*, pages 257–264, Vancouver, 2005. DOI: 10.3115/1220575.1220608 Cited on page(s) 92, 95

Caroline Sporleder and Alex Lascarides. Exploiting linguistic cues to classify rhetorical relations. In *Proc. of the Conference on Recent Advances in Natural Language Processing (RANLP)*, 2005. Cited on page(s) 111

Caroline Sporleder and Alex Lascarides. Using automatically labelled examples to classify rhetorical relations: An assessment. *Natural Language Engineering*, 14(3):369–416, 2008. DOI: 10.1017/S1351324906004451 Cited on page(s) 110, 112

Heather Stark. What do paragraph markers do? *Discourse Processes*, 11(3):275–304, 1988. DOI: 10.1080/01638538809544704 Cited on page(s) 18, 20

Manfred Stede. The Potsdam Commentary Corpus. In *Proc. of the ACL Workshop on Discourse Annotation*, pages 96–102, Barcelona, 2004. DOI: 10.3115/1608938.1608951 Cited on page(s) 110, 119, 126

Manfred Stede. RST revisited: Disentangling nuclearity. In Cathrine Fabricius-Hansen and Wiebke Ramm, editors, *'Subordination' versus 'coordination' in sentence and text*. John Benjamins, Amsterdam, 2008a. Cited on page(s) 86

Manfred Stede. Disambiguating rhetorical structure. *Research on Language and Computation*, 6(3): 311–332, 2008b. DOI: 10.1007/s11168-008-9053-7 Cited on page(s) 131

Manfred Stede and Kristin Irsig. Identifying complex connectives: Complications for local coherence analysis. In *Proc. of the 3rd Workshop on Constraints in Discourse (CID)*, Potsdam, 2008. Cited on page(s) 99

Manfred Stede and Carla Umbach. DiMLex: A lexicon of discourse markers for text generation and understanding. In *Proc. of the 17th International Conference on Computational Linguistics and 36th Annual Meeting of the Association for Computational Linguistics (COLING/ACL'98)*, pages 1238–1242, Montréal, Canada, 1998. Cited on page(s) 100, 102

Nicola Stokes, Joe Carthy, and Alan F. Smeaton. Select: a lexical cohesion based news story segmentation system. *AI Communication*, 17:3–12, 2004. Cited on page(s) 28, 29

Michael Strube, Stefan Rapp, and Christoph Müller. The influence of minimum edit distance on reference resolution. In *Proceedings of the Conference on Empirical Natural Language Processing*, pages 312–319, 2002. DOI: 10.3115/1118693.1118733 Cited on page(s) 67, 68

Roland Stuckardt. Design and enhanced evaluation of a robust anaphor resolution algorithm. *Computational Linguistics*, 27(4):479–506, 2001. DOI: 10.1162/089120101753342635 Cited on page(s) 59

Rajen Subba and Barbara Di Eugenio. Automatic discourse segmentation using neural networks. In *Proc. of the 11th Workshop on the Semantics and Pragmatics of Dialogue*, pages 189–190, Trento, Italy, 2007. Cited on page(s) 95

Rajen Subba and Barbara Di Eugenio. An effective discourse parser that uses rich linguistic information. In *Proc. of Human Language Technologies: The 2009 Annual Conference of the North American Chapter of the Association for Computational Linguistics*, pages 566–574, Boulder/CO, 2009. Association for Computational Linguistics. Cited on page(s) 110, 113, 119, 126

K. Sumita, K. Ono, T. Chino, T. Ukita, and S. Amano. A discourse structure analyzer for Japanese text. In *Proc. of the International Conference on Fifth Generation Computer Systems*, pages 1133–1140, 1992. Cited on page(s) 103, 107

Kristen Maria Summers. *Automatic discovery of logical document structure*. PhD thesis, Cornell University, 1998. Cited on page(s) 11, 12

John M. Swales. *Genre analysis: English in academic and research settings*. Cambridge University Press, Cambridge, 1990. Cited on page(s) 13

Maite Taboada. Discourse markers as signals (or not) of rhetorical relations. *Journal of Pragmatics*, 38(4):567–592, 2006. DOI: 10.1016/j.pragma.2005.09.010 Cited on page(s) 110

Maite Taboada and William Mann. Rhetorical Structure Theory: Looking back and moving ahead. *Discourse Studies*, 8(4):423–459, 2006a. DOI: 10.1177/1461445606061881 Cited on page(s) 83

Maite Taboada and William Mann. Applications of Rhetorical Structure Theory. *Discourse Studies*, 8(4):567–588, 2006b. DOI: 10.1177/1461445606064836 Cited on page(s) 83

Maite Taboada, Julian Brooke, and Manfred Stede. Genre-based paragraph classification for sentiment analysis. In *Proc. of the SIGDIAL 2009 Conference*, page 62–70, London, UK, September 2009. Association for Computational Linguistics. Cited on page(s) 9

Elke Teich and Peter Fankhauser. Exploring lexical patterns in text: Lexical cohesion analysis with WordNet. In *Heterogeneity in Focus: Creating and Using Linguistic Databases*, volume 2 of *Interdisciplinary studies in information structure*, pages 129–145, Potsdam, Germany, 2005. Cited on page(s) 24

Joel Tetreault. *Empirical evaluations of pronoun resolution*. PhD thesis, University of Rochester, 2005. Cited on page(s) 67

Simone Teufel and Marc Moens. Summarizing scientific articles – experiments with relevance and rhetorical status. *Computational Linguistics*, 28(4):409–445, 2002. DOI: 10.1162/089120102762671936 Cited on page(s) 13

Milan Tofiloski, Julian Brooke, and Maite Taboada. A syntactic and lexical-based discourse segmenter. In *Proc. of the Joint Conference of the 47th Annual Meeting of the ACL and the 4th International Joint Conference on Natural Language Processing of the AFNLP (Short Papers)*, pages 77–80, Suntec, Singapore, 2009. Association for Computational Linguistics. DOI: 10.3115/1667583.1667609 Cited on page(s) 89, 90, 93, 94

Masao Utiyama and Hitoshi Isahara. A statistical model for domain-independent text segmentation. In *Proc. of the 39th Annual Meeting of the Association for Computational Linguistics*, Toulouse/France, 2001. DOI: 10.3115/1073012.1073076 Cited on page(s) 34

Kees van Deemter and Rodger Kibble. On coreferring: Coreference in MUC and related annotation schemes. *Computational Linguistics*, 26(4):629–637, 2000. DOI: 10.1162/089120100750105966 Cited on page(s) 46, 48, 49

Yannick Versley, Simone Paolo Ponzetto, Massimo Poesio, Vladimir Eidelman, Alan Jern, Jason Smith, Xiaofeng Yang, and Alessandro Moschitti. BART: A modular toolkit for coreference resolution. In *Proc. of the 46th Annual Meeting of the ACL: Human Language Technologies Demo Session*, pages 9–12, Columbus, Ohio, 2008. Association for Computational Linguistics. Cited on page(s) 69

Renata Vieira and Massimo Poesio. An empirically based system for processing definite descriptions. *Computational Linguistics*, 26(4):539–593, 2001. DOI: 10.1162/089120100750105948 Cited on page(s) 55, 56, 62, 66

Renata Vieira and Simone Teufel. Towards resolution of bridging descriptions. In *Proc. of the 35th Annual Meeting of the Association for Computational Linguistics*, pages 522–524, Madrid, Spain, 1997. Association for Computational Linguistics. DOI: 10.3115/976909.979689 Cited on page(s) 45, 63

Marc Vilain, John Burger, John Aberdeen, Dennis Connolly, and Lynette Hirschman. A model-theoretic coreference scoring scheme. In *Proc. of the 6th Message Understanding Conference (MUC-

6), pages 45–52, San Mateo/CA, 1995. Morgan Kaufmann. DOI: 10.3115/1072399.1072405 Cited on page(s) 74

Marilyn Walker, Aravind Joshi, and Ellen Prince. *Centering in Discourse*. Oxford University Press, Oxford, 1998. Cited on page(s) 51

Marilyn A. Walker. Limited attention and discourse structure. *Computational Linguistics*, 22(2): 255–264, 1996. Cited on page(s) 73

Norman Walsh and Leonard Muellner. *DocBook: The definitive guide*. O'Reilly, Sebastopol/CA, 1999. Cited on page(s) 12

Ulli Waltinger, Alexander Mehler, and Maik Stührenberg. An integrated model of lexical chaining: Applications, resources and their format. In Angelika Storrer, Alexander Geyken, Alexander Siebert, and Kay-Michael Würzner, editors, *Proc. of KONVENS 2008 — Ergänzungsband Textressourcen und lexikalisches Wissen*, pages 59–70, 2008. Cited on page(s) 26, 27

Bonnie Webber. D-LTAG: extending lexicalized TAG to discourse. *Cognitive Science*, 28:751–779, 2004. DOI: 10.1207/s15516709cog2805_6 Cited on page(s) 83

Bonnie Webber, Alistair Knott, and Aravind Joshi. Multiple discourse connectives in a lexicalized grammar for discourse. In *3rd International Workshop on Computational Semantics (IWCS)*, NL-Tilburg, 1999. Cited on page(s) 123

Bonnie Webber, Matthew Stone, Aravind Joshi, and Alistair Knott. Anaphora and discourse structure. *Computational Linguistics*, 29(4):545–587, 2003. DOI: 10.1162/089120103322753347 Cited on page(s) 100

Bonnie Lynn Webber. *A formal approach to discourse anaphora*. Garland, New York/NY, 1979. Cited on page(s) 43

Ben Wellner and James Pustejovsky. Automatically identifying the arguments of discourse connectives. In *Proc. of the 2007 Joint Conference on Empirical Methods in Natural Language Processing and Computational Natural Language Learning (EMNLP-CoNLL)*, pages 92–101, Prague, Czech Republic, 2007. Association for Computational Linguistics. Cited on page(s) 108

Egon Werlich. *Typologie der Texte*. Quelle und Meyer, Heidelberg, 1975. Cited on page(s) 130

Janyce Wiebe, Theresa Wilson, and Claire Cardie. Annotating expressions of opinions and emotions in language. *Language Resources and Evaluation*, 39(2-3):165–210, 2005. DOI: 10.1007/s10579-005-7880-9 Cited on page(s) 91

Graham Wilcock. *Introduction to Linguistic Annotation and Text Analytics*, volume 3 of *Synthesis Lectures on Human Language Technologies*. Morgan and Claypool, 2009. DOI: 10.2200/S00194ED1V01Y200905HLT003 Cited on page(s) 4

Florian Wolf and Edward Gibson. Representing discourse coherence: a corpus-based study. *Computational Linguistics*, 31(2):249–287, 2005. DOI: 10.1162/0891201054223977 Cited on page(s) 124, 125

Gilbert Youmans. A new tool for discourse analysis: The vocabulary managment profile. *Language*, 67(4):763–789, 1991. DOI: 10.2307/415076 Cited on page(s) 29

Author's Biography

MANFRED STEDE

Manfred Stede is a professor of Applied Computational Linguistics at the University of Potsdam, Germany. He obtained his Ph.D. in Computer Science from the University of Toronto in 1996 with a thesis on language generation; in those years he studied discourse structure primarily for its role in text generation. After working for five years in a machine translation project at TU Berlin, he moved to Potsdam in 2001, where his interests shifted to text analysis. He conducted research projects on applications like information extraction and text summarization, and on more theoretical matters like the semantics and pragmatics of connectives. Thus, issues of discourse processing and discourse structure have been on his agenda for the past 20 years, with a focus on coherence relations and their linguistic signals.

Printed in the United States
by Baker & Taylor Publisher Services